Afrosofian Knowledge and Cheikh Anta Diop

PHILOSOPHY OF RACE

The Philosophy of Race book series publishes interdisciplinary projects that center upon the concept of race, a concept that continues to have very profound contemporary implications. Philosophers and other scholars, more generally, are strongly encouraged to submit book projects that seriously address race and the process of racialization as a deeply embodied, existential, political, social, and historical phenomenon. The series is open to examine monographs, edited collections, and revised dissertations that critically engage the concept of race from multiple perspectives: sociopolitical, feminist, existential, phenomenological, theological, and historical.

Recent Titles in the Series

Afrosofian Knowledge and Cheikh Anta Diop: Geo-Ethical and Political Implications, François Ngoa Kodena

Creating a Black Vernacular Philosophy, by Devonya N. Havis

The Making of American Whiteness: The Formation of Race in Seventeenth-Century Virginia, by Carmen P. Thompson

Racist, Not Racist, Antiracist: Language and the Dynamic Disaster of American Racism, by Leland Harper and Jennifer Kling

Ontological Branding: Power, Privilege, and White Supremacy in a Colorblind World, by Bonard Iván Molina García

Black Men from Behind the Veil: Ontological Interrogations, by George Yancy

White Educators Negotiating Complicity: Roadblocks Paved with Good Intentions, by Barbara Applebaum

White Ignorance and Complicit Responsibility: Transforming Collective Harm Beyond the Punishment Paradigm, by Eva Boodman

Iranian Identity, American Experience: Philosophical Reflections on Race, Rights, Capabilities, and Oppression, by Roksana Alavi

The Weight of Whiteness: A Feminist Engagement with Privilege, Race, and Ignorance, by Alison Bailey

The Logic of Racial Practice: Explorations in the Habituation of Racism, edited by Brock Bahler

Hip-Hop as Philosophical Text and Testimony: Can I Get a Witness?, by Lissa Skitolsky

The Blackness of Black: Key Concepts in Critical Discourse, by William David Hart

Afrosofian Knowledge and Cheikh Anta Diop

Geo-ethical and Political Implications

François Ngoa Kodena

LEXINGTON BOOKS
Lanham • Boulder • New York • London

Published by Lexington Books
An imprint of The Rowman & Littlefield Publishing Group, Inc.
4501 Forbes Boulevard, Suite 200, Lanham, Maryland 20706
www.rowman.com

86-90 Paul Street, London EC2A 4NE

British Library Cataloguing in Publication Information Available

Library of Congress Cataloging-in-Publication Data

Names: Kodena, François Ngoa, author.
Title: Afrosofian knowledge and Cheikh Anta Diop : geo-ethical and political implications / François Ngoa Kodena.
Description: Lanham : Lexington Books, [2023] | Series: Philosophy of race | Includes bibliographical references. | Summary: "Afrosofian Knowledge and Cheikh Anta Diop wrestles with the cultural, epistemological, ethical, and geopolitical conundrums of our contemporary world. It argues that sofia is a psychological, discursive, social, and civilizational sickle constantly sharpened to weed imperial-colonial, mental, linguistic, racist, and barbaric alienation"-- Provided by publisher.
Identifiers: LCCN 2023014524 (print) | LCCN 2023014525 (ebook) | ISBN 9781666909135 (cloth) | ISBN 9781666909142 (ebook)
Subjects: LCSH: Philosophy, African. | Africa--Civilization. | Pan-Africanism. | Knowledge, Theory of. | Diop, Cheikh Anta.
Classification: LCC B5310 .K63 2023 (print) | LCC B5310 (ebook) | DDC 199/.6--dc23/eng/20230424
LC record available at https://lccn.loc.gov/2023014524
LC ebook record available at https://lccn.loc.gov/2023014525

∞™ The paper used in this publication meets the minimum requirements of American National Standard for Information Sciences—Permanence of Paper for Printed Library Materials, ANSI/NISO Z39.48-1992.

To you, my Ankh-Scepters (Ancestors), for your solarizing legacy
To you, my parents Augustine NGONO and Jérôme
NGOA, for your constant love, care, and buoyancy
To you, my sisters, brothers, and friends, for your supportive presence
To you, my worldwide Afrikan torn-choked body, for your
agential resoluteness and enlivening resilience

Contents

List of Figures

Foreword

Molefi Kete Asante

François Ngoa Kodena has written a uniquely energetic quest into the nature of philosophy as seen in the context of the physical and geo-political spaces of Africa. I have found *Afrosofian Knowledge and Cheikh Anta Diop: Geo-ethical and Political Implications* an intelligent and dynamic read about how Africans can be taught to see the world from African perspectives.

Buttressed by the penetrating works of Cheikh Anta Diop, the most profoundly Afrocentric historian/linguist of the twentieth century, Kodena has given us a worthy study of the complexities of the search for knowledge, and, of course, wisdom.

Standing on the balcony of my hotel in Istanbul a couple of years before the 2020 outbreak of Covid 19, I saw glistening in the sunlight the Hagia Sophia and wondered why the Byzantines have spoken of it as "Holy Wisdom." Delving into the crevices of philosophical and etymological scholarship Kodena advances numerous avenues for interpreting the African concept of Afrosofia. Although Africologists have explained "Africology as the Afrocentric inquiry into phenomena from transgenerational and transcontinental perspective." Kodena, however, posits the view that "Afrikology" is the study of "black African civilizations" rather than a discipline with a particular methodology. He is clearly seeking to define, within the circle of his African conceptions, an African construction of philosophical thinking. This is why he calls the idea, Afrosofia.

The ancient Kemetic word, "Seba," from which Europeans developed *sophia* and *sapientia,* and the Coptics offered *sopi* and which is probably related to Arabic *sufi,* derived from mysticism, and the Arabic *hikma,* wisdom, are further extensions of the African original. In fact, following Miriam Lichtheim and others many Western thinkers claimed that the ancient Africans of Egypt created *sebayet,* wisdom teachings, as a way to separate ancient Africa from what they considered to be a Western creation, philosophy. Actually, the word *seba* appears during the reign of Antef 2 (2108–2059 BCE) on the stela of Antef Wahankh. Kodena's work does not seek to establish a Kemetic/Egyptian origin of *Sophia* as in Theophile Obenga's work. It seems to me that *sofia, Sophia*, and so forth are derived from the African *seba.* I offer this as a heuristic for additional points of inquiry for a very exciting work in the light of Cheikh Anta Diop.

The reader is struck by Kodena's easy flow between much Western thinking and some African ideas. He moves, for instance, from Plato and Aristotle to Mvettean zen, and is at home with discussing values, rationality, ethics, and geopolitical consciousness.

The Afrofuturist Reynaldo Anderson and the African Womanist, Nah Dove, both argue that we have not yet seen the gifts that Africa has to offer. Anderson, like Kodena, seeks to challenge the contemporary works that obscure or invisibilizes intellectuals like C. Tsehloane Keto who thought of space and time in relationship to Africa in the 1980s. On the other hand the group led by the African Womanist theorist Nah Dove seeks to adjust our thinking to an Afrosofia that would complement much of Kodena's work. I know that Dove's ideas, like those of Anderson, following Kodena, will burst forth in new futuristic ways with a strong and compelling womanist bent to bring complementarity between genders into the forefront. I think that Kodena has brought us a good way up the mountain of philosophical argumentation. Afrosofia is a ladder up that mountain and we shall study this work for classes and for the public as a part of the process of seeking African centered perspectives on reality. It is not a problem for us to understand Kodena's point if we are willing to accept the capability of all humans to reason from their own experiences, histories, and values.

Language is a key component to how we present what we think. In this profound work Kodena has introduced us to a new language of victory where Africa names itself, identifies its history as a usable trope for resurrecting the lost connections between Nile Valley civilizations and the productive capacity of African values in the Niger River valley as well as the emerging understandings provided by the Congo Basin ideas about society, relationships, and humanity.

When I published *The Afrocentric Manifesto* in 2007 I had already baked in the controversies and oppositions that I had received from those who did not see Africa as a continent and Africans as people who could create memes, ideas, and arguments based on African values. Kodena's work has aptly joined the fray with new ideas, innovative insights, and provocative appeals to a broad range of scholarship to explore the Afrocentric content in a powerful manner. I am certain that this book, once thoroughly understood, will have a profound impact on scholars in many fields.

Molefi Kete Asante is professor of Africology at Temple University. He is the author of 100 books, including *The History of Africa.*

Acknowledgments

Let me begin by expressing my deepest appreciation to each of you, valued brothers Molefi Kete Asante, Jay Lampert, Brian Cronin, George Yancy, Teodros Kiros, and Jean-Jacques Ngor Sène. Your outstanding insights patiently watered this book, gradually enhancing its growth and eventual maturation.

To you "mom" and "dad," I am wholeheartedly indebted, for your cultural and astronomic education.

My gratitude goes to you, Professor Pierre Oum Ndigi, for triggering my interest in Cheikh Anta Diop's scholarship.

To you, dear Spiritan confreres, I express my thanks.

I am extremely grateful to the ZENN Research Team. Your investigative companionship is here rewarded.

Many thanks to you, dear Baye Fall brother, Ndiaye Diagne, Founder and Curator of the Cheikh Ibra Fall Cultural Center in Dakar (Senegal). Your guidance yielded my informative encounters with the RND members Moustapha Diop and Abdoulaye Homar Seck, as well as with the Mouride Brotherhood in your Center, Thiès, and Caytu (Cheikh Anta Diop's native Home).

I am grateful to all the professors and library personnel I met at the University and IFAN Cheikh Anta Diop in Dakar.

My thanks also go to you, all my beloved siblings and friends, for your loving and continuing encouraging presence. Your energies sustain me along the way.

Introduction

This book[1] aims at clarifying, elucidating, and envisioning the geopolitical and ethical consequences of the enigmatic concept *(philo)sophia*[2] (causal knowledge)[3] from two convergent perspectives: the Antadiopian[4] and the Afrosofian. Both approaches, though potentially intricate to the reader due to their trans-disciplinarity, plurilingualism, and direct methodology, maintain that *sofia* qua enlightenment is inherently purposive, tasking, and at once rational (scientific), historical, cultural, ontological, ethical, and geopolitical. *Sofia* is a quest for a planetary civilization and, therefore, a transcendence of all forms of barbarism at personal and institutional levels. As *Femina/Homo sapiens sapiens,* ideally *sosŏ* or twice sapient (wise), we better ourselves and the world we live in, inasmuch as we strive to overcome the insanity of planetary barbarism through enlivening ways of thinking, writing, and living.

We are here in the sphere of geopolitical ferocity,[5] especially in its alienating and (neo)colonial overtones: geo-economic predation,[6] curricular soliloquies,[7] bad faith[8] in the Academy, and a worldwide bastardization of the masses through the geostrategic hand of corporate interests.

The disastrous result, in the second decade of the twenty-first century, has been the alarming pauperization of massive populations in Central America, the Middle East, and Afrika, faced with no other alternative than a desperate flight to "greener pastures," wherever they could be found. Thus, the perilous plight of a geostrategic chaos is more than ever present. Often orchestrated by the Western aisle of the "United Nations'" Security Council via its secular hands (NATO and AFRICOM),[9] geo-economic ferocity has been the enduring portion of people the world over, fueled by proxy military interventions[10] or still by transnational rogue groups like Boko Haram of the so-called Islamic State. As it were, the ontological disarray of the Other, the weak, the migrant, the worker, seems to arouse the geopolitical jouissance of the imperial corporatocracy.

Are Western communities/peoples/populations in America and beyond shielded from this pernicious leech of corporate imperium? The answer is both negative and alarming, hence Michael Parenti's warning:

> The goal of US Reactionary Rulers is the Third Worldization of the entire world including Europe and North America, a New World Order in which capital rules supreme with no public sector services or labor unions to speak of; no prosperous, literate, effectively organized working class or highly educated middle class with rising expectations and a strong sense of entitlement; no public medical care, pension funds, occupational safety, or environmental and consumer protections, or any of the other insufferable things that might cut into profits and lead to a more egalitarian distribution of life chances.[11]

What could human life mean in this torn global blueprint? Not much, unless the despoiled themselves resist the diluvian path of materialistic consumption and determinedly band together to bring about a more peaceful, stable, and sustainable world.

Such a tumultuous context calls for the reinvention of a human agential trajectory, grounded on a hospitable and transcultural education. It seems to me that neo-imperialism, understood as the fragmentation of humans alongside economic and ethnic lines, offers no future to global humanity. On the contrary, a Janusian precolonial and decolonial education challenges us, in this nascent twenty-first century, to work toward a civilization of sapientization, hospitality, and peace.

Therefore, through *Afrosofian Knowledge and Cheikh Anta Diop*, I endeavor to articulate how the latter concepts, namely wisdom (*sofia/sophia/sapientia)* and similar ones such as generosity, integrity, or truth constitute the very foundational prerequisite of the notion of knowledge in CAD. It will be shown that to know primarily means to strive to live out one's sapient nature. Such an analysis underscores the idea that knowledge, in both the Antadiopian and the Afrosofian perspectives, is ultimately about the socio-psychological formation and the achievement of a certain inspiring, noble, and heroic human type, namely the sapient, the highest type.

Thus perceived, *sofia* will prove to be a *Mvettean zen*, that is, a strenuous uplifting path/process of the human rational, ethical, and geopolitical consciousness toward its solarization. As it were, one's awakening and embodiment of this solar/cosmic consciousness, the Mvettean Tara (enlivening principle), will be the outcome of the adjectival cipher *sosǒ,*[12] which depicts the impeccable demiurgic human. Like the factorized apico-dental consonant "tt" of its ontological theory, the Mve*tt*,[13] the *So*[14] will embody the formal expansion of the generative *Atòm* Eyo[15] in sapient beings. It will express a hierophany of the maturing consciousness in its communion with Being (Eyo).

This striking find is geniusly highlighted by the cultural ontologists Robert Ndebi Biya[16] and Martin Heidegger.[17] Whereas the latter thinks and writes in German, the former, like me, is purposely Afrophone in his conceptual examination of be(com)ing as generation, though writing in French. But neither Ndebi Biya nor Heidegger unravel the etymological puzzle of *sophia* as I do.

This does not mean that the enigma of *sophia* is not of interest to contemporary thinkers. As we will see, many Afrikan philosophers on the continent and in the diaspora have shouldered the task. It is the case, for example, with CAD[18] himself, Théophile Obenga,[19] Pierre Oum Ndigi,[20] Ama Mazama, and Molefi Kete Asante.[21] These thinkers/authors provide resourceful analyses on the Kemetic concepts of philosophy and of philosophers, its practitioners. However, what they do not offer, as this study does, is some culturally compelling evidence of how present-day Afrikan concepts unravel the etymological conundrum of *sophia* in its ethical, geopolitical, and cosmic underpinnings. Why is it that "Egyptian philosophy was of a solar and cosmic orientation,"[22] as Obenga observes? Why would Frantz Fanon claim that *"l'homme est un OUI vibrant aux harmonies cosmiques?"*[23] Why does Plato compare the sun to the form of the good?[24]

Afrosofia elaborates on these questions. The first chapter discusses the panafrikan renaissance. The second addresses the concept Afrosofia, and unravels notions that seem semantically clear, and thus philosophically trivial, namely "Afrika," and "*sofia*." It also gives us the overall orientation of the project at hand. The book's title "Afrosofian Knowledge and Cheikh Anta Diop," is a prospective invitation for linguistic, conceptual, cultural, and geopolitical dialogue and cooperation in the academy and beyond. Universities, presumably, are institutions where the universe (global thinking) is awakened through questioning and persistent applied inquiry. Afrosofia problematizes the ontological question of each human being on earth. What does it mean for us to be *Femina/Homo sapiens sapiens?* Where do we come from? What is Afrika to us? It seems to me that these questions are relevant to the philosophical education to come; an education whose failure is certainly guarantied, if philosophers fail to problematize the connection between chronology, history, science, and ethics. Afrosofia inspires the production of asymptotic concepts such as "Asiasofia," "Eurosofia," "Americasofia," and related cultural and intellectual productions.

The third chapter deals with the current global predicament of cultural alienation.[25] It leads us, truth-seekers, to the crossroads of human history, with decisive options and missions ahead of us: shape, through our lifestyles and writings, a more agential and accommodating civilization grounded on what CAD calls "*une ouverture vers autrui.*"[26] To convey the same message, he uses other dynamic and visionary phrases like the "*progrès général de l'humanité*"[27] (general progress of humanity), or "*l'éclosion d'une ère d'entente universelle*"[28] (the emergence of an era of universal concord). Besides, the chapter challenges inquirers to detect the mechanisms of (neo) colonial alienation in our daily lives and in the production of knowledge, and to stand for academic integrity, scientific truth, intellectual creativity, and moral probity.

The fourth chapter examines how Afrosofia operates in CAD's methodology. It articulates the practical implications of such a process on the status of science, research, and innovation within a multi-polarized world. An interesting intuition in CAD's epistemology is his view that knowledge, especially in the current context of neocolonial education (which remains predominantly Eurocentric in its curricular orientation and contents) must be "direct." His favorite phrase is: "*la connaissance directe*"[29] (direct knowledge). The directness of this method is accounted for by its agential approach to science. To me, direct knowledge is of tremendous epistemic importance for two reasons. First, it captures the view that knowledge (scientific truth) involves independent thinking. Second, it constitutes the very springboard of my adoption of lithographic art as a writing system, and as a multi-millennial existential philosophy since the start of my field research in Kamerun and Senegal in 2016.[30] We are faced here with the Kantian conundrum of knowledge acquisition (*Critique of Pure Reason, B1*), through a conciliatory attempt between representationalist and constructivist theories.

The fifth chapter unfolds *sofia* as a solarizing process. The actualization of *sofia* [*Kheper* (Medu Neter), *šopi* (Coptic), *sopi* (Walaf)][31] requires a maturing process. In other words, with *sofia*, and probably with *sophia* too—defined by Plato as "the grasp of motion,"[32]—the acts of cultivation, change, and becoming are necessary steps toward one's social maturity and responsibility. Envisioned from this perspective, *sofia* is like an inner realm/land that each human should plow, for a bountiful socio-political harvest (thoughts, discourses, and actions) to ensue.

Sofia prepares the epistemic ground for the elaboration of a philosophic apparatus[33] geared toward Afrikology (study of black Afrikan civilizations). This is a prerequisite for cognitive renaissance, coupled with the reconciliation of humanity with its Afrikan future mediated by the past. The academic impact of this Antadiopian and Afrosofian visions are felt today in the growing emergence of Afrikan-oriented studies worldwide (Africana, Afrocentricity, Africology, African American, etc.). CAD is vindicated in his prediction that Kemet, "*[. . .] la mère lointaine de la science et de la culture occidentales,*"[34] "*[. . .] jouera, dans la culture africaine repensée et rénovée, le même rôle que les antiquités gréco-latines dans la culture occidentale*."[35] Humanity must investigate this heritage in all scientific domains in order to see how it could inflect, the quality of our fleeting corporeal life on earth.

NOTES

1. The multilinguistic title of the book alerts the reader that knowledge is achieved by sporting a trans-cultural cognitive jacket. That is a distinctive mark of this research's outlook. I am primarily a Beti speaker. The Beti is an Afrophone language spoken in Central Afrika. I think, it is valuable to learn to think primarily in one's mother language, while remaining open to the multiplicity of other world's languages, peoples, and cultures. Following this line of thought, the book aims at playing a fuse-like function, thus connecting the Beti, English, and French languages into a single semiotical network. I note from the outset that Cheikh Anta Diop (1923–1986) was a plurilinguist and trans-disciplinary Senegalese scholar. He spoke Wolof and French, and was knowledgeable in Medu Neter, Greek, Latin, English, and more. He was at once Egyptologist, historian, philosopher, geneticist, chemist, agronomist, jurist, anthropologist, linguist, politist, and physicist. Frantz Fanon's mentor, the Martinican poet Aimé Césaire, lauds C. A. Diop's first major work *Nations Nègres et Culture* as " . . . *le plus audacieux qu'un nègre ait jusqu'ici écrit et qui comptera, à n'en pas douter, dans le réveil de l'Afrique*." Translation from French: " . . . the most daring book ever written by a Negro and which, assuredly, will impact the awakening of Africa." See: Aimé Césaire, *Discours sur le Colonialisme* (Paris: Présence Africaine, 2004), 41.

2. The doxographer Diogenes Laertius (180–240 CE) reports, relying on Pythagoras' purported account, that *philosophia* was formerly called *sophia* (wisdom): Diogenes Laertius, *The Lives and Opinions of Eminent Philosophers*, Book I, §8, 5. But, to this day, the etymology of *sophia* (wisdom) remains unknown. See: Pierre Chantraine, *Dictionnaire Étymologique de la Langue Grecque* (Paris: Klincksieck, 2009), 1162 ; Plato, *Cratylus*, 412b.

3. Aristotle, *Metaphysics*, Book I, 982a2.

4. The adjective refers to Cheikh Anta Diop, abridged throughout the book as CAD.

5. William Blum, *Rogue State. A Guide to the World's Only Superpower* (Monroe, ME: Common Courage Press, 2005) and *America's Deadliest Export: Democracy—the Truth about US Foreign Policy and Everything Else* (London: Zed Books Ltd, 2014).

6. Dambisa Moyo, *Edge of Chaos. Why Democracy Is Failing to Deliver Economic Growth—and How to Fix It* (New York: Basic Books, 2018); Richard Peet, *Unholy Trinity. The IMF, World Band and WTO* (New York: Zed Books Ltd, 2010).

7. Curricular soliloquy leads to the fragmentation of students' cognitive openness and imaginary.

8. Cheikh Anta Diop, *Civilisation ou Barbarie* (Paris : Présence Africaine, 1981), 9; Jean Devisse in Prince Dika Akwa Nya Bonambela (Dir.), *Hommage du Cameroun au Professeur Cheikh Anta Diop* (Dakar Fann, Sénégal : Éditions Panafrika/

Silex/Nouvelles du Sud, 2006), 53; Théophile Obenga, *Le Sens de la Lutte contre l'Africanisme Eurocentriste* (Paris: L'Harmattan, 2006), 65, 108–9.

9. NATO is the North Atlantic Treaty Organization, whereas AFRICOM stands for the United States Africa Command.

10. We may mention the examples of Syria, Mali, Democratic Republic of Congo, Central African Republic, etc., and coup d'Ėtats in Ivory Coast (2011) or Libya (2011).

11. Michael Parenti, *The Face of Imperialism* (Boulder, CO: Paradigm Publishers, 2011), 35.

12. Philippe Laburthe-Tolra, *Initiations et Sociétés Secrètes au Cameroun. Essai sur la religion beti* (Paris: Karthala, 1985), 324.

13. Numerous philosophic works will be referenced on the Mvett. The verb *a vet* means to rise above or to transcend all forms of existential pessimism, nihilism, or that which is life-threatening. The Mvettean apothegm is *Bikalik!,* that is, let us not despair or give up! See: Steeve Elvis Ella, *Mvett ékang et le projet bikalik. Essai sur la condition humaine* (Paris: L'Harmattan, 2011), 232. The concept *bikalik* fittingly expresses what CAD calls "*un optimisme africain atavique*" (an Afrikan atavistic optimism) in *Civilisation ou Barbarie* (Paris: Présence Africaine, 1981), 16. The bikalization of consciousness is a victorious consciousness in the Mvettean agent. For her/him, the possibility of success qua triumph of civilization over barbarism is always a realistic utopia.

14. Philippe Laburthe-Tolra, *Initiations et Sociétés Secrètes au Cameroun, op. cit.,* 277–325.

15. As shall be evidenced in the book, Eyo is the mushrooming principle of all that is in the Beti ontology.

16. Robert Ndebi Biya, *L'Être Comme Génération. Essai critique d'une ontologie d'inspiration africaine* (Strasbourg: Cérit, 1995), 133.

17. Martin Heidegger, *Discourse on Thinking* (Trans. John M. Anderson and E. Hans Freund, New York: Harper & Row, 1966), 47–48.

18. Cheikh Anta Diop, *Civilisation ou Barbarie* (Paris : Présence Africaine, 1981), 389, 414, 425, 427–29, 431–33, 438, 446–47, 450.

19. Théophile Obenga, "Egypt: Ancient History of African Philosophy" in Kwasi Wiredu (Ed.), *A Companion to African Philosophy* (Malden, MA: Blackwell Publishing Ltd, 2004), 31–49.

20.Djasso Djasso, "L'Egyptologue OUM NDIGI nous explique l'œuvre de Wêre Wêre Liking selon le paradigme kamite" [Video]. *YouTube.* Retrieved January 17, 2020. https://www.youtube.com/watch?v=h-ZHnO_fNgI.

21. Molefi Kete Asante & Ama Mazama (Ed.), *Encyclopedia of African Religion* (Thousand Oaks, CA: Sage Publications, Inc., 2009), 596.

22. Théophile Obenga, "Egypt: Ancient History of African Philosophy," *op. cit.,* 40.

23. Frantz Fanon, *Peau noire, masques blancs* (Paris: Éditions du Seuil, 1952), 6. From French: "Man is a YES that vibrates to cosmic harmonies."

24. Plato, *Republic*, 508a–e.

25. I used the term alienation in the Beti sense of *akud*, that is, one's experience of cognitive dislocation, de-centeredness, and lack of existential agency. The

akud person lacks self-knowledge and would hardly think or act autonomously and creatively.

26. Cheikh Anta Diop, *Civilisation ou Barbarie, op. cit.*, 477. From French: " . . . an openness toward the Other." CAD's geopolitical philosophy of human collaboration opposes the view that knowledge is about hegemony and exploitation; that human civilizations cannot coexist peacefully without bellicose clashes. Likewise, CAD dismisses the incorrect phenotypic opinion that humans emerged from different parts of the world (polycentrism). He corrects the latter blueprint by emphasizing the scientific monogenetic theory, which holds that all humans emerged from black Afrika. Accordingly, human otherness ("yellow," "red," and "white" phenotypes) are just folds of black sameness and identity: we are all black Afrikans under the skin. In other words, there is a subtle unifying thread beneath human phenotypes, such that their genes are more homogeneous than distinct. Thus, to be opened to otherness is to mediate one's self-understanding by re-appropriating psychologically, not only the different hues of others as furtive shades of oneself, but more importantly, the cultural contributions of all humans toward civilization. Since humanity is one in origin, it can also unite in purpose, work toward peace and inclusive prosperity.

27. Cheikh Anta Diop, *Antériorité des Civilisations Nègres. Mythe ou Vérité Historique?* (Paris: Présence Africaine, [1967], 1993), 275.

28. *Ibid.*

29. Cheikh Anta Diop, *Civilisation ou Barbarie, op. cit.*, 16.

30. There are a few photographs of lithographic art at the end of chapter IV.

31. Cheikh Anta Diop, *Civilisation ou Barbarie, op. cit.*, 450 and 453. These linguistic morphemes are relevant for their convergent semantic reference to the notion of change.

32. Plato, *Cratylus*, 412b.

33. Such concepts include: "precolonial Africa," "cultural unity of black Africa," "anteriority of black civilizations," "scientific philosophy," "human reconciliation with itself," etc.

34. Cheikh Anta Diop, *Civilisation ou Barbarie, op. cit.*, 12. From French: " . . . the distant mother of Western science and civilization."

35. *Ibid.* From French: " . . . will play, in the reassessed and renovated African culture, the same role than the Greco-Roman antiquities in the Western civilization."

Chapter 1

For a Sofian Panafrikan Renaissance

On Friday evening, August 31, 2017, I meditatively walked along the busy Malcolm X Boulevard in Harlem, New York, when I came across a sidewalk book vendor, from whom a bought *Harlem on my mind*[1] and *The 101 Best Jazz Albums*.[2] My new finds were quite opportune. I had been pondering CAD's following vision of the Afrikan music to come: "*La musique africaine devra exprimer le chant de la forêt, la puissance des ténèbres et celle de la nature, la noblesse dans la souffrance avec toute la dignité humaine.*"[3]

What I was and am still concerned about is the very notion of music in its philosophic, ethical, and geo-political dimensions. Could philosophy be musical and capture the equivocality of the "*forêt*" (forest) or "*la puissance des ténèbres*" (the power of darkness) in the Antadiopian projection of the Afrikan music in the making? What could the notion of Afrikan music possibly mean, and how does it relate to "*la noblesse dans la souffrance avec toute la dignité humaine*" (nobleness and dignity in human suffering)? The Antadiopian quote does not address my concern. It even leaves the metaphors of forest and darkness in their ambiguous bareness.

But what is of interest in CAD's words, is their provocative character. As the French philosopher Paul Ricoeur (1913–2005) would argue about symbols,[4] the Antadiopian concept of music gives rise to thought. If we construe his analogies of forest and darkness in the sense of remoteness, inaccessibility, and uncertainty, his philosophic idea of music may sound irrelevant to the *sofian* purpose of this book. But if, on the contrary, we understand them, as I suggest, in their vitality and "irreducible opacity" as Édouard Glissant (1928–2011)[5] would say, then, the Antadiopian concept of Afrikan music becomes fruitful. Tropical forests are outstanding in biodiversity and in the regulation of global carbon cycles. This shows their crucial importance in the welfare of humanity. These opaque forests urge inquirers to think, heed, and embody, trans-linguistically, Afrika's philosophic significance and message/sound (energy/music) in the contemporary tempestuous world.

Music is pensive and ethical. It immerses melodious minds into the boundless realm of human creativity through rhythmic, agreeable, and harmonious sounds, both natural, vocal, and instrumental (voiceless). For Plato, wisdom (philosophy) is tuneful, because it joins the mind to the ethical "chorus,"[6] making it commune with the good (gods and good people).[7] This view is congruent, as will be evidenced in the book, with CAD's conciliatory philosophy, even if Plato sounds less ecological than CAD. This will be an interesting aspect of CAD's epistemology to investigate in my future research: *sofia* as ecology and mindfulness.

Coming back to my rewarding errand on Malcolm X Boulevard in Harlem, my interest in *Harlem on my mind* and *The 101 Best Jazz Albums* was all the more boosted by antecedent folds (layers) of reflective moments sprouting from my inquiries into the function of music and dance in contemporary history, and the idea of the mind as well. Three of such meditative events respectively found expression in Donny Elwood's masterful piece "*Négro et Beau*,"[8] Ray Charles' colorful[9] lyric "Georgia On My Mind," and Alain Locke's *The New Negro: Voices of the Harlem Renaissance.*[10]

Keeping in mind this notion of the renaissance in relation to our subject matter, *sofia,* I find Locke's book thought-provoking both in its title and content. My Antadiopian[11] sensitivity[12] is honed by Locke's contentious terminology with notions like the "New Negro" or the phrase "voices of the Harlem Renaissance" which, strikingly, are still fertile discursive grounds among contemporary thinkers like Achille Mbembe,[13] Têtêvi Godwin Tété-Adjalogo,[14] Stanislas Spero Adotevi,[15] Ngũgĩ wa Thiong'o,[16] Fantu Cheru,[17] Washington A. J. Okumu,[18] Doue Gnonsea[19] and many others, including CAD[20] himself.

Achille Mbembe, for example, understands the *Nègre* (Negro), not only as a series of historical discursive formations and practices,[21] but also more agentially as *"celui sur qui on n'a pas de prise; celui qui n'est pas là où on le dit, encore moins où on le cherche, mais plutôt là où il n'est pas pensé."*[22] The *Nègre*, in Mbembe, is at once elusive and specifically Other in her/his "irreducible opacity," to use Glissant's catchy phrase. Now, if the Antadiopian *Nègre*, like the Mbembean, has been discursively loaded over the centuries,[23] CAD dwells more on her/his precolonial connotation construed as cultural (civilizational), hence *Nations Nègres et Culture*.[24] To be *Nègre*, for CAD, is to be(come) civilized, as indicates the coordinating conjunction "*et*" (and) in the aforementioned title.

CAD's "Nègretude,"[25] which is not to be confounded with the Négritude movement of Aimé Césaire, Léon-Gontran Damas, and Léopold Sédar Senghor, is therefore more compelling than the Mbembean. In other words, the *Nègre* in CAD is the trope for the humanity to come, that is, the inner creative and demiurgic consciousness; the potential builder of nations who slumbers in each human being.[26]

This said, Professor Washington Okumu confronts the important question about the protagonists of the Afrikan re-appropriation of the historical initiative (re-naissance) in the making, suggesting that . . .

> . . . everyone has a role to play and each grouping must work out for itself how to contribute to an African Renaissance, as expressed in the values of hard work and integrity, in the development of the arts (painting, sculpture, design, music, poetry, literature), and in the development of science and technology, agriculture, business and financial growth.[27]

These are interesting ideas even if I wonder why Okumu, unlike CAD[28] and Th. Obenga,[29] does not envision federalism as a requisite to the said Afrikan renaissance.

In the American context, the awakening of the "New Negro," I guess, implies the demise of the colonial *Nègre*, culturally made moribund, subservient, and historically thingified, because in physical bondage, and consequently forced to toil gratis to death for the enslaver and the colonizer. It is from the pit of this existential "it-ness" and nothingness that the New Negro reclaims her humanity and creative agency. Thus, could be grasped the renascent turn and novelty brought about in and through the New Negro.

Alain Locke (1885–1954) himself, with an outstanding philosophic artistry, suggests in the book that the New Negro is a being of the "worlds of color";[30] the opaque "color" of the renascent and outreaching mind,[31] memorial and principled, which can spark truths and abiding meanings when set in motion by complex reasoning.[32] Furthermore, the New Negro pertains to inescapable waves of incisive question marks, framed subjectively from the practical loci of her experienced wretchedness in deportation. To be forcibly exiled can lead to ontological alienation and vagrancy. One loses the sense of homeness, historical location, and orientation.

It is therefore not surprising that the tropes Negro and Afrika be interwoven in the consciousness of the Harlem Renaissance protagonists. It is the case with Countee Cullen (1903–1946), who raises one of such dizzying concerns when he asks in his vivid poem *Heritage*: "What is Africa to me?"[33] I myself, like Cullen, address the Afrikan conundrum in the book. If the "me" refers to the Lockean New Negro, Cullen seems to be indicating that "Harlem," "Georgia," or any other toponym on one's mind remain groundless until they find the Afrikan sapient anchorage.

What then is Afrika to the rebirthing mind, if not this commitment to reason and to the unavoidable vertigo of grounded inquiry? The Cullenian Afrikan topos seems more intimately interrogative, addressing biting question marks in a personal and subjective manner. It is the situated being, the individual voice, the "me" that matters to Cullen. CAD is more general in his monocentric theory of Afrika as the cradle of sapient humanity. My Afrosofian contribution to this Afrikan conundrum is both genealogical, ethical, and more circumscribed around the uplifting ether of *Afiri* (Hope).

Locke signals that the semantic textures of the Afrikan question are unraveled and rediscovered whenever the New Negro thoughtfully "digs up"[34] the raison d'être of her historical presence in the world from the renascent scenes of her ancestral arts and scientific traditions. As this demanding investigation is carried out, the Afrikan Dream gradually glows with regal splendor in Cullen's cosmic mind, claimable by any demiurgic consciousness in these or similar terms:

> Copper sun, a scarlet sea, . . .
> Strong bronzed men and regal black
> Women from whose loins I sprang . . . [35]

Like a stream or a plant, renascent humanity springs, like Cullen, from this practical Afrikan-atomic-colorful world, at once made of "copper sun," "scarlet sea," and "strong bronzed men and regal black women." The vivid image of the "scarlet sea" is reminiscent of the "Atlantic Red Carpet," that is, the deported and torn Afrikana body, still heavily bleeding across the Atlantic Ocean through the neoliberal virus.[36]

As the second chapter of the book evidences, the *sofian* (sunny) inquirer, evoked in the Cullenian phrase "Copper sun," will examine and transgress the prevailing neocolonial (dis)order and the DuBoisian "color line"[37] of the current geo-economic and geopolitical dispensation. In so doing, she can uplift the epistemic, ethical, and social standards of our world. She can inspire people's lives and make them somewhat starry like a shining sun. Cullen, indeed, uses telluric, oceanic, and aerial metaphors for that purpose. His envisioned humanity, for the "wretched of the earth,"[38] is that of auto-determined and suntanned[39] "strong bronzed men and regal black women."

This ontological fabric equips the renascent woman/man with demiurgic powers such that the Poet can write: "Lord, I fashion dark gods, too."[40] Such gods, I think, are embodied in present-day creative minds, who struggle to reignite the fire of conscientious science in contemporary bluesy (tragic) societies. That is the sense in which Fanon writes that "each generation must discover its mission, fulfill it or betray it, in relative opacity."[41]

One of such opacities in the first two chapters that we are about to examine is less about the mission at hand for the New Negro, than about when and how her renaissance is to be brought to fruition. *"Quand pourra-t-on parler d'une renaissance africaine?"*[42] wonders CAD in his 1948 article. For him, as will be evidenced, the challenge ahead of contemporary humanity is to restore fraternal living worldwide.[43] But this Antadiopian vision runs the risk of remaining abstract.[44] This could explain, perhaps, why he married a French white woman in the person of Marie-Louise Diop-Maes.[45]

At any rate, the ferocious history of the past six centuries vis-à-vis the Afrikan seems to contradict and even cushion against the Antadiopian eschatological anthropology. Such is the current geopolitical dispensation, despite the mild will to international unity championed by the bellicose West in the aftermath of World Wars I and II through the "United Nations" creation in 1945. How can we experience fraternal living when a handful of states,[46] permanent members of the Security Council with the right to veto, unilaterally and undemocratically lord over the majoritarian rest of the world?

The chilling message seems unequivocal, as writes the Afrikan-Beninese philosopher Stanislas Spero Adotevi: *"tous les hommes ne sont pas frères."*[47] Of course, CAD would not agree with this idea on account of his monogenetic theory and conciliatory philosophy.

This said, one of the problems that confront CAD's critics and readers is that of direct knowledge, that is, the ability to read and question his transdisciplinary argumentation in the Wolof, Medu Neter, and French languages. This direct interaction with the Antadiopian documentation offers the advantage of lessening gross misrepresentations of his thought as is the case with the British anthropologist Christopher Stringer. Had he read the first chapter of CAD's *Civilisation ou Barbarie,*[48] he would certainly have referenced it and corrected his view that "the late Senegalese scientist Cheikh Anta Diop . . . argued that the first Cro-Magnons closely resembled present-day African populations."[49] Rather, what CAD writes is this:

> *La mutation du négroide en Cro-Magnon ne s'est pas faite en un jour! Il y eut une longue période de transition de plus de 15 000 ans, correspondant à l'apparition de plusieurs types intermédiaires entre le négroide et l'europoïde, sans qu'il puisse s'agir de métissage.*[50]

Another challenge that faces the Antadiopian critic and reader is to interact with him as a scientist-philosopher. It should be underscored that CAD earned a philosophic *Licence* (the equivalent of a master's degree)[51] at the Parisian Sorbonne. From this standpoint, he strongly advocates scientific leaps in philosophic inquiry and conversely.[52] In other words, science should remain a privileged source of inspiration for philosophy and vice versa.

More daringly, CAD considers that the scientific knowledge of Afrikan intellectual traditions, coupled with the genetic kinship between the Pharaonic Egyptian and Negro-Afrikan languages,[53] requires that the history of philosophy be rewritten.[54] Here again, the problematic of language resurfaces:

to philosophize is to think in language(s), and thinking is an act of speech. Théophile Obenga puts it differently: *"on ne peut pas dire sa pensée sans la dire concrètement dans une langue, dans sa langue de culture ou dans sa langue maternelle."*[55]

And since *"Ch. A. Diop n'a pas tout dit sur l'Afrique noire,"*[56] as Jean-Marc Ela rightly underlines, my constant endeavor in this book consists precisely in thinking in both my Beti mother tongue and in European ones (English and French). In attempting to address the subjective Cullenian question about the meaning of Afrika in its ontological, ethical, and socio-political overtones, I endeavor to "inpresent," that is, to inhabit and dwell in the aforementioned languages, so as to behold, listen, and then fashion meanings from the morphological components (phonemes and graphemes) of their concepts. It is the case, as we shall witness, with the concept of Afrosofia. I do so with the intention of contributing to the creative ongoing renaissance of global philosophy.

CAD, himself, assigns no other task to his epistemology than " . . . *réveiller le colosse qui dort dans la conscience de chaque Africain,*"[57] understood that Afrika is the trope for regenerative being, the Mother Land of all humans. The ethnocentric Martin Heidegger (1889–1976) is therefore right about the creative power of language when he opines: "Language is the house of Being. In its home man dwells. Those who think and those who create with words are the guardians of this home."[58]

It is my hope that my Afrosofian creative language will quench, even slightly, the thirst for culture, meaning, and unity within global humanity, both diagnosed through the setback of cultural alienation in chapter 2.

NOTES

1. Allon Schoener (Ed.), *Harlem On My Mind. Cultural Capital and Black America 1900–1978* (New York: Dell Publishing Co., Inc., 1979).

2. Len Lyons, *The 101 Best Jazz Albums. A History of Jazz on Records* (New York: William Morrow and Company, Inc., 1980).

3. Cheikh Anta Diop, *Nations Nègres et Culture. De l'antiquité nègre égyptienne aux problèmes culturels de l'Afrique Noire d'aujourd'hui* (Paris: Présence Africaine, 1979), 528. From French: "African music will have to express the song of the forest, the power of darkness and that of nature, nobleness in suffering with all human dignity."

4. Paul Ricoeur, *The Symbolism of Evil* (Trans. Emerson Buchanan, Boston: Beacon Press, 1969), 347–347.

5. Édouard Glissant, *Poetics of Relation* (Trans. Betsy Wing, Ann Arbor: The University of Michigan Press, 2010), 115.

6. Plato, *Laws,* II, 654a–b.

7. Plato, *Republic*, X, 607a.

8. Donny Elwood's classical piece can be pondered in its written and musical forms through the following link: Kamer Lyrics, "Donny Elwood: Négro et Beau" [Video]. *Youtube.* Accessed May 10, 2019. https://www.youtube.com/watch?v=zRgrgyq9BKs.

9. Ray Charles sings of "Georgia on my mind": "Georgia a song of you comes as sweet and clear a moonlight through the pines. . . . No peace I find," says he, "just an old sweet song keeps Georgia on my mind." Perhaps the "old sweet song" in question is that of a freedom won by a victorious mind, within the confines of an enslaving system that crushes the self-determination of the *Nègre*; the Afrikan in America and beyond through racism and imperial colonization.

10. Alain Locke, *The New Negro. Voices of the Harlem Renaissance* (New York: A Touchstone Book, 1997).

11. As already pointed out, the adjective Antadiopian stands for what is characteristic of Cheikh Anta Diop's epistemology.

12. The Antadiopian sensitivity is one which commits itself to the embodiment of a conciliatory personality for the sake of preventing various forms of barbarism worldwide. What is to be cultured is a lived theory of life geared toward a renascent humaneness within humanity. See: Cheikh Anta Diop, *Antériorité des Civilisations Nègres, op. cit.*, 278.

13. Achille Mbembe, *Critique de la Raison Nègre* (Paris: La Découverte, 2013).

14. Têtêvi Godwin Tété-Adjalogo, *La Question Nègre* (Paris: L'Harmattan, 2003).

15. Stanislas Spero Adotevi, *Négritude et Négrologues* (Bègles: Le Castor Astral, 1998).

16. Ngũgĩ wa Thiong'o, *Something Torn and New. An African Renaissance* (New York: Basic Civitas Books, 2009).

17. Fantu Cheru, *African Renaissance. Roadmaps to the Challenge of Globalization* (New York: Zed Books Ltd, 2002).

18. Washington A. J. Okumu, *The African Renaissance. History, Significance and Strategy* (Trenton, NJ: Africa World Press, Inc., 2002).

19. Doue Gnonsea, *Cheikh Anta Diop, Théophile Obenga: Combat pour la Re-naissance africaine* (Paris: L'Harmattan, 2003).

20. Cheikh Anta Diop, "Quand pourra-t-on parler d'une renaissance africaine?" in *Alerte sous les Tropiques* (Paris: Présence Africaine, 1990), 33–44.

21. Achille Mbembe, *Critique de la Raison Nègre, op. cit.,* 51.

22. *Ibid.*, 52. From French: "one over whom one has no control; one who is not where he is defined, still less where he is sought, but rather where he is not thought."

23. Cheikh Anta Diop, *Nations Nègres et Culture* (Paris: Présence Africaine, 1954), 49–58. This is the second chapter of the book titled *"Naissance du Mythe du Nègre"* (Birth of the Negro Myth).

24. *Ibid.*

25. The concept is mine.

26. Prince Dika Akwa Nya Bonambela (Dir.), *Hommage du Cameroun au Professeur Cheikh Anta Diop* (Dakar Fann. Sénégal: Éditions Panafrika, 2006), 43–44.

27. Washington A. J. Okumu, *The African Renaissance, op. cit.,* 259.

28. Cheikh Anta Diop, *Les Fondements Économiques et Culturels d'un État Fédéral d'Afrique Noire* (Paris: Présence Africaine, 1974).

29. Théophile Obenga, *L'État Fédéral d'Afrique Noire: La Seule Issue* (Paris: L'Harmattan, 2012).

30.Alain Locke, *The New Negro, op. cit.,* 383–414.

31. *Ibid.*, W.E.B. DuBois, "The Negro Mind Reaches Out," 385–414.

32. Reasoning can be carried out in various forms: abductive, deductive, inductive, intuitive, logical, verbal, etc.

33. Alain Locke, *The New Negro, Ibid.,* 250.

34. *Ibid.,* 229–69.

35. *Ibid.*, 250.

36. Samir Amin, *The Liberal Virus. Permanent War and the Americanization of the World* (New York: Monthly Review Press, 2004).

37. Alain Locke, *The New Negro, op. cit.*, 385.

38. Frantz Fanon, *The Wretched of the Earth* (Trans. Richard Philcox, New York: Grove Press, 2004).

39. The reader will witness the omnipresence of the sun in this research and on Afrikan thought in general. The sun stands for the generous outpourer of life on earth. The sun (generosity) is the Law and model of human living on earth. That is the reason why we, the Beti, call it Tara, that is, Mother-Father or, word for word, the sphere (territory) of Ra. Ptahhotep recommends: "Be generous as long as you live" in *The Teachings of Ptahhotep. The Oldest Book in the World* (Ed. Asa G. Hilliard III, Larry Williams and Nia Damali, Atlanta: Blackwood Press, 1987), 30.

40. Alain Locke, *The New Negro, op. cit.*, 252.

41. Frantz Fanon, *The Wretched of the Earth, op. cit.,* 145.

42. Cheikh Anta Diop, Alerte sous les Tropiques (Paris: Présence Africaine, 1990), 33–44.

43. Cheikh Anta Diop, *Antériorité des Civilisations Nègres. Mythe ou Vérité Historique?* (Paris: Présence Africaine, 1993), 275.

44. CAD does foresee the danger to defend some abstract humanism ("*l'humanisme abstrait*") through "*des expressions généreuses, mais sans contenu réel, ou applicable,*" that is, "generous expressions, but without any concrete or applicable content." *Ibid.*, 276.

45. Louise Marie Diop-Maes, *Afrique Noire. Démographie, Sol et Histoire* (Paris: Présence Africaine, 1996). In 2016 during my field research in Senegal, I visited both CAD's mausoleum and his wife's tomb in Caytou; CAD's village.

46. It is alleged that China, the Russian Federation, the United States, the United Kingdom, and France are privileged within the organization (United Nations) "because of their key roles in the establishment of the United Nations." See: United Nations, "Voting System." *United Nations Security Council* Retrieved: January 22, 2020. https://www.un.org/securitycouncil/content/voting-system.

47. Stanislas Spero Adotevi, *Négritude et Négrologues* (Paris: Le Castor Astral, 1998), 202. From French: "all humans are not siblings."

48. Cheikh Anta Diop, *Civilisation ou Barbarie* (Paris: Présence Africaine, 1981).

49. Christopher Stringer and Robin McKie, *African Exodus. The Origins of Modern Humanity* (New York: Henry Holt and Company, 1997), 246. These authors, however, share the Afrikan monogenetic theory of modern humanity with CAD.

50. Cheikh Anta Diop, *Civilisation ou Barbarie, op. cit.,* 70. From French: "The mutation from the Negroid to the Cro-Magnon did not occur in one day! There had been a long period of transition of more than 15,000 years, corresponding to the appearance of many intermediary types between the Negroid and the Europoid, without any type of métissage (crossbreeding)."

51. Cheikh M'Backé Diop, *Cheikh Anta Diop. L'homme et l'œuvre* (Paris: Présence Africaine, 2003), 32.

52. Cheikh Anta Diop, *Civilisation ou Barbarie, op. cit.,* 475–76.

53. Cheikh Anta Diop, *Parenté Génétique de l'Egyptien Pharaonique et des Langues Négro-Africaines* (IFAN-Dakar: Les Nouvelles Éditions Africaines, 1977).

54. Cheikh Anta Diop, *Sciences et Philosophie. Textes 1960–1986* (Dakar: Université Cheikh Anta Diop de Dakar, 1985), 187.

55. Théophile Obenga, *Cheikh Anta Diop, Volney et le Sphinx. Contribution de Cheikh Anta Diop à l'Historiographie mondiale* (Paris: Présence africaine, 1996), 284. From French: "One cannot express one's thought without concretely saying it in a language, in one's language of culture or in one's native language."

56. Jean-Marc Ela, *Cheikh Anta Diop ou l'honneur de penser* (Paris: L'Harmattan, 1989), 133. From French: "Ch. A. Diop did not say everything on black Africa."

57. Cheikh Anta Diop, *Antériorité des Civilisations Nègres, op. cit.*, 278. From French: "to awaken the giant who sleeps in the consciousness of every African."

58. Martin Heidegger, *Basic Writings* (Ed. David Farrell Krell, New York: Harper & Row, 1977), 193.

Chapter 2

Toward the Afrosofian and Antadiopian Epistemic Paradigm

True knowledge, through persistent inquiry, eventually leads to wisdom.[1] Accordingly, this chapter aims at providing us with an intelligibility of the unfolding current text, through an ontologico-ethical and geopolitical interpretation of Afrosofia, understood as a search for knowledge and *méthode chez* (method in) Cheikh Anta Diop.[2] This trans-linguistic phrase infers the possibility of any *homo loquens* (speaking human) to think and understand her complex condition[3] within the confines of the universe.

A good starting point, for the inquirer, would consist in sporting a trans-cultural cognitive jacket patched with a conciliatory blueprint. We are here on the pathway of human encounters and interactions, with their consequent eidetic (linguistic) transactions. This is important because multilingualism and cognitive openness certainly tool the thinker with a bigger, nuanced, and colorful picture of "reality." Perceiving the epistemic weight of this insight turns the researcher into a hunter of the "truth" behind the unfamiliar, the marginal, the foreign, and even what she thinks she knows.

Thus, leaning theoretically toward the "known" and the exotic is a distinctive mark of this research's outlook. I am primarily a Beti speaker. The Beti is an Afrophone language spoken in Central Afrika. It is certainly valuable to learn to think in one's mother language, while remaining open to the multiplicity of other world's languages, peoples, and cultures. Accordingly, the book aims at playing a fuse-like function, thus connecting the Beti, English, and French languages into a single semiotic chord.

I note from the onset, that plurilinguism and trans-disciplinary scholarship are key characteristics of Cheikh Anta Diop's epistemic outlook. The Afrikan-Senegalese, Cheikh Anta Diop (CAD: 1923–1986), spoke Wolof and French, and was knowledgeable in Medu Neter,[4] Greek, Latin, English, and more. He was at once Egyptologist, historian, philosopher, geneticist, chemist, agronomist, jurist, anthropologist, linguist, politist, and physicist.

Such a rich intellectual background radiates from his early work *Nations Nègres et Culture*, which Frantz Fanon's mentor, the Martinican poet Aimé Césaire (1913–2008), appraises as *"le plus audacieux qu'un nègre ait jusqu'ici écrit et qui comptera, à n'en pas douter, dans le réveil de l'Afrique."*[5]

But what could the (re)awakening of "Afrika" possibly mean to the contemporary scholar?[6] Could she securely[7] think the world from the cradle of sapient humanity, Afrika? In other words, regardless of her ethnicity or epistemic anchorage, can today's academic dig up her treasured utopia, her dreamed future *with* Afrikan present and past relevant cultural diggers, alongside Asian and Euro-American ones? What are those diggers? Is there any psychological, historical, or linguistic touchdown-take-off between her (the academic) and the Sphinx that Afrika is, according to the American poet Joaquin Miller?[8] If so, how can she tap the enlivening values emanating from it? In a word, how can she become Afrikan, Sphinx-like, exploring all possible avenues of human creativity and cooperation?

Though possibly discomforting, these questions are relevant for twenty-first century academia, in which the enduring systemic prejudice of the Du Boisian "color line"[9] adamantly persists. Professor Molefi Kete Asante stresses this point when he writes: "Education is no exception as a locus of confrontation where African Americans are up against curriculum and pedagogy that act to reduce agency."[10] The point here is that there is need for cultural diversity in contemporary academia in the United States of America, just as in continental Afrika. As the latter becomes a locus of epistemic attention, the hue prejudice gradually vanishes, ignorance of the human civilizing walk ceding the floor to informed precolonial human historical consciousness.

That is the therapeutic scientific remedy offered in CAD's *Nations Nègres et Culture*. But what is culture and is there any Afrikan culture? This question is deep and requires an elaborate answer, which is not my purpose at this point. Suffice it, for the time being, to say that a culture emerges from a people's geo-historical trajectory, both informing and modifying the ideals, aspirations, and life of the said people through concrete situations and events. The chapter endeavors to break down and defend an Afrosofian and Antadiopian universalist epistemic paradigm, as a fruitful alternative to the prevailing disjunctive Cartesian paradigm.[11] The latter, I argue, badly handicaps the flourishing of a geo-epistemic education and a culture of solidarity in the West and beyond.

To achieve the purpose assigned to this chapter, I will make use of pre-texts, that is, existing documents, mainly Antadiopian, that antedate the current text. Texts are cultural artifacts since they are produced by geo-historical individuals with specific epistemic and ethical motivations. Texts can be retrospective, circumstantial, and prospective reflections/answers (mirrors) of concrete and geographically situated peoples, to sporadic and perennial problems. In that sense, texts (discursive and symbolic) take charge of the conundrum of life, human and otherwise, in the universe. They provide the thinker, through mythic, scientific, graphic, and philosophic reason, with a perceptive armature for the comprehension of the human historical trajectory.

Thus, the universe, just like our world in its atomic, mineral, vegetal, and animal articulations, becomes a potential bio-archetype.[12] In the same vein, the spiral galactic Milky Way is viewed as a meaningful decryptable, but challenging "text" to our cognition. Similarly, our trans-physical[13] body itself can be approached as a still latent "script," deeper than present-day phenotypical descriptions, and their subsequent socio-political manipulations. The perspective is therefore to try, as much as I can, to envision a geographic, cultural, and universalist model of knowledge, likely to enrich us with a broader interconnected perception of humanity in the cosmos.

A point worth emphasizing in these introductory remarks is the intertextual continuity within a culture. The notion of continuity underscores the subtle presence of cultural artifacts such as language, psychology, or worldview in written data, such that texts potentially intersect and are not just isolated artifacts or disjointed and unconnected data. Rather, they emerge from a historical network of cosmological, aesthetic, linguistic, conceptual, scientific, axiological, psychological, and teleological transactions, because they are produced by socio-historical individuals. Even theoretical texts such as the Rhind and Moscow Mathematical Papyri, written by ancient Egyptian scribes in the second millennium BCE are contextual: using the symbolic notation of the mathematical jargon molded in the Kemetic language (Medu Neter), Ahmes[14] and other scribes address different geometrical problems like the volume of a pyramid's frustum.[15]

The argument here is that the actuality, the signifying presence of a text calls for a con-text. The context is the theoretico-practical setting which informs, enriches, and hosts the text. It ferments the text from within, giving it its epistemic breathing texture and existential breadth. But the context is also that which an author, a situated being,[16] wrestles with within her text. Weeding a context (epistemic or socio-political) through critical thinking in a text aims at improving its quality and upgrading its cognitive or ethical flaws for the advancement of science and the welfare of society. This is the task ahead of the "sofian" project at hand: further the geopolitical dignity of all humanity, beginning with its initial cradle; Afrikan humanity.

My argumentative style will be Eyoic,[17] that is, charged, invested, and infused with a symbolic and generative flavor, the reason being that the ex-pression, or the mere enunciation of theoretical concepts does not offer the necessary clarity intended by the writing process. Instead, it is the symbol, the metaphor, or the analogy, which sheds brighter rays on the cognitive "matter" under investigation. The foregoing argument is rightly captured by the Afrikan-Cameroonian artist, historian, and theologian Engelbert Mveng (1930–1995) in his following view that:

> *L'accès au langage symbolique passe par une connaissance scientifique du monde. La signification de l'objet symbolique est toujours une signification enrichie, comportant un extérieur et un dedans. C'est un passage permanent du phénomène au noumène. C'est au niveau du noumène que se situe le terrain propre de la symbolique.*[18]

Let us then begin, after these clarifications, by setting the anthropological platform around the thorny issue of wisdom.

ANTHROPOLOGICAL CONCERNS AROUND "WISDOM"

Striving to understanding one's presence and mission in the universe as an "instrument"[19] of life is certainly the noblest,[20] that is, the worthiest achievement of a sapient human being: it gives meaning and purpose to one's life, thoughts and actions in society, within the wider context of the cosmos. To be sure, thought cannot be indifferent to the motion of the latter, which brings about the alternation of seasons. We do enjoy the warm sunshine of the summertime in polar regions with their luxuriant verdure, just as we bear with the cold weather of the winter. Thus, we partner with the universe even after the decomposition of our physical body through "death," because our atoms will be recycled and conserved in "Matter."[21]

We can understand, from the preceding argument, why the Martinican philosopher and psychiatrist Frantz Fanon (1925–1961) argues for the need for humans to shoulder their cosmicity when he writes: "*Nous estimons qu'un individu doit tendre à assumer l'universalisme inhérent à la condition humaine.*"[22] The task of an individual, a scholar for example is, F. Fanon argues, to mirror the universe in her thought and life. And the universe is a manifold body; an ever-expanding diversity of interconnected stars grouped in galaxies.

Maintaining the same cosmic train of thought, F. Fanon unveils his inspiring anthropological outlook, declaring: "*L'homme est un OUI vibrant aux harmonies cosmiques.*"[23] For him, the nature of the cosmos and of humanity consists precisely in being coherently profuse, bountiful, and generous, despite the many corporeal or eidetic clashes that may occur between starry, telluric, and human "bodies." Hence the harmony of their "consensual"[24] togetherness, as is the case with the nine stars of our solar system.[25] At a bigger level, the universe coheres, cooperates and agrees in its multifariousness. This togetherness or coherent adherence can be envisioned as the included third, the synthetic evidence, and the proof of the inherent openness of apparent antithetic singulars within the universe's inner constitution. The universe "wills" and generates living "organs," perhaps out of necessity, else its expansion would be sheer randomness. But the universe seems to delight in the plural unity of its expressive forms, which are more diversified unity, more life.

So, the universe stretches and expands ad infinitum, such that its very life is the constant generation of harmonic abundant forms of "bodies." This explains why F. Fanon affirms the hyphenated (united) cosmic order as the existential paradigm of Afrikan humanism. Such a view sharply contrasts with the exclusivist and Faustian character of the Western humanism, as denounced in the forthcoming Sartrian, Zieglerian, and Deleuzian acerbic critiques.

For the French philosopher Jean-Paul Sartre (1905–1980), " . . . the only way the European could make himself man was by fabricating slaves and monsters,"[26] even though the latter are suicidal inventions, "which sooner or later the European will have to pay for,"[27] Sartre believes. Hence the inexorable ethical interrogation concerning the Euro-American historical raison-d'être:

> And that super-European monster, North America? What empty chatter: liberty, equality, fraternity, love, honor, country, and what else? This did not prevent us from making racist remarks at the same time: dirty nigger, filthy Jew, dirty Arab.[28]

Sartre is a prospective thinker, who does not just denounce the hegemonic geopolitical system of "white" supremacy. Rather, he wants us to confront the "super-European monster," the United States of America, in the specific area of its ethical nihilism. What must indeed be challenged by the despised-Rest, the so-called "dirty nigger, filthy Jew, dirty Arab," is the monstrosity, the ugliness and menacing character of a prevailing geopolitical space devoid of "liberty, equality, fraternity, love, honor, country," etc. Recourse to prejudice and name-calling only reveal the ethical anemia of the perceiver, whose mind becomes infested with negativity and pessimism to the point of construing otherness in his own image, that is, as an existential deformity.

But the despised-Rest fought for independence worldwide in the twentieth century, and still struggles against the global plutocratic establishment nowadays for its survival (epistemic, economic, political, etc.) and dignity. Thus, through a recursive reasoning knitted around the retributive rationale of reaping what one sows, Sartre predicts: " . . . our territory would have to be occupied by the formerly colonized and we would have to be starving to death."[29]

The imminent era of Western starvation, that is, the global dissenting *ras-le-bol* of the despised-Rest with the prevailing geopolitical culture of hegemony is accounted for by the hollowness of its ideals: liberty, love, equality, etc. As the American author John Perkins documents in *The Secret History of the American Empire*,[30] those empty ideals and similar ones[31] rather shield the international ruthless draining of world natural resources and environment by global corporations (ExxonMobil,[32] AREVA,[33] Bolloré,[34] etc.). Apparently, "wisdom" seems to be the arch-fiend of such Machiavellian geopolitics.

This pressing predicament of roguish terror confronting the international scene leads the French philosopher Jacques Derrida (1930–2004) to write indignantly:

> The first and most violent of rogue states are those that have ignored and continue to violate the very international law they claim to champion, the law in whose name they speak and in whose name they go to war against so-called rogue states each time their interests so dictate. The name of these states? The United States. . . . The most perverse, most violent, most destructive of rogue states.[35]

To be sure, this ethical vacuum in the "most destructive of rogue states," the United States of America, is symptomatic of a pressing need to rethink, as I try to do through the unfolding text, the human presence in the universe. Sartre does it in his own way, boldly lambasting Westerners: "Our noble souls are racist";[36] before thundering anxiously: " . . . we are the enemy of the human race."[37] Yet, this last pronouncement is neither marginal nor unique to Sartre. In effect, the Swiss sociologist Jean Ziegler expresses a similar view, confessing: "*Désormais, je reconnais ma culture d'origine comme ennemie; j'ai épousé l'univers africain comme une femme longtemps attendue.*"[38]

Western culture is considered by both Sartre and Ziegler as a malevolent and Sethean[39] pitfall. It is a "possession,"[40] a crippling destructive force, as Sartre writes. Nonetheless, though a "*déviation existentielle*"[41] (existential deviation), the West remains an integral part of the world, worth our epistemic attention. But we must endeavor to remain historically on track by revisiting our sapient nature from its inceptive Afrikan birthplace, since we are thoughtfully reminded by the French journalist and environmental activist Nicolas Hulot that: "*L'Afrique est un continent qui déborde de cette ressource qu'est la sagesse, tellement raréfiée chez nous*,"[42] that is, in the West.

Afrika possesses, in abundance, the "wisdom" that is deficient in the West, concedes N. Hulot. But what is the Afrikan "wisdom" alluded to here? It is perhaps the relational, "hyphenated," and theoretico-practical type of wisdom, which understands being (ontology) in terms of networks, connections, and included distinctions. The Antadiopian "Cheikh,"[43] who consistently defends an altruistic "anthropology without complacency,"[44] can be understood from this perspective when he urges us to labor earnestly and dutifully for Europe's ethical recovery.[45] What is her protracted illness? Imperial-colonialism is the answer. But is Europe ready to undergo the painful surgery? Can her misleaders renounce their worldwide predation in the name of democratic capital liberalism? I doubt.

CAD is commendable for mobilizing us toward the ethical recovery of Europe, the realm of ontological oblivion;[46] hence the necessity for a proper diagnosis of its exhaustion, which has mainly been colonial-imperial in recent centuries.[47] Presumably, the urgency to cure the sickly predacious West is the goal, which the French philosophers Gilles Deleuze (1925–1995) and Félix Guattari (1930–1992) jointly endeavor to achieve when they note alarmingly about the European "man": "It is obvious that 'man' holds the majority, even if he is less numerous than mosquitoes, children, women, blacks, peasants, homosexuals, etc."[48] Both authors suggest that the Western quandary stems from "man"; the hegemonic "majoritarian" urban heterosexual "white" male. This is "obvious," that is, plain factual reasoning, the authors conjecture.

However, the evidence that grounds the dominance of the Deleuzian-Guattarian "man" is not apodictic but rather hypothetical, since they argue: "Let us suppose that the constant or standard is the average adult-white-heterosexual-male-speaking a standard language."[49] It means that the social norms here painted in broad strokes (age, body hue, gender, "sexual orientation," and language) are just aleatory mainstays in the structure of power. A "standard language," for example, can be any language (Beti, Wolof, Lingala, Russian, Catalan, or Polish . . .). The take-away, however, in the Deleuzian-Guattarian argument, could consist in cautioning their reader against discriminatory anthropologies,[50] because they potentially ruin the intelligibility and appreciation of ethnic, cultural, and cosmic diversities.

Frantz Fanon on the contrary, as I noted earlier, strongly highlights the human connection with the universe. This assertion infers a simultaneous social unity in the making among humans themselves. Why emphasize the socio-cosmic ontological constitution of the human being? Fanon clarifies confidently: "*Alors? Alors, calmement, je réponds qu'il y a trop d'imbéciles sur terre.*"[51] The answer seems condescending, but sufficiently edifying: it is the human widespread cognitive insanity, which must be cured. That seems to be condition for our geo-ethical progress.

The psychiatrist Fanon, interestingly, models the human specific uniqueness on the quantum cosmic *mvende*[52] (constitution/order). In other words, he posits, like the physicists and philosophers CAD[53] and the Israeli Max

Jammer (1915–2010),[54] fluxes of boundless microphysical interactions (subatomic and atomic)[55] within the cosmic "matter" of which humans partake. Fanon interprets these subtle gravitational and electromagnetic interactions in terms of *"harmonies cosmiques"* (cosmic harmonies).

He suggests that what makes humans less "*imbéciles,*" that is, less prejudiced, misanthropic, or xenophobic in various social settings (family, street, office, church, etc.), is precisely our "*oui,*" meaning, our acquiescence and willingness to adjust our thinking, words, and actions to the anthropic universal principle. The task at hand consists in shouldering the responsibility to seek our life purpose in this earthly satellite of a "suburban" sun (our solar system) within the Milky Way. That purpose for the Afrikan (for whom the *Muntu* [human being] is an energetic living force),[56] as emphasized in Théophile Obenga[57] and Mbog Bassong[58] respectively, consists in one's identification with *Tara*[59] our sun, the igniferous "father" of every life.

With Fanon, we are in cosmological thinking, whereby the macrocosmic metaphysical "matter" (the cosmos)[60] mirrors the centripetal cognitive and ethical operations of the microcosmic physical complex (the human brain). He develops a complex epistemology of contact as a way for the human mind to host "reality," question, and scrutinize it patiently in view of its decipherment. By so doing, the universe becomes less enigmatic, and the inquisitive person hopefully journeys more securely in life. This would explain why Fanon addresses his "body" in an injunctive manner within the context of white misguidance (racism), entreating: *"O mon corps, fais de moi toujours un homme qui interroge!"*[61] Fanon here sublates the contrast between the body and the mind, and even auto-identifies with the "world" itself, elucidating successively: *"C'est que le corps pour nous n'est pas opposé à ce que vous appelez l'esprit,"*[62] because *"J'épouse le monde! Je suis le monde!"*[63]

This problem of the body (*corps*) will resurface in subsequent chapters through the Antadiopian categories of "matter," "alienation," or *"nègre"* (blackness). The "*corps-monde,*" (body-world) in the above Fanonian prayer, which concludes his anticolonial-imperial work *Peau noire, masques blancs,* is invested with a demiurgic capacity, that is, a generative and agential power to ignite existential interrogation. The notion of the *corps-monde* offers an interesting epistemic orientation, in that it throws an interpretative network beneath the multifariousness of "nature": everything is virtually interconnected in the cosmos.

Similarly, turning to the *corps-monde* in meditative thinking, within the present colonial-imperial dispensation of world affairs, also comes down to trailing, out of necessity, the arduous cliff of ongoing inquiry. What is sought is ultimate peaks (abiding answers) about what it means for us to interact as human beings (in our families, universities, societies) with different reigns (mineral, vegetal, animal) within the ecosystems of the biosphere.

In Fanon, the reach of such lofty pinnacles seems perpetually delayed, hence the "*toujours,*" (always), which certainly translates the restlessness of his geo-anthropological concern without racial prejudice: "*Je voulais tout simplement être un homme parmi d'autres hommes*,"[64] he writes. But behold, Fanon's defense of a humane world or quite simply his desire to be ("*être*") a human being among fellow humans and not an alienated being, is jeopardized by the omnipresent stranglehold of Western colonialism,[65] of which he writes:

> Colonialism obviously throws all the elements of native society into confusion. The dominant group arrives with its values and imposes them with such violence that the very life of the colonized can manifest itself only defensively, in a more or less clandestine way. Under these conditions, colonial domination distorts the very relations that the colonized maintains with his own culture.[66]

The psychiatrist Fanon diagnoses the Western colonial regime in narcissistic terms: colonialism wants the whole world for itself alone, and consequently proceeds by enslaving[67] it through geopolitical chaos and cultural distortion. Its brutal nature asphyxiates the very notions of human independence and dignity in oppressive institutional and ethical jungles, in which the dominated culture (languages, knowledges, histories, etc.) is forced into a "clandestine" and subaltern[68] existence.

It is from this dungeon of attempted acculturation by the colonial ferocious regime, that the Fanonian recurring injunctions (!!!) acquire their socio-political imperativeness. They seem to infer that something like an ethical "rain" should flow from "above," that is, from the "heavens" of human understanding to irrigate and impregnate the arid soil of social interactions, symbolized by the dots beneath the descending gushes.

Ultimately, what must be fertilized through right information, formal, and informal education is the moral consciousness of humanity. The gradual emergence of an informed international opinion via books, travels, the internet, social media, etc., augurs a progressive geopolitical openness of humans vis-à-vis one another. One can then hope that our increased awakening to human general history and to human lived experiences worldwide indicates the sure burgeoning of what CAD calls the era of a true humanity, of a new perception of the human being without ethnic factors.[69] The Antadiopian notion of a humanity beyond ethnocentrism contrasts with the Deleuzian-Guattari insulated "man" examined earlier.

More precisely, CAD delineates the steps toward the foregoing view, considering that the consciousness of modern man can only effectively progress if it is resolute in explicitly recognizing interpretative scientific errors, even in the very delicate field of history, to return to falsifications, and denounce legacy frustrations.[70]

Apart from reappraising scientific errors and willful historical distortions, as CAD recommends, I think that a decisive step toward the shaping of a more unitive humanity should consist, as I maintain here, in transcending the prevailing Eurocentric education in the West and beyond, through the promoting of trans-cultural curricula.

One hopefully understands, from what precedes, my unfolding argument that the inclusive "Afrosofian" and Antadiopian epistemic paradigm, can ethically invigorate the current eroding geopolitical dispensation. Without further ado, let us then begin the semantic exploration of "Afrosofia."

IN SEARCH OF *SOFIA:* THE EPISTEMIC *ATÓM*

Théophile Obenga's forthcoming epigraph suggests that the goal of human inquiry is ethical. In other words, "true knowledge" is a personal commitment to the lofty principle of "wisdom"; hence the following rhetorical question: "*La vraie connaissance n'est-elle pas celle qui aboutit à la sagesse?*"[71] Knowledge in Obenga, is the path to wisdom, such that the knower is recognized by her wisdom. But what is wisdom and how is it that we are capable of "true knowledge" (wisdom)? Who are we, and why are we called *Homo sapiens sapiens*?

Of the Sapient Human That We Are

The following analysis is informed by the Antadiopian theory of the cultural continuing unity of black Afrikan nations within the continent, dating from the emergence of the first Negroid[72] *Homo sapiens sapiens* in Afrika about -150,000 ago, up to their inter-continental diasporas started around -40,000.[73] How does CAD arrive at this conclusion? Is it a construction of his vivid imagination or the result of scientific investigations? CAD explains that his theory is built upon sciences such as prehistoric archeology, physical anthropology, and absolute chronology.[74] The latter science brought about a paleontological revolution from its discovery in the twentieth century,[75] in that it applies the radioactive method of Potassium-Argon dating on organic materials (hair, skin, bone, feather, rock, and so forth).

For CAD, then, the fortieth millennium before our era corresponds to the arrival of the Negroid Grimaldi in Europe, with his Aurignacian (industrial) culture.[76] Once there (in Europe), this migrant Grimaldi is faced with the austere climate of the declining last Würm Ice Age in the Alpine region, to which he must nevertheless adjust for survival. Thus far used to the sunny Afrikan weather and its luxuriant environment, the Grimaldi, in Europe, is forced into a quasi-underground life in caves, with little exposure to sunshine.

It follows that between -40,000–20,000, the Negroid Grimaldi undergoes a somatic and psychological mutation: his morphology, phenotype, and optimistic worldview[77] are modified. This is the monogenetic process through which the Europoid human type, the Cro-Magnon, came into being in CAD. He further argues that the Mongoloid type, which emerged in history from about -15,000, is a miscegenation between the Negroid Grimaldi and the Europoid Cro-Magnon.

Continuing his discussion on the cultural unity of the Afrikan populations living and migrating out of the continent over the past six millennia, CAD examines their interconnectedness under the following cultural traits: reverence for life and forebears, unitive cosmology, matriarchal social organization, psychological optimism, cultural creativity, common "paleo-African" language, totemism, circumcision, etc.";[78] hence the unambiguous title *Nations Nègres et Culture* (*Black Nations and Culture*).

The concept of "culture" in the singular highlights the point that there is a tangible underlying continuity between past (ancient Ethiopia, Meroitic Sudan, Kemet, Ghana, Mali, Songhai, Ndongo, Kuba, etc.) and present-day Afrikan nations worldwide. This argument runs through the Antadiopian *Antériorité des Civilisations Nègres,*[79] *Parenté Génétique de L'Égyptien Phaaraonique et des Langues Négro-Africianes,*[80] or *Civilisation ou Barbarie.*[81]

However, it is a "cultural unity"[82] nuanced and often obliterated by various alienations (psychological, religious, linguistic, historical, etc.), brought about by geopolitical imperialisms, and which considerably exhaust the revival[83] of the Afrikan inclusive ethos in different geographies and socio-political contexts.

The linguist CAD, like his Congolese and French peers Théophile Obenga and Lilias Homberger (1880–1969), defends the existence of a proto-Afrikan mother language, arguing that the Walaf, the Egyptian and the other African languages derive from a common mother tongue that could be called the paleo-African, the common African (L. Homburger) or the Negro-African (Th. Obenga).[84]

By inductive reasoning, if we consider the collaborative genetic research conducted in 2001 by the scientists A. Arnaiz-Villena *et al.* on the sub-Saharan origin of the Greeks,[85] we would reasonably argue that the chronological seniority (precedence) of the Antadiopian predialectal *"paléo-Africain"* surely impacted on both the ancient Greek language and the Pharaonic Egyptian[86] Mdw Ntr (Medu Neter).

Quite evidently, A. Arnaiz-Villena *et al.*'s research corroborates the Antadiopian monogenetic theory of the Negroid Afrikan origin of humanity. More importantly, they, like CAD, broaden our epistemic perspectives when it comes to questioning linguistic enigmas like the ancient Egyptian *Kheper* or *šopi* in Coptic,[87] the Beti *sofia,* the Walaf *sopi,*[88] and the Greek *sophia.*

What semantic and historic affinities could these concepts have in common? CAD envisions an insightful perspective to this question.

In an energetic style, he challenges contemporary academics to think and write with an Afrikan historical consciousness, meaning that they should endeavor to decipher epistemic problems from the broader angle of the cultural continuum between present-day black Afrikan nations and Pharaonic Egypt. But why must it be so? Why should the inquisitive mind, in the twenty-first century, not neglect the Afrikan enduring presence in world civilizations? CAD answers that it is contemporary Afrikans who can still demonstrate, in an exhaustive manner, their genetic cultural identity with Pharaonic Egyptians. Contrary to other humans (Indo-Europeans or Semites), they, alone, are still indubitably at home in the Egyptian cultural universe. This explains the crucial importance of the Nile Valley in Afrikological studies. Conversely, present-day Egyptology will recover from its secular sclerosis and textual hermeticism only when it determinedly turns to the Afrikan world.[89]

What is of interest in the foregoing perspective, is basically CAD's challenging recommendation to contemporary researchers to courageously transgress (transcend) the ideological boundaries, paradigmatic[90] and geopolitical,[91] that distance us from the still vivifying epistemic source that the Afrikan black world is. Through cultural ongoing sways along the Afrikan historical trajectory, scholars in any discipline can refresh their perspectives from that common human heritage. The reader should therefore be comfortable with the historical, cultural, linguistic, and semantic approaches used in this chapter, as I attempt to comprehend the enigma of *sofia*.

Of *Sofia*

The reader conversant with Western philosophy, could easily notice the morphological contrasts between the ancient Egyptian *Kheper* or *šopi* in Coptic, the Beti *sofia,* the Walaf *sopi,* and the Greek *sophia*. Yet, these concepts remain phonetically contiguous and semantically blurred, as if hazily pointing to some unknown *Atóm,*[92] or regulative virtue.[93] At any rate, if the Kemetic *Kheper* or *šopi* in Coptic, the Beti *sofia,* and the Walaf *sopi* remain semantically obscure at this point,[94] the Greek *sophia,* at least, seems definitionally less vague, especially when we consult dictionaries. They indicate that *sophia* respectively means "wisdom, skill, acquaintance with, or knowledge of"[95] something. The inference here is that *sophia* is an ethical (realistic?) utopia since it connotes the theoretical aspect of wisdom and not its practical embodiment in sapient persons (*sophoi*).

Sophia in Plato and Aristotle

We find the latter opinion expressed in the Greek philosopher Pythagoras (-570–495), who learnt the Egyptian language in Egypt,[96] and of whom the biographer Diogenes Laertius (180–240) reports to have said that "no man ought to be called wise, but only God."[97] Wisdom would then be a luring ideal that escapes the grip of the concrete human. Thus, the Greek *sophia,* which arguably became *philosophia*[98] later, seems more reflective than pragmatic. Though a human "skill," it rather mirrors something beyond ordinary human life, which should perhaps constitute the focus of "true cognition" under the synonymous names of "being" or "matter"[99] at individual, domestic, and international levels.

Like Pythagoras, the Greek philosopher Plato (-428–347) shows a great deal of epistemic closeness with ancient Egypt. He considers that wisdom is a Kemetic "way of life," that is, a culture (language, ideals and ideas, institutions, customs, acquired and lived experiences, knowledge, industry, etc.) through which children become "more alert and resourceful persons."[100] I underline the important Platonic observation that wisdom is tantamount to culture in ancient Egypt. Therein, unlike in Greece, wisdom (culture) trains the human mind from childhood, to become diligent and creative as it investigates matters, theoretical and practical.

Plato is quite critical vis-à-vis Greek education. He characterizes it as a "swinish stupidity," which makes him blush not only for himself, "but for Greeks in general."[101] Plato blushes over Greek education because he considers that it teaches calculation, elementary arithmetic, and geometry improperly. That is the reason behind his following recommendation: "So we should insist that gentlemen should study each of these subjects to at least the same level as very many children in Egypt, who acquire such knowledge at the same time as they learn to read and write."[102]

The Platonic propensity toward the Egyptian wisdom (way of life/culture) would explain his further caution that: "As for 'wisdom' ('*sophia*'), it signifies the grasp of motion. But it is rather obscure and non-Attic."[103] Where lies the said obscurity which makes wisdom non-Greek? One could hypothesize that it is the very etymology of the word *"sophia,"* which is problematic. The French linguist Pierre Chantraine (1899–1974) observes in his etymological dictionary of the Greek language that *sophia* has no Greek etymology.[104] But if we consider the precious Platonic idea that wisdom is the Egyptian "way of life," meaning the Egyptian culture, then the obscurity dissipates: culture is not a static given. Its contents (language, ideals and ideas, institutions, customs, acquired and lived experiences, knowledges, and industry, etc.) are rather processed, repetitively, or creatively, by each generation in its own historical context. That is how cultures evolve, stagnate, or regress.

For Plato still, wisdom is also the principle "of the world order," as well as a "system of social order."[105] It harmonizes the cosmos, just as it brings about social cohesion by tuning the individual's will and character to the social and cosmic choruses.[106] Such a sapient (cultural) adjustment requires a long time of maturation. This explains why wisdom is presumably attained by mature people, trained in "the good," and aged at least fifty.[107]

For the meantime, as we turn to another Greek philosopher, Aristotle (384–322 BCE), we find the very same view that wisdom is the peak of knowledge. Aristotle rightly suggests that "[. . .] philosophy should be called knowledge of the truth," the latter (truth) being the end of theoretical knowledge,[108] just as "the good" is for Plato. In the Aristotelian chain of causality, when the inquisitive mind regressively ascends the stairs of agential origins (material, formal, efficient, and final) to hit the primary unmoved "matter";[109] God, knowledge is achieved, and wisdom displayed. For Aristotle, assuredly, "[. . .] wisdom is knowledge about certain causes and principles."[110]

It follows, in Aristotle, that thinking the ultimate origin of things (God/wisdom), perceiving it clearly, and making it one's existential abode, is the goal of research. Such a possession determines one's intellectual and social ethics. In other words, wisdom is not to be regarded as hypostatized in a hollow and congealed series of isolated letters (w-i-s-d-o-m) with no practical consistence: it must rather guide and pacify communal human living, unless God be construed as a chaotic principle.

So, epistemology and ontology mirror ethics and conversely. The truth attained through scientific and philosophic means becomes the shared dwelling-place of epistemology and ethics. Consequently, the process of constant inquiry about what is essential to thought and action (wisdom, the good, or God), the search for what really matters and is of value for ourselves and the human community, turns into a refreshing spring that spurs our sapient nature as *Homo sapiens sapiens*, and makes our lives worth living, as Socrates (470–399 BCE) argues.[111] At this point, let us then examine the Afrosofian and Antadiopian epistemic paradigm.

WHAT IS A PARADIGM?

I define a paradigm as a sort of cognitive outlook which informs one's way of thinking, seeing, doing things, feeling, living, writing, speaking, or relating with one's living environment. etc. A paradigm is a sort of intellectual framework shaped by one's opinions, ideas and ideals, education, profession, aspirations, values, and existential blueprint (*mvende.)*[112] A paradigm determines the type of world (inclusive or exclusive) one wants to live in and bring about.

Now if, in my understanding, the essence of a paradigm consists, not in deteriorating, but rather in bettering geopolitical contexts, it means that a paradigm is existential, socially and geopolitically engaging. However, there are scholars like the French philosopher Edgar Morin, who tend to lean more on its speculative side. Morin considers, for example that *"un paradigme est un type de relation logique (inclusion, conjonction, disjonction, exclusion) entre un certain nombre de notions ou catégories maîtresses."*[113] But E. Morin is a complex thinker with an intricate perception of the mind's interconnection with reality.

In the above quote, he distinguishes four types of paradigms (inclusion, conjunction, disjunction, exclusion), which could also be collapsed into two: the exclusive and the inclusive. To the latter belongs Afrosofia.

Of Afrosofia

We have examined earlier the Antadiopian unitive epistemic paradigm through the theses of the monogenetic origin of the human species and the cultural unity of black nations, which both impact on the emergence and spread of civilization worldwide. That is the angle from which statements like Egypt is the distant mother of Western science and culture[114] should be understood. Additionally, as evidenced, for example, in *L'Unité Culturelle de l'Afrique Noire*[115] and *Les Fondements Ėconomiques et Culturels d'un Ėtat Fédéral d'Afrique Noire*,[116] CAD's scholarship reveals that black Afrikan and pharaonic Egyptian cultures can serve as reciprocal systems of reference.[117] What the author means by reciprocal systems of reference (*systèmes de référence réciproques*) is that Afrika explains ancient Egypt and conversely. Accordingly, the unity of Afrikan culture makes it possible to envision, as I will show in the fifth chapter, semantic connections between the Beti *sofia*, the Kemetic *sebayit*[118] and *Kheper* or *šopi* in Coptic, and the Walaf *sopi,* all five concepts expressing the idea of wisdom.

But before even moving to the fifth chapter, the following sections attempt to test CAD's foregoing theses by examining, from an endogenous perspective, the cultural and linguistic congruence or dissonance of what the Beti people say about themselves relatively to "Afrika," with a "k" at the end rather than a "c." What could have *sofia* meant to them, and how could it be interpreted today? Did the Beti forebears live with an "Afrikan" historical consciousness that could help the contemporary researcher enrich her understanding of the concept "Afrika?"[119] These are some of the questions that I will endeavor to answer through the compound concept "Afrosofia," using the Beti language and genealogy.

The term Afrosofia is coined from the particle "Afro," which stands for the Beti proper name Af(i)ri-Ka(ra)[120] or Afri-ka, and the common Beti substantive *sofia.* As seen in the last endnote of the previous paragraph, many semantic hypotheses have been propounded to decipher what the continental name Afrika could possibly mean. In tune with those theories describing Afrika as the sunny birthplace of humanity, the English writer Gerald Massey (1828–1907) argues that Afrika comes from the Egyptian word *af-rui-ka*, meaning "to turn toward the opening of the Ka," that is, toward a "Womb" or a birthplace. Accordingly, Afrika would mean "the birthplace."[121] Bearing in mind CAD's human monogenetic theory, confirmed once again by the discovery in 2001 of Toumai (Hope of Life)[122] in Chad, G. Massey's notion of Afrika as a home is convincing. The paleontological and genetic evidence shows thus far that Afrika is the cradle of sapient humanity.

For his part, the Afrikan-Cameroonian linguist and Egyptologist Pierre Oum Ndigi, who taught me Egyptology and influenced my orientation to Afrikan studies reveals, in his article *"Les sources égypto-nubiennes authentiques de l'unité africaine,"* that Afrika means "black,"[123] just like *kem*[124] in ancient Egyptian. The important point in Oum Ndigi's insight is the semantic correspondence between Afrika and the philosopheme "black" which, as evidenced in the present and subsequent chapters, is recurrent in CAD.

Like the other continents, Afrika is a vast spot of emerged telluric "matter" amidst watery matter. Her (in)visible "blackness," that is, her (un)seen deferral of self-revelation would suggest something enigmatic about the very nature of "matter" (starry, gross, or (sub)atomistic). As exemplified by the Milky Way in the infinite dark cosmic "sheet" above with its glaring stars,[125] matter confronts us with the haziness of visibility and cognoscibility regarding ourselves and the nature of things.[126] Perhaps we, humans, ought to see ourselves as puzzling microcosms (cosmoses in miniature) with the potential to illumine social life with the beam of our skills. *"L'Afrique noire"*[127] (black Afrika) reminds us of the etiological thread between humans. It is still toward a reconciled humanity to come that CAD's conciliatory epistemology points to.

Now, Af(i)ri Kara, in the Beti genealogy, is the name of the proto-ancestor who named the Afrikan continent after himself.[128] The idea of genealogy entails the dimension of origin, of "birthplace" underlined above by G. Massey. Af(i)ri Kara (Afrika), for the Beti people of Central Afrika, is the progenitor of humanity. As such, his descendants, contemporary humanity, should concern themselves with the fate of his legacy: Afrika-humanity. The reader could perhaps perceive and feel, at this juncture, the intricate cosmic and genetic connection that exists between her, the sun, and the birthplace, Afrika. What is the latter to her, the reader?

At a deeper level, one could say that Afrika is a federating concept that could bridge life segments (cosmic, telluric, and human) in the inquirer:

without the sun, telluric life (vegetal, animal, and human) would be illusory. The sun is the source of life on earth and is rightly sought by the Beti initiates to the "*so*" mysteries for its energy, as I observed earlier. They call it metaphorically *Tara* ("Father"). The sun being a vital source, identifying with it would mean furthering in deeds the coming of a different world where life is sought and valued; a world in which "*l'homme est un OUI vibrant aux harmonies cosmiques.*"[129] Having seen that Afiri-Kara, in the Beti genealogy, is the name of the proto-ancestor who named the Afrikan continent after himself, let us now proceed by examining its semantics in relation to us, concrete humans of the twenty-first century.

Afiri is a proper Beti name which literally means reverence, respect, self-reliance, confidence, or hope. In Afiri itself, we have the vocative "*a,*" which is a responsive affirmation of the self in a social context. The word *firi,* in turn, can be used either as a noun, or as a verb. When used as a substantive, *firi* refers to (char)coal, which is black. Used as a verb, *firi* conveys the respective meanings of trusting in, crushing, or grinding something.

Considering the geopolitical orientation of the present text, what could be of interest in the philosopheme Afiri is the notion of hope (resilient confidence): the type of militant hope that turns one's social life and daily activities (thinking, writing, reading, etc.) into a struggle for human dignity in this predatory world, all too cynical, unabatedly colonial-imperial.

As for the suffix *kara,* it literally refers to the crab, which is an amphibian crustacean known for its adaptability in water and land, and its trenchant protective pair of claws. In Kemet, *Kheper,*[130] the principle of mutation, transformation, and becoming in matter was represented by the scarab. Interpreted geo-economically, the *kara*-like characteristics of adjustment, transmutation, and self-defense could incite present-day oppressed humanity at large, and Afrikans (continental and diasporic) in particular, to become geopolitically more assertive *(kara-kara)*. How could Afrika, for example, retrieve her centeredness?

A sixth additional chapter to this work would show that the steps toward Afrika's agential recovery have been successively delineated, for example, by CAD,[131] Kwame Nkrumah (1909–1972),[132] and Théophile Obenga.[133] The three authors conjointly argue for the creation of one Afrikan federal state. Its task would consist in reconciling the continent with its vital and creative culture and shield it from the predatory imperial West and its indigenous satellites. That is how Afrika would hopefully defend humanity's geopolitical "health" (welfare), and stop its relentless waning by global corporations, the discriminatory "United" Nations' Security Council, the World Bank, and the "International" Monetary Fund (IFM) foxy policies.[134]

There are further semantic intricacies in the concept *kara.* It expresses one's discontent with unbearable situations, and the subsequent decision to confront them once and for all. In the context of present-day academy, *kara* could serve as a prospective category for curricular inclusiveness and diversity. It enjoins univers-(c)ities to become more global and multicultural in their approach to "knowledge." As the psychologist Edward Bruce Bynum rightly enjoins us, we would certainly be better off as inquirers when we enlarge our perspectives not only to "Rome, Paris, and Europe, but" also to "Alexandria, Abydos, and Egypt,"[135] and Tibet, Yaoundé, Baltimore, São Paulo, and more.

Furthermore, *kara* is a composite of *ka* and *ra.* The verb *ka* in Beti respectively means to liberate, to rescue, to help someone out. When used as a noun, it means either "sister" or "pangolin." Both notions are quite revealing: the term "sister" is relational. It conveys the ideas of familyhood, connection, kinship, affinity, and commonality between individuals. Additionally, when alive and at rest, a distinguishing feature of a pangolin is its spiraling shape. The pangolin rolls onto itself, as if instantiating the enneadic form of the Milky Way. By so doing, it encapsulates the antinomic principle of motion and rest expressed in the Hermopolitan *Noun.*[136]

It could then be said, from a numerological perspective, that the *ka* (pangolin) represents the enneadic unity of being in the expanding universe. As CAD puts it, writing from the perspective of Kemetic Arithmetic, 9 is indeed the number of the Heliopolitan ennead, that is, the eight primordial deities created by Ra, the demiurge himself.[137] The ennead (9) then encapsulates the following ogdoadic cosmos under Ra: Schou-Tefnut (air-water), Geb-Nut (earth-fire), Osiris-Isis (man-woman), Seth-Nephtys (sterile couple).

In Kemetic philosophy, the *ka* represents the immortal principle in the human being. There is no corporeal acting being without a *ka.* The *ka* confers "life" to the physical body as its empowering sibling, as its "double," its invisible "twin," or its "sister." The philosophical import from this analysis is the important connection between the *ka* and "life." Life is a sort of *ka*; it matters and must be valued. The time is certainly coming when wisdom lovers (philosophers) transmute into lovers of life in its multifarious forms (vegetal, animal, human). What is needed is a holistic (re)education in the art of living, that is, of nurturing life in and around oneself.

As I pointed out shortly, the concept *ka* in Beti does connote the notion of help. So, as will be argued in a moment by the Afrikan-Cameroonian theologian Engelbert Mveng (1930–1995), Afri-*ka* could rightly inspire and help us reconnect with the cosmic living whole. Our *ka* (life principle), if awakened through the initiation process (holistic education),[138] would align us with the cosmic energy breathed out by the demiurgic *atòm* Ra, whom the Beti name Ta-Ra.[139] For Mveng then, the initiation process transforms the initiate, making him

> *[. . .] le rendez-vous de toutes les forces vitales: il est le caillou, il est la rivière, il est l'océan, il est firmament, avec tout le flamboiement de l'armée des étoiles, il est bête des champs, il est oiseau du ciel, il est œil solaire et sourire nocturne de la lune. En l'homme, l'univers se fait biologiquement humain.*[140]

Now that we have an idea of the hermeneutic subtleties involved in the concept Afiri-Kara, it is also convenient to say a preliminary[141] word on the Beti telluric term *"sofia."* The latter concept has to do with human activities on nature though agriculture. Farming goes hand in hand with agronomic and astronomic knowledge because the nature of the soil, the luminosity, humidity, and the density of the ecosystem are the basics taken into consideration by any farmer. In the literal sense, *sofia* is the care with which the farmer handles her plantation to yield a bountiful harvest. In other words, *sofia* is a toilsome agrarian process toward the production of food, wealth, and economic prosperity. Farming is a technical activity enshrined in the knowledge of one's environment. The peasant's mind is restless until the purpose of her work is achieved.

On a deeper level, *sofia* requires good health of body and mind. *Sofia* could be assimilated to the activity of the creative mind within a specific context. The *sofia* agent (*mbo sofia*) must wrestle with the problems of her social environment. The peasant is familiar with her farming ecosystem, the weather, and the climate. She presumably knows what to grow, when and where to sow it, and the reason for its planting. The *mbo sofia* is a sort of environmentalist, a beautician of nature, a creator of what is lasting and productive: she perceives what must be weeded out of the farm and what is to be preserved, for a good harvest to ensue.

Furthermore, the "farm" that is to be cared for by the *mbo sofia* can be at once objective and subjective. At the objective level, the spatiality symbolized by the "farm" can be grasped as one's cultural productions (family, education, economy, military, politics, law, religion, health, entertainment, etc.). These are vital fields from which life-threatening discourses, policies, and practices must be weeded out through the trenchant epistemic sickle of *sofia*. Similarly, the space to be protected by the *mbo sofia* can be primarily interpreted as her ontological habitat (*maa)*[142] amidst threats of existential nihilism (Western arrogance and imperial barbarism).

So, as we are about to step into the third chapter dealing with the predicament of colonial alienation, the foregoing analysis on the Afrosofian and Antadiopian epistemic paradigm has endeavored to provide us with a broader etiological, unified, and teleological understanding of our historical trajectory as humans. CAD, a strong defender of scientific philosophy,[143] recounts our historical kinship from what is most intimate and hidden in us: our genes; hence his monogenetic theory of humanity.

Figure 2.1. The author in front of Cheikh Anta Diop's mausoleum in Caytu-Senegal. Photo taken by François Ngoa Kodena.

"What we know today," confirms the clinical psychologist E. Bruce Bynum, "is that the deep and shared memory of all peoples is rooted in our genetic and DNA inheritance. We are all permutations of that primogenitor of our species, the first *Homo sapiens sapiens*, the African."[144] But we are primarily offshoots of a cosmic evolution: we emerged from and live in a solar system within the Milky Way. These truths should urge us to explore more earnestly the organizing principle *(maa)*[145] behind the cosmos we live in, provided we *"sofia"* (weed out) the exclusivist colonial paradigm of our time and learn the spiraling[146] "language" of the universe and its organic implications. To live according to *maa* is perhaps what Th. Obenga drives at when he questions rhetorically: *"La vraie connaissance n'est-elle pas celle qui aboutit à la sagesse?"*[147]

NOTES

1. Théophile Obenga, *La philosophie africaine de la période pharaonique: 2780–330 avant notre ère* (Paris: L'Harmattan, 1990), 180: *"La vraie connaissance n'est-elle pas celle qui aboutit à la sagesse?"* From French: "Is true knowledge not that which leads to wisdom?"

2. I will be using the adjective "Antadiopian," instead of Diopian, to refer to Cheikh Anta Diop. There are actually many Diop in Senegal; Diop being a proper name. For the elementary meaning of the Beti concepts used throughout the text, the reader will fruitfully consult the following dictionary: Siméon Basile Atangana Ondigui, *Le Nouveau Dictionnaire Ewondo* (Condé-sur-Noireau (France): Les Éditions Terre Africaine, 2007).

3. As will be explained in the third chapter, it is the Antadiopian view that such a condition should be analyzed through a cultural spectrum, at once historical, psychological, and linguistic.

4. *Medu Neter* (the word of God) is the language of Kemet, ancient Egypt. We, the Beti people of central Afrika, call it *"Medzo me Nti,"* meaning "Divine Words." The name infers that language is the compressed form of all value. It is the means through which the human being and the universe itself eject being from themselves. Thus, the word *"adzo,"* participates in this creative process. It is an operation deriving from *Nti,* the creative agent. That is the reason why the word is *Nti*'s possession. *Nti* means "Lord," or "God."

5. Translation from French: "the most daring book ever written by a Negro and which, assuredly, will impact the awakening of Africa." See: Aimé Césaire, *Discours sur le Colonialisme* (Paris: Présence Africaine, 2004), 41.

6. This question is reminiscent of Countee Cullen's recurrent interrogation in his poem "Heritage." The Harlem renaissance poet Countee Cullen (1903–1946) meditatively questions: "what is Africa to me?" An intersubjective answer seems to be required, when he writes at the end of the third stanza, as if addressing an invisible interlocutor: "Stubborn heart and rebel head. Have you not yet realized You and I are civilized?" See: Alain Locke (Ed.), *The New Negro. Voices from the Harlem Renaissance* (New York: Touchstone Edition, 1997), 251.

7. That is, by examining the available historical data, such as the Sphinx of Giza, the pyramid and hieroglyphic texts, and the pyramids themselves. Such texts are presented and analyzed in Théophile Obenga, *La Philosophie Africaine de la Période Pharaonique: 2780–330 avant notre ère* (Paris: L'Harmattan, 1990).

8. Joaquin Miller (1837–1913) does indeed declare at the beginning of the fourth stanza of his poem "Africa": "Behold! The Sphinx is Africa." See: Joaquin Miller, "Africa." *Poetry Atlas.* Retrieved April 10, 2018. http://www.poetryatlas.com/poetry/poem/4501/africa.html. I suggest that Afrika, the Sphinx, be perceived as the concrete riddle of being, that is, as the hospitable host of all that is to be (re)discovered and explored. The ancient black Afrikan totemic Sphinx of Giza has a stony anomalous body, suggesting the idea that thought must be abiding and heteroclite in nature; at once opened to the existential, cosmographic, geo-ethical, and geopolitical hassles of human history. The Sphinx' "hospitality" is exercised in a telluric-sandy-luminous-airy-pyramidal locus, as if to insinuate the inherent heterogeneity of deep thought.

9. W. E. B. Dubois, *The Souls of Black Folk* (New York: Dover Publications, Inc., 1994), v. The phrase "color line" stands for racism or "white" supremacy, that is, the Caucasoid systemic prejudice against darker peoples in the United States of America and beyond.

10. Molefi Kete Asante, *Revolutionary Pedagogy. Primer for Teachers of Black Children* (Brooklyn, NY: Universal Write Publications LLC, 2017), 106.

11. Descartes does well to distinguish and endeavor to articulate the uniqueness of subjectivity in the acquisition of knowledge. Yet, there seems to be no recursion in his dualistic blueprint, since the subject, the thinking substance, or the *res cogitans* is somewhat estranged from the *res extensa*, the corporeal substance. One would have hoped to get enough room for cooperation and (retro)interactions in the thinking-body.

12. "Potential" because the scientific adventure is still at its threshold. The sub-atomic study of matter surely extends the comprehension of what could be expressed through the notion of "life."

13. The invisibility of the air that humans, animals, and plants breathe in and out is a good indication of something puzzling about their bodies. Besides, healing practices through silent meditation or mere energetic contact of the healer with a human sick-ened body in many spiritual traditions do suggest the existence of met(a)-empirical "strata" in the human body. There are also parapsychological phenomena such as apparitional experiences, clairvoyance, near-death experiences, precognition, rein-carnation, telepathy, and more, which hint at the trans-physicality of the human body.

14. Ahmes is the scribe who wrote the Rhind papyrus in the middle of the 17th CBCE.

15. Problem no. 14 of the Moscow Papyrus: Egypt Forever, "The Moscow Papy-rus." *Egypt Forever.* Retrieved April 12, 2018. http://www.egyptforever.hu/en/articles/about-ancient-egypt/the-moscow-papyrus.html. Mathematical knowledge was cer-tainly not meant to remain theoretical for the ancient Afrikans: it served in practical life, especially in engineering (the building of the pyramids, the Sphinx of Giza, or the numerous Kemetic temples visited by the French philologist Jean-François Cham-pollion (1790–1832) during his trip to Egypt and Nubia between 1828 and 1929. See: Jean-François Champollion, "Les Lettres écrites d'Égypte et de Nubie en 1828 et 1829." *Bibliothèque Nationale de France.* Retrieved April 12, 2018. https://www.sapili.org/livros/fr/gu010764.pdf..

16. Locality should be understood here more like a swerve: it can be ethical (ten-sional commitment of one's life to certain values and principles such as human dig-nity, benevolence, freedom, etc.), experiential and physical (related to "space-time"), as well as psychological (the case of empathy) and paradigmatic.

17. In the Beti cosmology, the bio-archetype "Eyo" is the generative Principle, which "vomits" all that is the universe from Itself. See: Grégoire Biyogo, *Adieu à Tsira Ndong Ndoutoume. Hommage à l'inventeur de la raison graphique du Mvett* (Paris: L'Harmattan, 2006), 67–68. I am primarily a Beti speaker. The Beti are a trans-national people living around the Equatorial regions of central Africa. Beti is the plural form of Nti.

18. Engelbert Mveng, "La symbolique dans l'art africain" in *Racines Bantu*, 201; cited by Mbog Bassong, *Les Fondements de la Philosophie Africaine* (Québec: Kiyikaat Editions, 2014), 50. From French: "Access to the symbolic language passes through the scientific knowledge of the world. The signification of the symbolic object is always an enriched signification, comprising an exterior and an inside. It is

a permanent move from the phenomenon to the noumenon. It is at the level of the noumenon that is located the proper terrain of the noumenon."

19. This notion of instrument will be explored in the fourth chapter, when examining the *mvettean* Antadiopian method. Suffice it, in the meantime, to say that the mvett is the struggle for life, that is, for immortality among the Ekang (the Beti). See: Tsira Ndong Ndoutoume, *Le Mvett. L'homme, la Mort et l'Immortalité* (Paris: L'Harmattan, 1993).

20. The nobility meant here is ethical. It implies decency and integrity. These virtues differ from the Nietzschean hierarchical and predatory socio-political nobility, of which he writes: "At the beginning, the noble caste was always the barbarian caste . . . these were the more complete human beings (which at every level also means the 'more complete beasts.')" See: Friedrich Nietzsche, *Beyond Good and Evil. Prelude to a philosophy of the Future,* 257.

21. I will come back to this notion of "matter" in the fourth chapter.

22. Frantz Fanon, *Peau noire, masques blancs* (Paris: Éditions du Seuil, 1952), 8. From French: "We consider that an individual must aim at assuming the universalism inherent to the human condition."

23. *Ibid.*, 6. From French: "Man is a vibrant YES to cosmic harmonies." Fanon adopts the cosmic principle of unity in diversity to address the enduring predicament of racism ("white" supremacy), which has imposed an existential deviation (alienation) on human interactions around the world over the past six centuries.

24. Consensual because they abide by the laws of motion as the 17th century German astronomer Johannes Kepler (1571–1630) has argued in his three laws of planetary motion. See: The Editors of Encyclopaedia Britannica, "Kepler's laws of planetary motion." *Encyclopaedia Britannica.* Retrieved April 13, 2018. https://www.britannica.com/science/Keplers-laws-of-planetary-motion.

25. The stars of our solar system are the following: Mercury, Venus, Earth, Mars, Jupiter, Saturn, Uranus, Neptune, and Pluto.

26. Frantz Fanon, *The Wretched of the Earth* (Trans. from the French by Richard Philcox, New York: Grove Press, 2004), lviii.

27. *Ibid.*, li.

28. *Ibid.*

29. *Ibid.*, lxi.

30. John Perkins, *The Secret History of the American Empire. The Truth About Economic Hit Men, Jackals, and How to Change the World* (New York: A Plume Book, 2008).

31. "Representative Democracy" is a fitting example of such hollow notions. The question is who "represents" whom and how does the representation come about? Are social categories (women, men, students, workers, farmers, traders, intellectuals, etc.) represented by their own colleagues or just by professional "politicians"? At any rate, the *demos* ("people") remains an ambiguous political and juridical category in so-called representative democracies. It presumably refers to the political body of a specific nation, which detains and exercises the *kratos* (power) of self-government through the processes of informed consenting delegation called "elections." But the "vote" is too often a mercantile and narcotic mechanism for plutocratic elites under

the mantle of political factions (religious sects, ethnic group(s), corporations, left/right parties, etc.) to rise to power. Once the electoral process is over, the "elected" minority, the rulers, can then juridically, economically, politically, and militarily lord over the former electorate through the vague constitutional "We" as "We the people." Such a masqueraded dictatorship (representative democracy) calls for a re-appropriation of alternative forms of governmental apparatuses such as the Afrikan bicameral version of direct democracy. See: Cheikh Anta Diop, *Les Fondements Économiques et Culturels d'un État Fédéral d'Afrique Noire* (Paris: Présence Africaine, 1974), 53–55. In this system, popular interdependent and decentralized congresses formed by women on the one hand, and men on the other, could co-run the country through constructive debates on specific and general socio-geopolitical issues at different geographic level.

32. Etikkrädet for Statens Pensjonsfond utland, "Recommendation to use the climate criterion to exclude ExxonMobil from the Government Pension Fund Global (GPFG)." *The Norwegian Climate Foundation.* Retrieved April 13, 2018. http://klimastiftelsen.no/wp-content/uploads/2017/03/Letter-to-Council-on-Ethics-Exxon-and-climate-change.pdf.

33. WikiLeaks, "The New Dirty War for Africa's uranium and mineral rights." *WikiLeaks.* Retrieved April 13, 2018. https://wikileaks.org/car-mining/..

34. Greenpeace France, "Africa's forests under threat: Socfin's plantations in Cameroon and Liberia." *Greenpeace.* Retrieved April 13, 2018. https://www.greenpeace.org/africa/Global/africa/publications/forests/2016/AFRICA%27S_FORESTS_UNDER_THREAT_1.pdf.

35. Jacques Derrida, *Rogues. Two Essays on Reason* (Trans. from the French by Pascale-Anne Brault and Michael Naas, Stanford, CA: Stanford University Press, 2005), 96–97.

36. *Ibid.*, lv.

37. *Ibid.*, lix.

38. Jean Ziegler, *Les vivants et la mort. Essai de sociologie* (Coll. Esprit, Paris: Seuil, 1975), 10. From French: "Henceforth, I perceive my culture of origin as enemy; I have embraced the African world as a long awaited woman."

39. In Kemetic cosmology, the dialectical union of the syzygy Seth and Nephtys represents the barren couple which introduced "evil" in human history, out of jealousy for the fertile proto-human couple Osiris and Isis (Adam and Eve), which generated the whole of humanity. See: Cheikh Anta Diop, *Civilisation ou Barbarie. Anthropologie sans Complaisance* (Paris: Présence Africaine, 1981), 390; John G. Jackson, *Christianity Before Christ* (Cranford, NJ: American Atheist Press, 2002), 106.

40. Frantz Fanon, *The Wretched of the Earth, op. cit.*, liii.

41. Frantz Fanon, *Peau noire, masques blancs, op. cit.*, 11.

42. Mbog Bassong, *Le Savoir Africain. Essai sur la théorie avancée de la connaissance* (Québec: Kiyikaat Editions, 2013), 42. From French: "Africa is a continent which overflows with the resource that wisdom is, so rarefied in us."

43. In West Afrika and in Arabic, the name "Cheikh" means leader, scholar, wise, learned, or full of wisdom.

44. Cheikh Anta Diop, *Civilisation ou Barbarie. op. cit.*

45. Cheikh Anta Diop, *Nations Nègres et Culture* (Paris: Présence Africaine, [1954] 1979), 22.

46. Martin Heidegger, *Being and Time* (Trans. from German by John Macquarrie & Edward Robinson, Oxford: Basil Blackwell, 1978), 2.

47. *Les conquérants* (the conquerors), a poem by the Cuban-born French poet José-Maria de Heredia (1842–1905), is a telling parable of the Western colonial imperial blueprint. See: José-Maria de Heredia, "Les Conquérants." *Étudeslittéraires.* Retrieved April 15, 2018. http://poesie.webnet.fr/lesgrandsclassiques/poemes/jose_maria_de_heredia/les_conquerants.html.

48. Gilles Deleuze & Félix Guattari, *A Thousand Plateaus. Capitalism and Schizophrenia* (Trans. from French by Brian Massumi, Minneapolis: University of Minnesota Press, 2001), 105.

49. *Ibid.*

50. Emmanuel Chukwedi Eze (Ed.), *Race and the Enlightenment. A Reader* (Malden, Massachusetts: Blackwell Publishers Inc., 1997).

51. Frantz Fanon, *Peau noire, masques blancs, op. cit*, 5. From French: "So? So, quietly, I answer that there are too many imbeciles on this earth."

52. The Beti concept *mvende* means "law" or "commandment." It also refers to that which is ontologically prior to anything else.

53. See CAD's analysis of parapsychology in *Civilisation ou Barbarie, op. cit.*, 465–76.

54. *Ibid.*, 467.

55. Such interactions concern energy mediating particles called "bosons" like quarks (top and bottom, up and down, and charm and strange) and leptons (electron and electron neutrino, muon and muon neutrino, and tau and tau neutrino).

56. Placide Tempels, *Bantu Philosophy* (Paris: Présence Africaine, 1969), 97.

57. Théophile Obenga, *La Philosophie Africaine de la Période Pharaonique, op. cit.*, 511. For Obenga, Pharaonic black Egyptian astronomy aimed at identifying human cognition with the force and power of the sun, upon which life on earth is predicated.

58. Mbog Bassong, *La Religion Africaine. De la Cosmologie Quantique à la Symbolique de Dieu* (Québec: Kiyikaat Editions, 2013), 32.

59. The Beti initiates in the *So* mysteries outstretch their hands toward the sun shouting *"Tara!"* ("Father!"). By calling the sun their "Father," the Beti initiates express their will to become sun-like, that is, to identify with its strength and power upon which life on earth is predicated. See: Philippe Laburthe-Tolra, *Initiations et Sociétés Secrètes au Cameroun. Essai sur la religion beti* (Paris: Karthala, 1985), 37. On the *So* mysteries themselves, read pages 229–326 of this same book.

60. The physicist CAD observes that "matter," in our solar system, ordinarily presents itself as a "void" that can hardly be seen by the naked eye. See: Cheikh Anta Diop, *Civilisation ou Barbarie, op. cit.*, 394. It is the case, for example, with Sirius' invisible companion called *põ tolo* in Dogon astronomy, or *tolo* among the Beti. During my 2016–2017 field research in Senegal and Cameroon, my mother Augustine Ngono often tutored me, as we beheld the starry firmament at night, on how the "white" invisible dwarf star *tolo,* and sets of other stars, could impact the inner

functioning of the human body. The Beti verb *tole* means to burst or to explode. This explains, perhaps, why *tolo* (an explosive?) affects the human body with its invisible "energetic" blasts, as my mother explained to me. Tolo is also a Beti proper name. On the Beti astronomic *tolo*: Philippe Laburthe-Tolra, *Initiations et Sociétés Secrètes au Cameroun, op. cit.*, 37.

61. Frantz Fanon, *Peau noire, masques blancs, op. cit.,* 188. From French: "O my body, make of me always a man who questions!"

62. *Ibid.*, 102. From French: "That is because for us the body is not something opposed to what you call the mind."

63. *Ibid.*, "I espouse the world! I am the world!"

64. *Ibid.*, 91. From French: "All I wanted was to be a man among other men."

65. Frantz Fanon, *A Dying Colonialism* (New York: Grove Press, INC., 1965).

66. *Ibid.*, 130.

67. *Ibid.*, 103.

68. Walter D. Mignolo, *Local Histories/Global Designs. Coloniality, Subaltern Knowledges, and Border Thinking* (Princeton, NJ: Princeton University Press, 2000).

69. Cheikh Anta Diop, *Civilisation ou Barbarie, op. cit.*, 477. In French: *"l'ère d'une humanité véritable, d'une nouvelle perception de l'homme sans coordonnées ethniques."*

70. Cheikh Anta Diop, *Antériorité des Civilisations Nègres. Mythe ou Vérité Historique?* (Paris: Présence Africaine, 1993), 12. In French: "*La conscience de l'homme moderne ne peut progresser réellement que si elle est résolue à reconnaître explicitement les erreurs d'interprétations scientifiques, même dans le domaine très délicat de l'Histoire, à revenir sur les falsifications, à dénoncer les frustrations de patrimoines.*"

71. Théophile Obenga, *La philosophie africaine de la période pharaonique op. cit.*, 180. From French: "Is true knowledge not that which leads to wisdom?"

72. The phenotype *"Nègre"* (Negro) describes, in CAD, " . . . *un être humain dont la peau est noire, à plus forte raison quand il a les cheveux crépus.*" From French: " . . . a human being whose skin color is black, even more so when his hair is curled," meaning spiral in shape. See: *Nations Nègres et Culture, op. cit.*, 207. More importantly, as will be shown in the fourth chapter (on the Afrosofian-Antadiopian methodology), the category of *Nègre* is equally epistemologically pregnant in CAD. He reads it historically and turns it into a "*concept scientifique opératoire*" ("operative scientific concept"), that is, a factual trigger toward the awakening of the Afrikan and worldwide historical consciousness. See: *Civilisation ou Barbarie, op. cit.,* 10. This perspective would explain the black color on most covers of the Antadiopian works, as well as the representation of human phenotypes on the covers of *Nations Nègres et Culture* and *Parenté Génétique de L'Égyptien Phaaraonique et des Langues Négro-Africianes* (IFAN-Dakar: Les Nouvelles Éditions Africaines, 1977).

73. Cheik Anta Diop, *Civilisation ou Barbarie, op. cit.*, 37. See also: Abdias Do Nascimento & Elisa Larkin Nascimento, *Africans in Brazil. A Pan-African Perspective* (Trenton, NJ: Africa World Press, Inc., 1992); Ivan Van Sertima, *They Came Before Columbus. The African Presence in Ancient America* (New York: Random House, 2003); Christopher Stringer & Robin McKie, *African Exodus. The Origins of Modern Humanity* (New York: Henry Holt and Company, Inc., 1996).

74. Cheikh Anta Diop, *Civilisation ou Barbarie, op. cit.*, 14.

75. *Ibid.*, 25. As a trained chemist (with two diplomas in general and applied chemistry) and physicist, CAD creates, from 1961–3, the first radiocarbon 14 laboratory in black Afrika at the IFAN (*Institut Fondamental d'Afrique Noire*), which is located in the CAD Dakarian university.

76. *Ibid.*, 58–69. The Aurignacian culture of the Negroid of Grimaldi in Europe (Meridional France and Spain probably) concerns the first lithic industry of the European upper Paleolithic. *Ibid.*, 25, 71. It will be instructive for further research, to date my finds (Figures at the end of chapter V) through carbon 14, to see whether they belong to the Paleolithic or Neolithic Age. At any rate, such dating will provide a further grasp of the lithic industry of the Negroid Afrikan Grimaldi.

77. The geographic mutation of the Afrikan Negroid Grimaldi to the Europoid Cro-Magnon accounts for CAD's Two-Cradle Theory: the Afrikan sedentary and matriarchal cradle and the European nomadic and patriarchal cradle. See: Cheikh Anta Diop, *Antériorité des Civilisations Nègres, op. cit.*, 117–93; and *L'Unité Culturelle de l'Afrique Noire* (Paris: Présence Africaine, 1982). But it is not my purpose to examine these two cradles at this point.

78. Cheikh Anta Diop, *Nations Nègres et Culture*, *op. cit.*, 204–335.

79. Cheikh Anta Diop, *Antériorité des Civilisations Nègres. op. cit.*

80. Cheikh Anta Diop, *Parenté Génétique de L'Égyptien Phaaraonique et des Langues Négro-Africianes, op. cit.*

81. Cheikh Anta Diop, *op. cit.*

82. Cheikh Anta Diop, *L'Unité Culturelle de L'Afrique Noire* (Paris: Présence Africaine, 1982).

83. The second chapter will examine the Antadiopian interrogation on the Afrikan renaissance.

84. Cheikh Anta Diop, *Parenté Génétique de L'Égyptien Phaaraonique et des Langues Négro-Africianes, op. cit.*, xxv. In French: *"Le walaf, l'égyptien et les autres langues africaines dérivent d'une langue mère commune que l'on peut appeler le paléo-africain, l'africain commun ou le Négro-africain de L. Homberger ou de Th. Obenga."* See: Théophile Obenga, *Origine Commune de l'Egyptien Ancien, du Copte et des Langues Negro-Africaines Modernes. Introduction à la Linguistique Historique Africaine* (Paris: L'Harmattan, 1993), 9.

85. Arnaiz-Villena et al., "HLA genes in Macedonians and the Sub-Saharan Origin of the Greeks" in *Tissue Antigens* (No. 57, 2001), 118–27.

86. Jean-Claude Mboli holds the view that the proto-Indo-European and the proto-Semitic should be considered as forms of Creoles, whose lexical base is Negro-Egyptian. See: Jean-Claude Mboli, *Origine des Langues Africaines* (Paris: L'Harmattan, 2010), 612.

87. Cheikh Anta Diop, *Civilisation ou Barbarie, op. cit.*, 431, 450, 453.

88. *Ibid.*

89. Cheikh Anta Diop, *Antériorité des Civilisations Nègres. op. cit.*, 12.

90. Mary Lefkowitz, *Not Out of Africa. How Afrocentrism became an excuse to teach myth as history* (New York: BasicBooks, 1996). Despite the Eurocentric orientation of this work, it is nonetheless interesting in that it discusses the scholarship of

those that Professor Lefkowitz indistinctively calls "extreme Afrocentrists," "Afrocentrist," and "Afrocentric" writers on pages 1, 2, 5–11, 14, etc. The book also evokes relevant philosophic categories such as "black Africa," "history," "myth," "evidence," and more. The following works are essential for a fair grasp of the Afrocentric paradigm: Molefi Kete Asante, *Afrocentricity. The Theory of Social Change* (Chicago: African American Images, 2003) and Ama Mazama (Ed.), *The Afrocentric Paradigm* (Trenton, NJ: Africa World Press, Inc., 2003).

91. These are politics of cognitive geographies, which either consolidate the expansion of human consciousness through autodidactic ongoing (in)formation or quenches the fire of human understanding through cultural alienation. The latter process leads to a gradual menticide (brainwashing) in social agents. See: Tom Burrell, *Brainwashed. Challenging the Myth of Black Inferiority* (New York: SmileyBooks, 2010); Makhily Gassama (Dir.), *L'Afrique répond à Sarkozy. Contre le discours de Dakar* (Paris: Éditions Philippe Rey, 2008).

92. The concept *atóm*, in Beti, literally refers to a tree that produces edible sweet small black fruits called *tóm*. Interestingly enough, the English actions of jumping, leaping, or jerking are expressed in Beti by the verb *tom,* which also means, in the injunction *"Tom nyõl!"* be alert, brave, and courageous! *Atóm* can then rightly be understood, in the philosophical sense, as the Principle of becoming, action, and motion. This intuition would then clarify the puzzle raised by Socrates about the non-Attic word "wisdom," ("*sophia*" in Greek). He wonders why wisdom "signifies the grasp of motion." See: Plato, *Cratylus*, 412b. Mbog Bassong hypothesizes that the Kemetic generative concept Atum was Grecized as *atomos*, through epistemological contamination. See: Mbog Bassong, *Le Savoir Africain: Essai sur la théorie avancée de la connaissance* (Québec: Kiyikaat Editions, 2013), 21. Bassong's explanation seems plausible when we consider Th. Obenga's view that Atum (Ra), is a demiurgic emanation from a flux of free atoms called by the enigmatic name of "Noun" by the ancient Egyptians. See: Th. Obenga, *La Philosophie Africaine de la Période Pharaonique. 2780–330 avant notre ère* (Paris: L'Harmattan, 1990), 32. I give a material "portrait" of the inceptive "matter" on Figure 5.8.

93. Plato, *Republic, IV*, 445c and VII, 540a. Plato understands the "good" as the form of forms. It is the inner constitution, or the model of order in the philosopher.

94. I will elaborate on them in the fifth chapter.

95. Online Etymology Dictionary, "Philosophy." *Online Etymology Dictionary*. Retrieved, April 20, 2018. https://www.etymonline.com/search?q=wisdom.

96. Diogenes Laertius, *The Lives and Opinions of Eminent Philosophers*, Book VIII.3.

97. *Ibid.*, Book I.8.

98. *Ibid.*

99. Cheikh Anta Diop, *Civilisation ou Barbarie, op. cit.*, 429 and 462.

100. Plato, *Republic*, VII, 819c.

101. Plato, *Laws*, VII, 819d–e.

102. *Ibid.*, 819b.

103. Plato, *Cratylus,* 412b.

104. Pierre Chantraine, *Dictionnaire étymologique de la langue grecque. Histoire des mots* (Paris: Éditions Klincksieck, 2009), 1162.

105. Plato, *Timaeus,* 24b–c & *Republic,* VII, 540a–b.

106. Plato is a lover of music, rhythm, and harmony, which he connects to the Egyptian religion. See: *Ibid*., 798d–799b.

107. Plato, *Republic,* VII, 540a.

108. Aristotle, *Metaphysics*, A2, 993b, 20–21.

109. Aristotle defends the unknowability of "matter" (sensible or intelligible) in itself. See: *Ibid.,* Z7, 1036a, 8.

110. *Ibid*., A1, 982a, 1–2.

111. Plato, *Apology*, 38a.

112. In Beti, *mvende* literally means "law." The law plays a fuse-like function in society, influencing the various actual and potential interactions of its members. So, the law aims at being both circumstantial and proactive.

113. Edgar Morin, *Introduction à la pensée complexe* (Paris: Éditions du Seuil, 2005), 147. From French: "A paradigm is a type of logical relationship (inclusion, conjunction, disjunction, exclusion) between a certain number of notions or key categories."

114. Cheikh Anta Diop, *Civilisation ou Barbarie, op. cit.,* 12. These are CAD's words: *"l'Ėgypte est la mère lointaine de la science et de la culture occidentales."*

115. Cheikh Anta Diop, *L'Unité Culturelle de l'Afrique Noire* (Paris: Présence Africaine, [1959] 1982).

116. Cheikh Anta Diop, *Les Fondements Ėconomiques et Culturels d'un Ėtat Fédéral d'Afrique Noire* (Paris: Présence Africaine, [1960] 1974).

117. Cheikh Anta Diop, *Antériorité des Civilisations Nègres, op. cit.,* 12. In French: "*peuvent servir de systèmes de référence réciproques*."

118. Théophile Obenga, "Egypt: Ancient History of African Philosophy" in Kwasi Wiredu (Ed.), *A Companion to African Philosophy* (Malden, MA: Blackwell Publishing Ltd, 2004), 33–35.

119. Many linguistic perspectives attempt to unravel the meaning of the concept "Afrika." It is the case, for example, with the Greek and Latin adjectives *"aphrike"* (without cold) and *"aprica"* (sunny), both conveying the convergent idea of the sunny environment that continental Afrika actually is. The epithet "Alkebu-lan" (Mother of humanity) is also said to have been used by indigenous populations (Nubians, Ethiopians, Moors, etc.) to refer to Afrika. See: Wikipedia, "Africa." *Wikipedia The Free Encyclopedia.* Retrieved May 3, 2018. https://en.wikipedia.org/wiki/Africa.

120. Marie-Rose Abomo-Maurin, *Les pérégrinations des descendants d'Afri Kara* (Paris: L'Harmattan, 2012).

121. Website, *op. cit.*

122. Toumaï is the oldest known human ancestor. The name Toumaï comes from the local Daza language of Chad in Central Afrika. See: Wikipedia, "Sahelanthropus." *Wikipedia, The Free Encyclopedia*. Retrieved May 3, 2018. https://en.wikipedia.org/wiki/Sahelanthropus. Before Toumaï, Lucy was discovered in Ethiopia in 1974.

123. https://www.pambazuhka.org/fr/governance/les-sources-égypto-nubiennes-authentiques-de-lunité-africaine. Retrieved: June 13, 2017.

124. Cheikh Anta Diop, *Nations Nègres et Culture, op. cit.*, 277.

125. Edward Bruce Bynum, *Dark Light Consciousness. Melanin, Serpent Power, and the Luminous Matrix of Reality* (Rochester, VT: Inner Traditions, 2012).

126. I will discuss the notion of matter in the fifth chapter, since it traverses the entire history of philosophic thought from Afrikan ancient Egypt with the notion of the Noun, through Greco-Roman atomism with Democritus, Epicurus, or Lucretius' *The Nature of things* (Trans. A. E. Stallings, New York: Penguin Books, 2007).

127. Cheikh Anta Diop, *Les Fondements Économiques et Culturels d'un État Fédéral d'Afrique Noire* (Paris: Présence Africaine, [1960] 1974); *L'Unité Culturelle de L'Afrique Noire* (Paris: Présence Africaine, 1982).

128. Marie-Rose Abomo-Maurin, *Les pérégrinations, op. cit.*, 7.

129. Frantz Fanon, *Peau noire, masques blancs, op. cit.*, 6. From French: "Man is a vibrant YES to cosmic harmonies." Fanon adopts the cosmic principle of unity in diversity to address the enduring predicament of racism ("white" supremacy), which has imposed an existential deviation (alienation) on human interactions around the world over the past six centuries.

130. Cheikh Anta Diop, *Civilisation ou Barbarie, op. cit.*, 450.

131. Cheikh Anta Diop, *Les Fondements Économiques et Culturels d'un État Fédéral d'Afrique Noire, op. cit.*

132. Kwame Nkrumah, *Africa Must Unite* (London: Heinemann, 1963).

133. Théophile Obenga, *L'État Fédéral d'Afrique Noire. La Seule Issue* (Paris: L'Harmattan, 2012).

134. Birgit Brock-Utne, *Whose Education for All? The Recolonization of the African Mind* (New York: Falmer Press, 2000). See also John Perkins' two books, *Confessions of an Economic Hit Man* (New York: Plume, 2004); and *The Secret History of the American Empire* (New York: Plume, 2008).

135. Edward Bruce Bynum, *Dark Light Consciousness. Melanin, Serpent Power, and the Luminous Matrix of Reality* (Rochester, VT: Inner Traditions, 2012), 7.

136. Cheikh Anta Diop, *Civilisation ou Barbarie, op. cit.*, 446.

137. *Ibid.*, 440–441. In French: *"le 9 est bel et bien le chiffre de l'ennéade héliopolitaine, c'est-à-dire des huit divinités primordiales créées par Ra, le démiurge lui-même,."*

138. Philippe Laburthe-Tolra, *Initiations et Sociétés Secrètes au Cameroun. Essai sur la religion beti* (Paris: Karthala, 1985). For the initiate that the writer is, the initiation process culminates in one's identification with the "cosmic eye," *Tara*, the sun. The initiate learns that he is primarily a creator of life like *Tara*, before defending it in concrete social situations.

139. *Ibid.*, 37.

140. Engelbert Mveng, *L'art d'Afrique noire. Liturgie cosmique et langage religieux* (Yaoundé: Clé, 1994), 39. From French: " . . . the rendezvous of all vital forces: he is the pebble, he is the river, he is the ocean, he is the firmament, with all the flare of the army of stars, he is beasts in the fields, he is birds in the sky, he is solar eye and nocturnal smile of the moon. In the human being, the universe becomes biologically human."

141. The fifth chapter will deal with the concept and the practice of *sofia* in human history.

142. The Beti concept *maa* literally means "luck," "blessing," or "happiness." The Afrikan-Congolese philosopher Théophile Obenga understands it as "the real," "reality," that is, that which is genuine and authentic as opposed to artificial or spurious. See: Théophile Obenga, "Egypt: Ancient History of African Philosophy," in Kwasi Wiredu (Ed.), *A Companion to African Philosophy* (Malden, MA: Blackwell Publishing Ltd, 2004), 47.

143. Cheikh Anta Diop, *Civilisation ou Barbarie, op. cit.*, 475–76.

144. Edward Bruce Bynum, *Dark Light Consciousness, op. cit.*, 11.

145. I will elaborate on this concept in the fifth chapter.

146. Spiraling forms are present in the human body (DNA, fetus, Afro-textured hair, etc.) as well as in nature (Milky Way, pangolins, snails, and more).

147. Théophile Obenga, *La philosophie africaine de la période pharaonique, op. cit.*, 180. From French: "Is true knowledge not that which leads to wisdom?"

Chapter 3

Kara Olere

Up From Colonial Aliénation!

Deep questions are compelling. With finesse, they mobilize the inquiring mind toward a restless quest for answers. Thus, as I start knitting this contentious chapter on colonial *aliénation*, I raise anew Césaire's following biting query, and echo his subsequent serious warning to contemporary global imperial powers spearheaded by the United States these past decades:

> *Où veux-je en venir? À cette idée: que nul ne colonise innocemment, que nul non plus ne colonise impunément; qu'une nation qui colonise, qu'une civilisation qui justifie la colonisation—donc la force—est déjà une civilisation malade, une civilisation moralement atteinte, qui, irrésistiblement, de conséquence en conséquence, de reniement en reniement, appelle son Hitler, je veux dire son châtiment.*[1]

The second chapter has attempted to tool us with an inclusive (cosmic) epistemological blueprint, doubly articulated: the Afrosofian, and the Antadiopian. The argument was about underscoring the implicative practicality of *sofia,* which demands the active deployment of the sapient practitioner *(mbo sofia)* in her lived world, from a generative *sens,*[2] ethical in meaning, social and geopolitical in scope. The *mbo sofia*'s struggle for a shared life (mineral, vegetal, animal), I argued, must prevail over death (human failure to perceive and advocate human and cosmic oneness). That was the substance of the inclusive paradigm. As I will emphasize in the subsequent chapters, generativity is about the donation of qualitative life through one's inner ascent and intimate communication with Eyo, the birthing *Atòm* (Principle).

This third chapter deepens the preceding paradigm. As we gradually proceed in the analysis, it will become clearer that the chapter defends the inalienability of human culture and dignity, so reified by the current geopolitical dispensation, analyzed, and denounced with verve in the Antadiopian epistemology through the category of colonial *aliénation*. The latter is captured in the above title by the phrase *kara olere*.

After exploring the separate and mutual subtleties of the two locutions that I just enunciated, namely colonial[3] *alienation* and *kara olere*, the chapter challenges us to introspect, psycho-analyze our life and writing *à la* Plotinus, ultimately "act as does the creator of a statue that is to be made beautiful."[4] We are here in a reflective process, whereby the *mbo sofia*'s inclusive blueprint presumably illumines her multifarious interactions with herself and the outer world through writing.

Though apparently idyllic, the Plotinian beautifying vision orients us toward an inward aesthetic-ontological, anthropological, and geopolitical peak from which we can gauge the *sens* (meaning, direction, and *telos*) of our epistemic acts such as perceiving, interpreting, listening, feeling, writing, reading, thinking, seeing, etc. The axis of our discussion, however, will be the following important question raised by CAD in 1948: "*Pourquoi et pour qui écrivons -nous?*"[5] The inquiry is undertaken within the general framework of a pertinent article titled: "*Quand pourra-t-on parler d'une renaissance africaine?*,"[6] which will be the mainstay of an elaborate chapter in my future research.

WHAT IS *KARA OLERE*?

In the second chapter, I dealt with the morpheme "kara," as I explained the compound concept Afro-sofia. I argued that "Afro" is an abbreviation of the anthroponym "Afiri Kara," who is the eponymous forebear who named the Afrikan continent after himself.[7] However, the Beti[8] genealogy connects Afiri Kara himself to Ma'a Ngô[9] the Proto-ancestor of sapient humanity, explaining: "*Afiri Kara 'qui a donné son nom à l'Afrique' est le fils de Kara Kuba, fils de Kuba Ta, fils de Ta Ma'a, fils de Ma'a Ngô 'qui est le père de la race nègre.*'"[10]

Though it is not my purpose here to undertake an in-depth interpretation of the various Beti philosophemes enumerated in the above quote, it is important, nonetheless, to cursorily stress their semantic elongation. Of course, the semantic stratum itself must be grasped as being constitutive of a larger cultural complex; at once trans-genealogical, ethical, mythical, and ontological. As will be made explicit in the chapter, humanity and the cosmic whole are both predicated upon the timeless generative *Atòm* (Principle of principles) Eyo. Accordingly, to be human would mean to be not only in connection, but most importantly in harmony with Eyo, by emulating Her in thought, speech, and behavior. What is Eyo's activity? Eyo "vomits" or "spits out" (*yo)* life,[11] and so should Her closest "shadow," the sapient human. That is the ethical ascent inferred in the quote closing the previous paragraph, and which I now clarify.

1. Afiri Kara[12] literally means "Hopeful Resilient." This category seems to prescribe an attitude of hope and resilience to humans, whenever they are faced with choking constraints such as imperialism and colonialism in their historical trajectory. What is needed in such ontological divagations, is a tenacious will in the struggle to bring about a more humane existential paradigm.
2. Kara Kuba[13] stands for "Resilient Fount." It is a philosopheme that could represent one's endeavor to "spread out" (promote and achieve) certain ideals and goals in life.
3. Kuba Ta[14] signifies "Sprinkler Spreader" or Nation Builder. This name connotes a patriotic inclination and existential blueprint in its bearer.
4. Ta Ma'a means the Home of Blessings/Happiness.
5. Ma'a[15] Ngô designates the Blessed Merciful.

These genealogical anthroponyms suggest something profoundly trans-physical and cultural about the interconnection between language, axiology, epistemology, history, and the becoming truly human of their respective bearers. There is an ontology (worldview) of lineage immersion that gives meaning to language and naming, here understood as existentially programmatic. It means that names are sorts of "hyphens" that connect their bearers to the abiding reality Eyo. Thus, the philosopheme Afiri Kara ultimately leads to Ma'a Ngô, and to Eyo, the blueprint of a full-grown human. Afiri Kara becomes like a philosophical imperative, an existential "must" to actualize the human fundamental make-up, which is harmony with Eyo.

Writing or constructing knowledge, from this line of thought, comes down to enhancing and mediating Life (Eyo), and not distancing oneself from It or threatening It in a *kara olere* (scorpion-like) manner. Presumably, that is what Af(i)ri-Ka(ra)n (Afrikan) writers endeavor to do as they imprint their thoughts through visual symbols such as words, graphs, pictograms, or ideograms on physical matters (human body, paper, cloth, aircraft, rock, etc.). They use the enlivening cultural[16] layer of language to channel their epistemic paradigm (inclusive/exclusive). This makes language, in academia, a privileged path which leads writers and readers alike to the ontological, ethical, and semantic vicinities of concepts, especially when used creatively.

So, all language being epistemic[17] in the quest for knowledge, the plurality of linguistic media within humanity presents the academy, if inclusive in outlook, with an overwhelming wealth of graphic, phonetic, semantic, and philosophic nuances and perspectives. Such is not the case, regrettably, in colonial contexts, where the invader's language(s) choke the local public sphere, including the education system and academia. That is the general geopolitical dispensation in which Pan-Afrika,[18] in particular, has been trapped before and after the colonial inter-European 1884–1885 Berlin Conference.

Such a linguicide, I call *kara olere,* which is the Beti word for the scorpion. Contrary to the edible and nutritious (life-enhancing) *kara* (crab), the *kara olere* (scorpion) is poisonous and shunned. It can sting and kill its prey, once poisoned. Metaphorically speaking, a *kara olere* infrastructure, person, or language is understood as highly harmful or deadly. The scorpion-like language of the colonial system cannibalizes subdued ones, alienating and ostracizing the latter from the public life (educative, administrative, economic, etc.) of the nation.

KARA OLERE AND LINGUICIDE

I had a *kara olere* lived experience with European languages (English and French) languages in elementary school. Afrikan languages were censured and silenced on campus, where they could only be whispered furtively, if we were to escape the symbols; derisive necklaces aimed at making us culturally Afrophobic and psychologically Europhile. Neither promoted, appreciated, nor even tolerated by the system, our languages were blatantly mirrored to us as vile "patois" to be dropped outside the school fence in the morning and picked up in the evening on our way back home, if necessary.

To speak "patois" was construed in the school milieu as an affront to the normative English and French. Such a challenge was censured by a scornful "necklace"; a symbol. As we joined secondary school, we were to add either German or Spanish to the two "official" languages spoken throughout Kam-Heru/Kamalon (Cameroon). That is how I came to learn German.

It was obvious to us then, that for obscure reasons, the neocolonial school disdained us, and yet seemed to need us. Quite precociously, many classmates like Mengue, Kom, or Bell, unmasked some macabre project behind the school complex: it covertly attempted to make us exclusively Europhile and Europhone, thereby bleaching our Afrikan memory (existential paradigm, ideals, conception and purpose of life, etc.). By so doing, the neocolonial school crippled the "promotion of research, science, and technology in Afrikan languages."[19] It aimed at bastardizing the latter. And yet, just like the Afrikan-Kenyan writer Ngũgĩ wa Thiong'o, we somewhat knew that "memory resides in language and is clarified by language."[20] This probably explains why some schoolmates cherished *l'école buissonnière,* heartily skipping school.

Looking at our predicament retrospectively, it is my sense that, since the colonial school paralyzed our Afrophone self-exploration and expression, it sowed the germs of its stagnation and eventual demise in the long run. It purposely failed to boost the endogenous background of young inquisitive minds, certainly hoping that we should alienate ourselves from the culture of self-love and knowledge handed to us by our parents in our respective homes.

But the zest of independence that blew over Afrika, America, and Asia from the 1960s onward was too fresh in our minds. Around the 1980s, "*Indépendance Cha Cha*" of the Afrikan-Kongolese Joseph Kabasele Tshamala was still the musical "hit" of the day, expressive and soaring. Besides, we regularly heard from our parents about the anti-colonial struggle of freedom fighters such as Ruben Um Nyobe, Patrice Lumumba, Kwame Nkrumah, Malcolm X, Steve Biko, and many others. We had been for a long time under siege and yet, our parents were faced with the awkward quandary of enrolling us in the neo-colonial school. It was, in the words of the Afrikan-Senegalese writer Cheikh Hamidou Kane, an *aventure ambiguë*[21] ("ambiguous adventure") we embarked on, leading either to our liberation, or to our perdition. We could liberate ourselves by reclaiming our Af(r)i-ka(ra)n (Afrikan) culture of oneness and ongoing dialogue with Eyo, the enlivening Whole, and Her concrete manifestations in culture and nature. The obverse perspective consisted in alienating and distancing ourselves from Eyo, subsequently undergoing an ontological dislocation, and adopting an attitude of animosity vis-à-vis ourselves and otherness.

The neocolonial school system in Kam-Heru/Kamalon (Cameroon) and beyond fostered this second attitude. Perhaps it feared that curricular and linguistic diversity in academic institutions might jeopardize the socio-political cohesion and stability of neocolonial nations. Presumably, the danger could be that every linguistic community become insular, and perhaps claim its independence from the rest of the nation. But this argument is somewhat weak, considering the precolonial existence of pluri-linguistic Afrikan nations and empires (Mali, Ghana, Songhai, Ndongo, etc.). Additionally, as CAD rightly observes, Europe does not think its unity based on its monolingualism; Europe is rather a conglomerate of at least "*360 langues et dialectes*"[22] (languages and dialects). So, autochthonous languages are not a setback to national cohesion, unless they are construed and instrumentalized as such for geo-economic and political reasons. This reasoning is even more pertinent when we consider the cultural unity binding Pan-Afrikan nations together.[23]

The real fear of the neocolonial regime, one might suspect, is that the adoption of a transcultural education possibly ousts the normative dictatorship of linguistic tycoons such as English, French, Portuguese, Spanish, and more. For these reasons and similar ones, ongoing worldwide linguicides appear as the safest way to cosmetic unity. Such a unity is cosmetic because what lies behind the above views, is surely the will to cultural stagnation and alienation. *Stricto sensu,* it is neither cultures nor languages (*minkòbò* in Beti), *per se*, which threaten domestic and geopolitical peace. As I will contend shortly, what disrupts and destroys human relationships and pollutes our psycho-physical environment is rather cultural *aliénation,* carried out through the holocaust of colonialism.

From the historical standpoint, languages are genealogical and genetic. In comparing them synchronically and diachronically with one another as the linguists CAD,[24] Théophile Obenga,[25] or Jean-Claude Mboli[26] have respectively done, languages reveal an intrinsic genetic kindship between themselves. In the case of Afrikan languages, the comparative method in historical linguistics based on lexical (vocabulary), grammatical (forms of words), and phonological (sounds of words) elements leads to the factual Antadiopian conclusion that the Egyptian and other contemporary Afrikan languages derive from a common mother tongue that one could call the paleo-African, the common African (L. Homburger) or the Negro-African (Th. Obenga).[27]

The convergent argument between the Afrikan linguists CAD and Théophile Obenga and their European peer, the French linguist Lilias Homburger (1880–1969), is the attestation of the existence of a proto-Afrikan language. In other words, when contrasted diachronically with one another, Afrikan languages, ancient and contemporary, manifest an obvious monogenetic origin. They all flow from a common mother tongue respectively called "*paléo-africain*" (paleo-African), "*le Négro-africain*" (the Negro-African), and "*l'africain commun*" (the common African) by CAD, Théophile Obenga, and L. Homburger. What is the underlying insight of such a fundamental discovery about research? My response is that the intelligibility of the "*babilonian*"[28] (complex) Afrikan concepts, like the Beti ones in this text, certainly becomes epistemically startling, especially when approached from the perspective of retrospective (comparative and historic) linguistics. They can then help the researcher clarify etymologies of words such as "philosophy," still reckoned in Western dictionaries[29] as "unknown."

Moreover, the comparative study of languages could tool "scientific philosophers"[30] with a philological "torch," surely more appropriate for the intelligibility of concepts such as matter (cosmos), "being," or "becoming." Ahead of us, then, lies the promise that if studious in our quest for inclusive knowledge, we can become polyglots and thereby savor the conceptual sap (wisdom) inherent to each language. But that is hardly the epistemic perspective of the current worldwide neocolonial dispensation, hence *aliénation*.

OF COLONIAL *ALIENATION*

I use the terms coloniality[31] and *aliénation*[32] to describe the domineering Western geopolitical system of capitalist-imperialism, in which its predatory "elite"[33] has plunged and "jailed"[34] the rest of humanity over the last six centuries. This definition underscores the violent structuring principle behind the exclusivist colonial worldview, and that principle is monopoly; the appropriation of the world for oneself alone. That is the sense in which Frantz Fanon observes: "The White person wants the world; he wants it for himself alone. He discovers himself the predestined master of this world. He enslaves it. An appropriative relation is established between the world and him."[35]

Fanon's words should be understood from the perspective of a human being undergoing what he calls "*l'expérience vécue du Noir*" (the lived experience of the Black person) under white masks. The title of the work itself is telling: *Peau noire, masques blancs* (Black body, white masks). Perhaps one should talk about the "blackened person," a title which would put in perspective the person doing the blackening, his intentions, and objectives. From this angle, the "*masques blancs*" (white masks) will certainly be unmasked, unveiling the psychological sphere behind the masks. It seems to me that it is the lived experience of a psyche haunted (colonized) by its creation, the essentialist "Black person," that Fanon conveys. In other words, Fanon does not just express theoretical ideas. He functions, rather, on the practical field, within the concrete realm of the human cognitive space and its outer (inter, counter, and retro)-actions. He throws his reader into the real world of thoughts and praxis; in the sphere of human greed, prejudice, oppression, and struggle for liberation.

And so, his view that the "*Blanc*" (White person) covets the world in an exclusive manner, that the *Blanc* "*asservit*" (enslaves) the world has profound implications for an adequate understanding of alienation in the current colonial dispensation, with its geopolitical, geo-economic, and geo-ethical ramifications. The colonial regime monopolizes space (psyches, bodies, lands, natural resources, etc.) and the means of production (finance capital through banks and industrialists), thereby estranging humans from one another and from nature.

It means, more clearly, that the world, beginning with the West, is being transformed into a global colony ruled by a few enriched individuals.[36] As will be clarified in the subsequent development with CAD's exegesis of the capitalist-colonial-imperial complex, the latter has primarily revolved around a discursive objectivation of humans and nature (land, water, air). According to the French philosophers René Descartes (1596–1650) and Michel Foucault (1926[37]–1984), the rise of the scientific-capitalist era inaugurated a geo-economic production, possession, transformation, and exploitation of both the environment and human mind-bodies.

In his *Discours de la Méthode* (*Partie* 6, §2), R. Descartes critiques both the speculative sciences and philosophy, and rather defends utilitarian knowledges[38] and practical philosophy in the following terms:

> *[. . .] et qu'au lieu de cette philosophie spéculative, qu'on enseigne dans les écoles, on en peut trouver une pratique, par laquelle, connaissant la force et les actions du feu, de l'eau, de l'air, des astres, des cieux et de tous les autres corps qui nous environnent, aussi distinctement que nous connaissons les divers métiers de nos artisans, nous les pourrions employer en même façon à tous les usages auxquels ils sont propres, et ainsi nous rendre comme maîtres et possesseurs de la Nature.*[39]

In R. Descartes' view, the renascent European scientific-capitalist surge (from the sixteenth century onward) nurtured an anthropocentric project that construed Nature, not as a partner, not as a living body to reckon with and care for, but as a "thing" to possess (haunt, own, and subjugate). Nature and her various "*corps*" (bodies: water, air, fire, etc.) were to be dompted by human "*maîtres*" (masters) and squeezed restlessly for material profit, according to "*tous les usages auxquels ils sont propres*" (all the usages for which they are suited). Worse, the system assumed a quasi-perennial stature, knitting its strength ("*force*") and "*actions*" with the "metastatic kerygma" (spreading belief) that material development was tantamount to territorial, maritime, and aerial conquests and exploitation, mindless of environmental pollution and ecosystems' deterioration.

It is therefore not surprising to witness, in our own time, the relative cacophony and the lack of global consensus around the thorny issue of climate change and global warming. Meanwhile, geo-economic and strategic "wars" through international corporations (World Bank, International Monetary Fund *et al.*),[40] non-governmental organizations (NGOs),[41] and military invasions and conquests of lands, seas, and aerial space continue unabatedly, perpetuating the cycle of human migrations and holocausts (psychic, linguistic, religious, economic, physical, etc.)[42] around the globe. The hunt for human resources through immigration policies (Green Card, *Immigration Choisie*[43]); the race for minerals (coltan, uranium, diamond, gold etc.), land, and fossil energy sources (coal, oil, natural gaz) has turned Afrika, for example, into a geo-strategic battleground of foreign military bases (American,[44] European, Chinese, etc.). Djibouti, located in the Horn of Africa, is a telling case in this regard.[45]

These are facts, not too hyperbolic to make colonial *aliénation* antonymous to a worldwide pauperizing penitentiary, whereby "the West and the rest of us"[46] from other parts of the world, and "the rich and the rest of us"[47] in the so-called lower and middle economic "classes," are asymptotically confined without any existential contiguity. As if these geographic and economic divisions within humanity were not endangering enough, a supplementary anthropological barrier was erected since 1681, with the juridical invention of the "white" hue:[48] racism (white supremacy) thus settled as a system of governance in the United States of America and beyond.

Considering the preceding observations, we are justified to analogize the predatory colonial-imperial worldview with the Foucauldian carceral system. M. Foucault presents us with an insightful genealogical analysis of the carceral institution in the West. He sees the rise of the prison system as a controlling Eye (police, cameras, curricula, etc.) or a sort of panopticon, "at once surveillance and observation, security and knowledge, individualization and totalization, isolation and transparency."[49] Additionally, M. Foucault portrays the prison as an "apparatus for transforming individuals."[50] It is also "the penalty par excellence"[51] and an economic asset shaped as a "political anatomy," whose aim is to discipline and produce "subjected and practiced bodies, 'docile' bodies. Discipline increases the forces of the body (in economic terms of obedience),"[52] maintains he.

In a lengthier quote, M. Foucault writes that the prison aims at:

> Distributing individuals, fixing them in space, classifying them, extracting from them the maximum in time and forces, training their bodies, coding their continuous behavior, maintaining them in perfect visibility, forming around them an apparatus of observation, registration and recording, constituting on them a body of knowledge that is accumulated and centralized.[53]

It is curious that M. Foucault, who impressively theorized on power structures[54] wrote no book on Western colonialism in Afrika and beyond, remaining circumspect on the matter.[55] He kept a Eurocentric topical stance, addressing rather epistemic and cultural problems related to language, power constructs, and sexuality. Nevertheless, his theory of the prison system relative to the exploitative politics and economics of bodies could serve as a theoretical framework for the deactivation of the colonial alienating machine. Instead of forging corrective, inquisitive, and creative individuals, the latter turns them rather into submissive, malleable, and obedient bodies.

Viewed from the trans-linguistic (Beti-English-French) perspective of this text, the French concept *aliénation*[56] reveals a morphological and phonetic chasm between its Beti and English respective synonyms, namely *okukud/akud* and alienation. However, if *aliénation* and alienation are graphically and semantically asymptotic, both conveying the idea of estrangement, *okukud* and *akud* are more alarming in their semantics. The notion of *okukud* jointly expresses the ideas of existential disorder (behavioral insanity) and psychological dislocation, made visible through one's defective judgement and comportment. Similarly, the *akud* person is one who lacks knowledge (*feg*) and functions, subsequently, with a silly, that is, flawed worldview. Let us now examine how the conundrum of colonial alienation is tackled in the Antadiopian query about the location, purpose. and audience of scholarship in de-colonial contexts, namely the Afrikan one.

CONTEXT AND TEXT

A *con*text can be defined as that which is coextensive to a text. The context is the biotope of a document. It ferments a text from without, giving it its epistemic breathing texture and existential breadth. That is why the overall "sofian" context of this work, is the coming geopolitical renascent dignity of all humanity, beginning with the Pan-Afrikan contemporary humanity.

Talking about contexts, one can object that they are epiphenomenal to texts which, in turn, enjoy the epistemic status of autonomy. After all, is a text not intelligible without any extra-textual reference? For example, can a book not make sense if its author and the conditions that led to its production are silenced? Would it falter in inner coherence and meaning, if its contextual setting and historical emergence are obliterated? To take another example, as we drive through cities or countryside, does a stop sign beside the road need any additional contextual information to be interpreted by the trained and sound driver? We may be dubious in our answers and perhaps respond in the negative, since our driving does not require that we know, for instance, when the stop signpost was placed there and by whom.

Nevertheless, the notion of "context" is determinant for the comprehensive intelligibility of a given text. It denotes the ideas of textual setting, situatedness, and proliferating relationships around and within a text. The text itself is a conjunction of form and content. The form is the cultural shell (style, language, paradigm, etc.) with which the message (content) is wrapped and conveyed to the audience.

To be sure, a text is never a-temporal or even extemporaneous. Rather, it is a conscious perspective and purposive production of an author, that is, of a cultural being who lives in space and time. Her writing, that is, her visual system of sound representation through symbols (colors, letters, pictures, etc.) is informed and surrounded by a wider "environment" (geo-spiritual, sociological, ontological, psychological, axiological, intellectual, technological, economic, historical, geopolitical, etc.), which constitutes its germinative setting.

This trans-layered background (context) is the humus of one's writing. It connects to virtually everything: the way we understand ourselves in society, the manner with which we relate to one another, the food we eat, the water we drink, the air we breathe, the sounds we hear around us, etc. These are all symbiotic lines of a specific environment, evoking, in regress, a web of interconnected issues. The Antadiopian question "*Pourquoi et pour qui écrivons-nous?*" (Why and for whom do we write?) is an exemplar of the foregoing train of reasoning.

THE COLONIAL-IMPERIAL CONTEXT OF THE ANTADIOPIAN INTERROGATION

"*Pourquoi et pour qui écrivons-nous?*" CAD raises the latter question in 1948, that is, three years after World War II (1939–1945), during which Adolf Hitler (1889–1945?),[57] the *Führer* ("leader"),[58] undertook to ingest Euro-America[59] and Afrika afterwards[60] in the German *Reich* (empire). But was Hitler a historical coincidence or a colonial exception? Could Hitler have become an imperial *Führer* without the instigation and support of the many German colonial capitalists (industrialists[61] and bankers[62]) and the various organizations[63] grouped under the KORAG (*Koloniale Reichsarbeitsgemeinschaft*)? My sense is that the colonial question, that is, the global expansion of the German *Reich* is at the very heart of Hitler's rise to power. This view is confirmed by Kum'a N'dumbe III, who writes:

> *Lorsque Hitler accédera au pouvoir en 1933, il trouvera un vaste mouvement colonial organisé et dynamique, où seront représentés la plupart des tendances politiques de Weimar et surtout ceux qui seront plus tard les compagnons politiques les plus fidèles du Führer.*[64]

Hitler's own speech before the *Reichstag* (parliament) on March 7, 1936, questioning namely the 1919 Treaty of Versailles[65] also corroborates the foregoing perspective. It appears therefore plausible that Hitler is an outgrowth of a long and pervading Occidental tradition of human servitude[66] and racist contempt.[67] This hegemonic blueprint was particularly exacerbated by German and French theorists such as Johann Friedrich Blumenbach (1752–1840), Arthur Comte de Gobineau (1816–1882),[68] and the anthropo-sociologist Georges Vacher de Lapouge (1854–1936).[69] In the line of these notorious "apostles" of racial prejudice, Hitler immersed Nazi Germany into the chauvinistic fantasy of Aryan superiority over the rest of humanity. He believed that *Deutschland* was *über alles*, meaning that the Aryan predatory culture was presumably *über* (above) human intrinsic and autonomous dignity.

How could Germany, the land of the Deutsch, possibly be "above" other lands, peoples, and nations, if not merely from an ideological point of view?

Surely, countries are not literally superposed, like floors in a building, on one another. It is true that a country can naturally be wealthier or run by a wilder propagandistic-imperialist administrative machine than another. It can even possess an "army" of "scientific" demagogues, a horde of countless military troops, or a huge battery of epistemic and chemical weapons. But do these deadly systemic and cultural productions constitute compelling rational arguments likely to vindicate "superiority" and hegemony? In other words, would the thinking individual, who aims at *ati*[70] (worthy, decent, and upright) ideals in herself fail, at least, to hypothesize that such could also be the case in the Other's self-perception, be she disabled or from a different cultural background?

If so, would then the subject construed as such; the so-called "outsider" or "alien" not be likely to retain some ontological residue in and for herself? Is the stranger epistemologically transparent, ontologically void, or geopolitically endangering? Could she not rather be the ruler, the yardstick of the colonialist's own humanity, openness, and will to knowledge? Why is it that Hitler did not see Otherness as his own mediate image? Could corporeal dissemblance and phenotypical aloofness not halt or perhaps caution him against any rushed excluding and biased judgement on the Other? Did it occur to him that he would be ferociously opposed in his unrestrained campaign of empire expansion?

These are open questions. At any rate, as if deaf to the language of nature, which factually wills diversity by producing different stars through motion (gravitation and expansion), various shades in mineral, vegetal, and animal (including human) physiognomies, Hitler shut his intellective gaze to both likeness and difference. He could not see a fellow human and still less a friend to respect and learn from in the non-Aryan. For lack of a sound and conciliatory anthropology, his flawed ideology of domination eventually metastasized worldwide, bringing about the Japanese holocaust caused by the American successive atomic annihilations of Hiroshima and Nagasaki on August 6 and 9, 1945.

The nightmare was consumed: the Japanese had drunk the cataclysmic hemlock of Western colonial madness after the Europeans themselves, the American Indians,[71] and the Afrikans[72] before them. With the emergence of the United Nations on October 24, 1945, and its commitment to protect "the dignity and worth of the human person" (preamble of its charter),[73] one would have hoped that, having been briefly subjugated by Hitler to the very enslaving methods they had been "crippling" other peoples with worldwide, colonial Euro-America would abhor colonialism and rethink its relationship with global humanity once and for all.

Such a hope could be explained by two factors. First, World War II (WWII) could have been interpreted as a shock therapy for the colonial Occident or, at the very least, as a warning sign for the possible disastrous resurgence of the Hitler within, that is, the Westerner who fights the West. Why envision such an eventuality? One could argue that WWII smashed, perhaps for good, the European racist pride in its alienating colonial system upheld in the name of "civilization," which was rather, in the case of Pan-Afrika for example, the "black man's burden."[74]

But the load was even heavier on Europe itself, for if a civilization ridicules its own foundational principles (liberty, equality, fraternity, trust in God, etc.), how can it stand? When such values, which are supposed to propel a civilization toward cohesion and creativity become fleeting shadows and shameless lies in the homeland, then the likelier downward path is cultural suicide, decay, and regression.

This brings us to the second point: WWII laid bare both the absurdity and the ethical bankruptcy of colonization. Instead of bargaining its return to the geopolitical arena discursively after losing World War I, Nazi Germany rather transformed Europe into a horrific field of competing egos (Adolf Hitler, Charles de Gaulle,[75] Benito A. A. Mussolini, to name but a few). Thus, the world witnessed, at the very heart of Europe, an unprecedented display of barbarism. With the imminent decolonization of the "Mother Land"[76] from the late 1950s onward, CAD, unhesitatingly, thought the dawn of the Afrikan renaissance finally at hand.[77]

Thus, ahead of Afrikan academics, laid the demanding task of a decolonial epistemology, at once critical and corrective of the Eurocentric exclusivist paradigm.[78] Writing in the latter took the confessional and creedal orientation of colonial vindication, silencing human precolonial history, or reconfiguring it in the image of the victors of the moment. That is the regressive and misleading process denounced at length by CAD in the following disturbing remark:

> *Ainsi l'impérialisme, tel le chasseur de la préhistoire, tue d'abord spirituellement et culturellement l'être, avant de chercher à l'éliminer physiquement. La négation de l'histoire et des réalisations intellectuelles des peuples africains noirs est le meurtre culturel, mental, qui a déjà précédé et préparé le génocide ici et là dans le monde. De telle sorte que dans les années 1946 et 1954—où s'est élaboré notre projet de restitution de l'histoire africaine authentique, de réconciliation des civilisations africaines avec l'histoire, l'optique déformante des œillères du colonialisme avait si profondément faussé les regards des intellectuels sur le passé africain que nous éprouvions les plus grandes difficultés, même à l'égard des Africains, à faire admettre les idées qui aujourd'hui sont en passe de devenir de lieux communs. On imagine à peine ce que pouvait être le degré d'aliénation des Africains d'alors.*[79]

It is precisely, during the momentous 1946 and 1954 interludes, geared toward the "*projet de restitution de l'histoire africaine authentique, de réconciliation des civilisations africaines avec l'histoire,*"[80] that CAD addresses the predicament of the "*degré d'aliénation de Africains d'alors*" ("level of alienation of the Africans of that time"). He undertakes the project to restore the authentic place of the Afrikan precolonial history and civilizations within human general history, with the intention of deworming the Pan-Afrikan intellectual community from the rampant cultural alienation of Western subjugation and control. The endogenous psychic therapy, CAD envisions, is to reconcile the Pan-Afrikan community with history, which is an agential and creative trajectory.

We would have understood that the key problem with *kara olere* colonial *aliénation* is cultural alienating mimesis, as recurrent in Afrikan literary, linguistic, epistemic, and artistic productions before and after CAD' 1948 question "*Pourquoi et pour qui écrivons-nous?*" raised within the larger context of the Pan-Afrikan renaissance.

WRITING: ORIGIN AND PURPOSE

Writing can be defined as a cultural means through which humans, for millennia, have been inscribing their reading (perception) of themselves and of the universe around them on rocks, bones, bodies, clothes, caves, papyri, paper, drums, buildings, pyramids, and obelisks, etc. It is the case, for example, with the cryptic mathematical Ishango Bone,[81] with the generative Akoa Mfula and Fotna,[82] or with the Great Kemetic Sphinx of Giza, characterized by its Bantu profile.[83]

These engravings of human thought in the "book" of nature should not, however, make us oblivious of the fact that the production of knowledge extends far beyond the confines of graphemes and ideograms. Oral knowledge, as propounded for example in Plato's Socrates, flows from the human phenomenal and remarkable memory. Oral knowledge is a form of intellective expression of the universe, such that philosophies, myths, proverbs, proper names, toponyms, ethnonyms, etc., all become relevant epistemic channels to be deciphered, just as the arts (dance, music, architecture, poetry, and more) are. Socrates cherishes orality and does not write. However, that does not make him less philosopher than CAD[84] or Ama Mazama.[85] He readily leans toward the verbal and dialogical forms of knowledge production than to written ones, as evidenced by Plato's dialogues, especially the *Phaedrus.*[86]

Therein, Socrates values the interactive epistemic method. He delights in the liveliness of thoughtful conversations. With his interlocutors, he actively discusses, with the view of begetting something true, minutely surveyed by inquiring minds. For him, knowledge, or the thorough examination of human lives[87] and things, flows from inside out, and not the contrary. Thus, discussions yield centripetal and centrifugal arguments expounded and rephrased at will, for the surge of truth. It is the latter (truth), that is, one's personal capacity to filter facts from opinions, which ascertains the validity of philosophic inquiry.

It is worth underscoring that writing, from the Socratic outlook, is an Afrikan invention,[88] whose purpose is to remind people of things already known through recollection.[89] In other words, written documents, in themselves, are neither sapient and memorial, nor self-explanatory. They are just anamnestic, that is, they help the reader remember what is stored in their natural "hard disc"; their memory. However, the recollective function put aside, written data have an inconvenience. They often leave the reader with more questions than answers. Sometimes, they seem to freeze meanings, rather ceding the gymnastics of argumentative justifications and interpretations to their readers.

Assuming the foregoing view to be true, it must nonetheless be reminded that writing, understood as the outpouring of thought on a material surface (paper, ground, wall, etc.) through symbols and letters, connotes the ability to convey and (re)read what one writes. And to read means to cognitively merge the stored cultural data and signs (linguistic, iconic, symbolic, artistic, etc.) of one's potential galactic (vast) memory with outer ones in a logical, colorful, and meaningful manner. This supposes some sort of literacy in the writing system in which a document is written. Thus, reading, just like writing, synchronizes memorial, affective, and existential impressions in the mind through sight or touch (like in the case of braille and computing).

The problem, when it comes to reading and writing, is often that of the subject's relative analphabetism. Unless one is initiated into specific cultural forms of writing such as the Congolese *Mandombe*, the Bamun script (Cameroon), or the Kemetic "*Medzo me Nti*"[90] (*Medu Neter*), it becomes difficult to transcribe and decode what is seen and heard: symbols and signs remain weird, mute, and meaningless.

But even in writing systems familiar to the reader, parallel difficulties still surface, stimulating further inquiry, since writing and reading denote the capacity to enliven language through the creation of concepts, as well as the audacity to interrogate the content and purpose of the documents one reads, including their authors. This critical attitude enables the reader/writer decrypt discursive, linguistic, artistic, and symbolic materials, besides those of the artful book that the universe (trans-galactic whole) is.

Writing, then, is a cultural artifact, whose signification participates in a vital series of interconnections. Its activity constantly challenges the writing circle (authors, readers, critics) to strive to listen, see, and raise humanity to its greatest heights. Writing, on could say, is an enterprise that connects the writing circle to the joys, beauties, pressing geopolitical and ethical fears, anxieties, screams, cries, sorrows, dreams, and hopes of the "wretched of the earth,"[91] both the unconscious and the conscious ones. I will return to these two qualifications shortly.

In the meantime, it could be objected that the above optimistic view of writing can rightly be downplayed, especially if we consider Claude Lévi-Strauss' argument in the eighteen chapter of his *Tristes Tropiques,* titled "A Writing Lesson," that:

> the primary function of written communication is to facilitate slavery. The use of writing for disinterested purposes, and as a source of intellectual and aesthetic pleasure, is a secondary result, and more often than not it may even be turned into a means of strengthening, justifying or concealing the other.[92]

Though highlighting the possibility of exceptions to his hypothesis beyond the Western hemisphere, the French anthropologist Cl. Lévi-Strauss (1908–2009) is adamant: writing aims at deceit, thirst for power, prestige, and dominion by one or a few individuals at the expense of the multitude. He explains further:

> If we look at the situation nearer home, we see that the systematic development of compulsory education in the European countries goes hand in hand with the extension of military service and proletarianization. The fight against illiteracy is therefore connected with an increase in governmental authority over the citizens. Everyone must be able to read, so that the government can say: Ignorance of the law is no excuse.[93]

Lévi-Strauss alerts us here of the necessity to critically appraise our epistemic and educational documentation, which is mediated by written documents. They may be infested with ideological-geopolitical tricks and ethical lies, which possibly brainwash readers, instead of leading them to a greater awareness of their existential situations and creative potentialities. Thus, writing with the purpose of deceiving others and concealing the truth, whose ". . . production is thoroughly imbued with relations of power,"[94] according to Michel Foucault, is what CAD denounces as "bad faith"[95] in Afrikanist scholarship.

To me, bad faith scholars operate from the weak point of an unconscious wretchedness, because they seem not yet really awakened to the compelling nature of factual truth, and to the evanescent character of intentional pseudo-science. Such an approach to scholarship is self-deceptive and shortsighted because it cannot resist the test of time. Rather, human history attests to the fact that the quest for what is abiding (truth) in human civilizations, the yearn for personal expression, creativity, and freedom are enduring constants of epistemic and geopolitical struggles. These are worthy ideals that guide the conscious wretched in this world, that is, the impoverished multitude of humans, who eventually think and understand the socio-historical meanders of their present miserable condition, and wrestle "by any means necessary"[96] to get out of it.

Having said this, the Antadiopian question persists: why and for whom do we write? The concern is deeply reflective. The "we," I suggest, is neither anonymous nor restrictive to a given epistemic community. Rather, the query may be read as expressing a deeply subjective and intersubjective worry. Why do "we," academics, write in this colonial-imperial world? Why do I write this Afrosofian text, and why did CAD dedicate his adult life to writing?

AFROSOFIAN AND ANTADIOPIAN EPISTEMIC PURPOSES AND AUDIENCES

Before turning to CAD's epistemic motives, my personal response to his question is that I want my writing and life to spark and witness something sofian, refined, *ati* (decent/noble), and excellent in global humanity. I want my writing to be a vital part of human deepest insights, foresights, and fulfilment; a gesture and component of humanity's struggle for liberation and healing: healing from despicable oppressive worldviews and alienating cultural followership. That is the reason why my epistemic anchor is precolonial and Pan-Afrikan, that is, leaned on a humanity that antedates the ambient Afrophobia of the colonial-imperial worldview. Since sapient humanity is Afrikan in origin,[97] my writing aims at awakening the continuing Afrikan enlivening presence and passion for oneness in the human global.[98]

What I mean is that we are inheritors of the *Homo sapiens sapiens*, insofar as we strive to rethink our Afrikanness beyond the DuBoisian "color-line"[99] enduring predicament, which nature knows not.[100] We can do this by orienting our writing toward the betterment of human relationships and with the environment in which we live; hence my federating concept Afrosofia. In arguing from the perspective of the Beti-Afrikan inclusive presence in global humanity, I hold that we, humans, do share a sapient, thinking nature, whose unique thread is to vibrate,[101] enliven, and stimulate all that is *ati* (virtuous, honest, and noble) in us. The ethical goal here is to become individually and collectively *ati ati*; which means, always targeting the ultimate, the outstanding, and the supreme in us.

This vision captures my epistemic posture and goal, fleshing out the instructive comment from the French philosopher Paul Ricoeur (1913–2005) that:

> nobody writes from nowhere . . . It is a great illusion to think that one could make himself a pure spectator, without weight, without memory, without perspective, and regard everything with equal sympathy. Such indifference, in the strict sense of the word, destroys the possibility of appropriation.[102]

It is indeed in appropriating the existential condition of the conscious wretched, within current humanity, that the responsibility to think our identity, mission, and raison d'être in a predatory geopolitical world (dis)order becomes pressing. Therefore, it is my hope that, in rethinking the primeval Pan-Afrikan presence in global humanity as a challenging call to integrity in the current *kara olere* world, I hasten the eradication of the unconscious wretched (colonial-imperialism), which delays the age of lasting peace, creative freedom, and inclusive prosperity on earth.

To be sure, these are some of the values that also govern CAD's militant writing. The author of *Alerte sous les Tropiques* envisions his life and scholarly activity as telling witnesses of the truth about the human presence on earth. As we saw in the first chapter, CAD's epistemology is conciliatory in outlook: the language of "reconciliation" of humanity with itself is one of its recurring themes. As a person, generosity and moral uprightness were endearing ideals for CAD. He sought them not only in himself, but also in others.

This explains why he dedicates, for example, his work *Parenté Génétique de l'Égyptien Pharaonique et des Langues Négro-Africaines* to the then General Secretary of the Dakarian University, Mahady Diallo by name, "*pour ses éminentes qualités morales et professionnelles et pour les services exceptionnels qu'il a rendus à la recherche africaine pendant les années où il a dirigé le secrétariat de l'IFAN.*"[103]

For CAD, it is capital for a human being to wrestle, precisely, with the conundrum of her being on earth by subjectively appropriating the following questions: Why am I in the universe? How did I come about in this world? What is my purpose for being human and not something else within this cosmos? Such questions are important because they give meaning to one's ethical, social, and intellectual lives. That was the case with Alioune Diop, the founder of "*Présence Africaine*,"[104] which is the corporation where CAD published his works. As we see after the next paragraph, the author of *Civilisation ou Barbarie* dedicates the latter work to Alioune Diop, praising his qualitative inner self, at once altruistic and generous.

It is certainly challenging for someone, whose life's blueprint is individualistic and capitalistic,[105] to become, out of love and self-giving, a hospitable ground for alterity. The capitalist individual, because preoccupied with material and pecuniary profit, tends to lessen the relevance and ontological worth of Otherness. He is inclined to function with a narcissistic view of himself in society, viewing values like generosity or altruism as too communitarian, and therefore dangerous to individual autonomy. It is the "I," the Ego, the solipsistic individual with his dreams, fears, and hopes who really matters. Otherness, here understood in terms of culture, citizenship, ethnicity, ideology (political, religious), and gender, etc., is rather epiphenomenal to such a person. The question, however, is to know whether a society can perdure when construed as a mere juxtaposition of isolated individuals?

The search for a responsible functioning of the social-individual is constitutive of the ontological and socio-political nodal approached with different epistemic emphases by CAD himself, Jean-Paul Sartre, or Martin Heidegger, after the ancient Afrikans and Greeks.[106] But, it is not my purpose here to delve into their respective subtleties. Nevertheless, as far as the Antadiopian political philosophy is concerned, it aims at grounding humans, geopolitically, in a symbiotic and interactive existential trajectory with their human and natural environment. That is its advantage which, nevertheless, requires an earnest disposition to draw inspiration from *ati* (decent) people such as Alioune Diop, of whom CAD writes:

> *Alioune, tu savais ce que tu étais venu faire sur la terre: Une vie entièrement consacrée aux autres, rien pour soi, tout pour autrui, un cœur rempli de bonté et de générosité, une âme pétrie de noblesse, un esprit toujours serein, la simplicité personnifiée! Le demiurge voulait-il nous proposer, en exemple, un idéal de perfection, en t'appelant à l'existence?*[107]

For CAD, the Afrikan-Senegalese Alioune Diop (1910–1980), who died a year before the publication of *Civilisation ou Barbarie* in 1981, found his existential purpose in the cosmos. He knew or rather discovered what he was on earth for. His life and writing were not about segregating, isolating, or oppressing his fellow humans. Rather, in CAD's words, Alioune Diop saw himself as a sheltering gift for all humanity: "*Une vie entièrement consacrée aux autres, rien pour soi, tout pour autrui, un coeur rempli de bonté et de générosité*" ("A life entirely consecrated to others, nothing for oneself, everything for others, a heart filled with goodness and with generosity").

CAD's meditative reading of Alioune Diop's character consists in attempting to understand the deeper meaning of such a life for contemporary humanity. In the rhetorical question "*Le demiurge voulait-il nous proposer, en exemple, un idéal de perfection, en t'appelant à l'existence?*" ("Did the demiurge want to propose us, as an example, an ideal of perfection, in calling you into existence?" CAD affirms the presence of an abiding value in Alioune Diop: perfection. We are here in the transcendent realm of spiritual *sofia*, where the acting human gradually fuses with her *ati* (divine) character by awakening her social self.

From this perspective, the demiurgic intellectual is one who commits her life and writing to truth telling: her writing is not conditioned by any prevailing hegemonic ideology. Concomitantly, like Alioune Diop, she finds fulfilment in what is ethically beautiful (goodness, generosity, altruism, serenity, and simplicity). What is of interest, however, is that in writing such words about Alioune Diop, CAD seems to be indicating the dormant existence of something sublime and great, albeit divine in each human being, which is to be remembered and awakened. Alioune Diop, according to CAD, successfully revived those noble (decent) qualities in himself, embodying them as his character. Consequently, the founder of *Présence Africaine* is viewed by the man of Caytu[108] as a lived sample of a worthy ideal; perfection, excellence, and brilliance in one's dealings with fellow humans.

It can then be said, without exaggeration, that CAD writes and lives with the view of perfecting and fine-tuning what is still deficient in the human contemporary character, namely civilization, which is a heritage of sociality, freedom, and creativity. It is a reversal of history which is operated in the Antadiopian epistemology: humans, divided by centuries of Western capitalistic exploitation through "white supremacy" (racism), must rediscover their Afrikan monogenetic origin, and learn anew the art of communal living at domestic and international levels.

With CAD, we are on the verge of a prospective and renewed Afrikan humanism in international relations. He could become, for the United Nations, a prophetic voice to celebrate worldwide, since he defends a geopolitical order based on dialogue. That is the reason why the spiritual language of "*réconciliation*"[109] is recurrent in his writing. Reconciling humanity with itself would mean interconnecting the world around a common vision of human dignity and respect. It is about building bridges and not walls between individuals, cultures, nations, and continents. *Réconciliation* should then be a significant stratum of academic productions.

After centuries of speechless barbarism spearheaded by a Western geo-economic, ethical, political, and hegemonic misguidance, CAD envisions a writing geared toward the urgent renaissance of a Pan-African ontology spelled out in the following words:

> *L'Africain qui nous a compris est celui-là qui, après la lecture de nos ouvrages, aura senti naître en lui un autre homme, animé d'une conscience historique, un vrai créateur, un Prométhée porteur d'une nouvelle civilisation et parfaitement conscient de ce que la terre entière doit à son génie ancestral dans tous les domaines de la science, de la culture et de la religion.*[110]

The foregoing words announce a possibility of inner metanoia in CAD's reader, provided she understands his epistemic intention, which is about the burgeoning of a creative human type, endowed with a sound Afrikan precolonial and historical consciousness.[111] What does this mean?

Simply that Afrikan civilization is the legacy of all humans in the *realms "de la science, de la culture et de la religion"* ("of science, of culture and of religion." Why emphasize this continuing scientific, cultural, and religious Afrikan heritage as the property of all humanity? The reason is that Africanist and Americano-Eurocentric circles, are often obliterated with sententious publications such as *Not Out of Africa,* which ironically restricts "truly African features of Egyptian culture" to "the practice of elaborate rhythmic hand-clapping at festivals."[112]

These words are from Professor Mary Lefkowitz, who subtly defends, through her words, the incorrect Africanist dogma that the black Afrikan Nile Valley civilization was a white production. She still talks about "truly African features of Egyptian culture" in 1996, that is, 42 years after the publication of CAD's *Nations Nègres et Culture*, which does not feature in her bibliography. Perhaps she never heard about the book or never read it. If she had, she would have examined the extensive dialectical evidence[113] provided by the author in favor of the black Afrikanness of the Kemetic civilization, as confirmed by the 1974 International Egyptological symposium held in Cairo,[114] in its conclusion that:

> Although the preparatory working paper sent out by Unesco gave particulars of what was desired, not all participants had prepared communications comparable with the painstakingly researched contributions of Professors Cheikh Anta Diop and Obenga. There was consequently a real lack of balance in the discussions.[115]

Though I disagree, for example, with CAD's dichotomic understanding of "philosophy" and "myth," as will be shown further down in the book, there is a real danger of misrepresenting and distorting his thought, as does his colleague, the French historian Jean Devisse when he alleges that CAD considers " . . . *matriarcat la caractéristique des sociétés européennes et méditerranéennes.*"[116] It is rather the contrary view that CAD holds in his Two Cradle Theory, arguing that the matriarchate is Afrikan, and the patriarchate Western.[117]

Taking the Antadiopian substantive "*Africain*" (Afrikan) as an inceptive matrix and an ethical trope, that is, as a sapient (wise) and reasonable human being who values factual truth, creativity, freedom, and communal living in her life, CAD underscores the necessity to understand the ontological focus behind his overall discursive project. What is at stake in his writing is the surge of a strong sense of moral consciousness and communal responsibility in the individual, nurtured by a true scientific knowledge sheltered from scientific "bad faith."

In other words, the purpose of the Antadiopian epistemology is to achieve the individual's conscious embeddedness in human history; the mobilization of her creative genius; her genuine mindfulness and eagerness to bring about a new civilization through her acute awareness of the Afrikan determining contributions to science, culture, and religion worldwide.

This view constitutes, for me, an exciting gnoseological challenge to every citizen of this world, and more importantly to academics and students in the field of liberal arts and beyond. They must look for the religious, cultural, and scientific reasons that motivate the necessity of the "*nouvelle civilisation*" (new civilization) that CAD talks about. The implicit argument of his claim seems to be that contemporary humanity must awaken from the dying "*ancienne civilisation*" (ancient civilization) in which it still dangerously wags; hence the need for something novel and energizing, namely a paradigmatic shift from the Nordic to the Meridional cradle.

Many questions can be addressed to the epistemological turn advocated by CAD. To begin with, why does he want us to discontinue the Nordic cradle? What is so special and of scientific interest about the Meridional cradle he envisions for us, academics? Why must the scholar capitalize on the said Meridional (Afrikan) cradle today?

CAD sharply replies that no thought or ideology is, by essence, foreign to Afrika, which was their birthplace.[118] He continues, explaining that ideas sometimes viewed as foreign are often mere images (blurred, reversed, modified, or perfected) and creations of our Afrikan ancestors. It is the case with Judaism, Christianity, Islam, dialectics, the theory of being, exact sciences, arithmetic, geometry, mechanics, astronomy, medicine, literature (novel, poetry, drama), architecture, arts, etc.[119]

Such a decisive paradigm turn, in my view, will certainly enrich academics with a fertile scientific land to critically plow and draw inspiration from in their multifarious investigations. That is what I attempt to do in the present text. By engaging Afrika in our epistemologies, we would hopefully have an articulate foreground from which we can appraise the tumultuous geopolitical context of CAD's writing, as well as ours, including his timely call that all nations band together to build a planetary civilization instead of sinking into barbarism.[120]

CONCLUSION

The argument running through this chapter has been that our epistemic pursuit defends a unitive blueprint. That is the message of the Afrosofian and Antadiopian paradigm to the decolonial worldwide audience. In asking academics to examine their epistemic motives, and to determine their addressees,

CAD's scholarly corpus intents academic pursuit as a shining lamp around which humanity can gather, each people speaking its own language, thinking in its concepts, and yet dialoguing with others and earnestly working toward a planetary civilization of human reconciliation with itself. The fourth chapter on the Afrosofian-Antadiopian direct methodology prolongs the latter reflection through the promotion of what CAD terms "scientific philosophy."

NOTES

1. Aimé Césaire, *Discours sur le Colonialisme* (Paris: Présence Africaine, [1955], 2004), 18. From French: "What am I driving at? At this idea: that no one colonizes innocently, that no one colonizes with impunity either; that a nation which colonizes, that a civilization which justifies colonization—and therefore force—is already a sick civilization, a civilization which is morally diseased, which irresistibly, progressing from one consequence to another, one denial to another, calls for its Hitler, I mean its punishment."

2. The French substantive "*sens*" connotes the mutual imbrication of embodiment (the five senses: touch, sight, smell, hearing, and taste), meaning, and purpose in *the mbo sofia*'s production of knowledge. Without the human body and its sapient "tool" the brain, the heart, or both, depending on cultures, critical thought, the pursuit of excellence, and intuition (innate capacity to apprehend reality) are hardly conceivable. It is the human being who, from her self-perception as thoughtful, social, cosmic, and ethical, actively projects herself toward the personal embodiment of worthy ideals such as wisdom, beauty, love, generosity, etc. As indicated in the first chapter, most Beti concepts used in the present text can be retrieved in Siméon Basile Atangana Ondigui, *Le Nouveau Dictionnaire Ewondo, op. cit.*

3. In this text, colonialism will also encompass its neo-version, neocolonialism.

4. Plotinus, *Ennead* I, VI.9.

5. *Ibid.*, 34. From French: "Why and for whom do we write?"

6. Cheikh Anta Diop, *Alerte sous les tropiques* (Paris: Présence Africaine, 1990), 33–44. From French: "When shall we talk about an African Renaissance?"

7. Marie-Rose Abomo-Maurin, *Les pérégrinations des descendants d'Afri Kara* (Paris: L'Harmattan, 2012), 7; Angèle Christine Ondo, *Mvett Ekang: Forme et Sens. L'épique dévoile le sens* (Paris: L'Harmattan, 2014), 11.

8. The Beti are also called Ekang, meaning "Rays of light" or "Initiates." See: Alain Elloué-Engoune, *Du Sphinx au Mvett. Connaissance et sagesse de l'Afrique* (Paris: L'Harmattan, 2008), 23 and 47.

9. The surnames Ma'a, Ngo'o, Afiri, Kara, Ta Ma'a, Kuba, etc., are still very common among the Beti of central Afrika today.

10. Pierre Alexandre et Jacques Binet, *Le Groupe dit Pahouin (Fang-Boulou-Beti)* (Paris: Puf, 1958), 16.

My translation: "Afira Kara 'who gave his name to Africa' is the son of Kara Kuba, son of Kuba Ta, son of Ta Ma'a, son of Ma'a Ngô 'who is the father of the Negro race.'"

11. Angèle Christine Ondo, *Mvett Ekang, op. cit.,* 159.

12. From Afiri (Hope) and Kara (Crab). Crabs have pincers that help nourish and defend themselves if attacked. Accordingly, a *kara kara* person is metaphorically understood as resilient, tough, and strong. For complementary information on the anthroponym Afiri, one could consult the thought-provoking ethnonym *Afrim,* dealt with by the Afrikan Ghanaian historian Nana Banchie Darkwah. His linguistic and cultural research on the Afrikan writers of the Bible leads him to the view that the *Afrim* are an Ancient Egyptian people that migrated to "Europe to become the Jews and Hebrews," through the so-called Biblical Exodus. See: Nana Banchie Darkwah, *The Africans Who Wrote the Bible. Ancient Secrets Africa and Christianity Have Never Told* (Orlando, FL: HBC Publications, 2018), 177–229.

13. Kuba comes from the verb *kub*, meaning to lavish, sprinkle, impart, or pour some liquid or blessing on someone or something.

14. From the verb *ta* or *te*, meaning to spread out. But the substantive *ta(n)* means "village" or "geographic origin" in Eton, which is a spoken modification within the Beti language.

15. From the concept *ma'a/maa* (blessing, luck, wellbeing), the Beti coin the ethical word "*ntotomama*" Or "*ntotomamaa*," meaning "That which confers true happiness." *Totoe*, indeed, means "truly."

16. In CAD, culture is a wider notion than that of nation. A people's culture permeates national and continental borders. That is the argument behind the titles of his magna opuses *Nations Nègres et Culture*, *op. cit.;* and *L'Unité Culturelle de l'Afrique Noire* (Paris: Présence Africaine, [1959] 1982).

17. Molefi Kete Asante, *Afrocentricity. The Theory of Social Change* (Chicago: African American Images, 2003), 42.

18. Pan-Afrika designates, in the context of the past six centuries, not only the forced geographic dislocation of modern continental Afrikans throughout the world because of Western enslavement and colonial holocausts, but also their ongoing struggle to regain their historical protagonism (agency).

19. Ngũgĩ wa Thiong'o, *Something Torn and New. An African Renaissance* (New York: Basic*Civitas* Books, 2009), 93. See also: SpringerLink, "Asmara Declaration on African Languages and Litteratures (2000)." *Springer Nature*. Retrieved May 15, 2018. https://www0.sun.ac.za/taalsentrum/assets/files/Asmara%20Declaration.pdf.

20. Ngũgĩ wa Thiong'o, *Something Torn and New*, *op. cit.,* 113.

21. Cheikh Hamidou Kane, *L'Aventure Ambiguë* (Paris: Union générale d'éditions, 1971).

22. Cheikh Anta Diop, *Civilisation ou Barbarie, op. cit.,* 275.

23. Cheikh Anta Diop, *L'Unité Culturelle de l'Afrique Noire, op. cit.*; Molefi Kete Asante & Kariamu Welsh Asante (Ed.), *African Culture. The Rhythms of Unity* (Trenton, NJ: Africa World Press, Inc., 1996).

24. Cheikh Anta Diop, *Parenté Génétique de l'Égyptien Pharaonique et des Langues Négro-Africaines* (IFAN-Dakar: Les Nouvelles Éditions Africaines, 1977).

25. Théophile Obenga, *Origine Commune de l'Égyptien Ancien, du Copte et des Langues Négro-Africaines Modernes. Introduction à la Linguistique Historique Africaine* (Paris: L'Harmattan, 1993).

26. Jean-Claude Mboli, *Origine des Langues Africaines* (Paris: L'Harmattan, 2010).

27. Cheikh Anta Diop, *Parenté Génétique . . . , op. cit.*, xxv. In French: "*l'égyptien et les autres langues africaines dérivent d'une langue mère commune que l'on peut appeler le paléo-africain, l'africain commun ou le Négro-africain de L. Homburger ou de Th. Obenga.*"

28. This adjective is an example of linguistic diffraction. Those familiar with biblical literature, especially Genesis 10: 8–10 would certainly call to mind the Ethiopian Nimrod, son of Kush (Ethiopia), builder of the civilization of southern Mesopotamia (Babylon), when they see the substantive "*Babilon*" occur in my writing. The Tower of Babel (confusion in Hebrew), in the biblical account, stands for the etiology of language confusion and diversity, hence the name Babylon. In Beti, however, *babilon* is a compound of the adjective "*babi*" (near, wounded) and of the tree "*elon*," endowed with mystical properties. The syneresis between "i" in *babi* and "e" in *elon* gives the diphthong "i" between both terms. Accordingly, the adjective "babilonian" suggests the idea of something quite mysterious.

29. Pierre Chantraine, *Dictionnaire Étymologique de la Langue Grecque* (Paris: Éditions Klincksieck, 1984), 1031.

30. Scientific philosophy builds its discourse from the finds of contemporary sciences (quantum mechanics, physics, biology, etc.).

31. Coloniality expresses the fact of being colonized, that is, psychologically and culturally hunted by the mortiferous geopolitical ideology of predation (anthropological and environmental).

32. The concept of alienation has received different epistemic overtones in thinkers like CAD, Frances Cress Welsing (1935–2016), Karl Marx (1818–1883), or Sigmund Freud (1856–1939). I will expatiate on CAD's theory of alienation in my analysis. Frances Cress Welsing insightfully discusses the root causes of alienation in Karl Marx and Freud, assenting with their respective dynamic analyses of the phenomenon. However, she rejects the Marxian economic theory that alienation comes from of the capitalists' private ownership of the means of production, and their subsequent expropriation of the worker's labor. Likewise, she opposes Freud's view that alienation results from the unresolved psychological conflict in the individual between the conscious and unconscious strata. Hers is the view that white skin is a form of albinism, which accounts for "white" people's alienation toward themselves and melaninated people alike. It is this inner hate and hostility in relation to oneself, known as white supremacy/Western civilization/racism, she contends, that surfaces worldwide in the albino mutants' destructive and aggressive behavioral patterns vis-à-vis "black" people. See: Frances Cress Welsing, *The Isis Papers. The Keys to the Colors* (Washington, DC: C. W. Publishing, 2004), 17–38.

33. I am not here making the hyperbolic claim that the whole Western "elite" is predatory.

34. Michel Foucault, *Discipline & Punish. The Birth of the Prison* (Trans. from the French by Alan Sheridan, New York: Vintage Books, 1995).

35. Frantz Fanon, *Peau noire, masques blancs, op.*, 103. In French: "*Le Blanc veut le monde; il le veut pour lui tout seul. Il se découvre le maître prédestiné de ce monde. Il l'asservit. Il s'établit entre le monde et lui un rapport appropriatif.*"

36. Tavis Smiley and Cornel West, *The Rich and the Rest of Us. A Poverty Manifesto* (New York: SmileyBooks, 2012).

37. René Descartes, *Discours de la Méthode pour bien conduire sa raison et chercher la vérité dans les sciences* (Paris: L. Berthier, 1894).

38. He speaks of " . . . *des connaissances qui soient fort utiles à la vie*" (knowledges that be very useful to life).

39. *Ibid.*, 102. From French: " . . . and instead of this speculative philosophy, that is taught in schools, a practical one could be found, through which, knowing the power and the actions of fire, of water, of the air, of stars, of the heavens and of all the other bodies that surround us, as distinctly as we know the various jobs of our artisans, we would use them in similar fashion for all the usages for which they are suited, and thus make us like masters and possessors of nature."

40. Birgit Brock-Utne, "Education Policies for Sub-Saharan Africa as Viewed by the World Bank," in her book titled *Whose Education for All? The Recolonization of the African Mind* (New York: Falmer Press, 2000), 35–68.

41. John Perkins, *The Secret History of the American Empire. The Truth About Economic Hit Men, Jackals, and How to Change the World* (New York: A Plume Book, 2008), 253–55.

42. Adam Hochschild, *King Leopold's Ghost. A Story of Greed, Terror, and Heroism in Colonial Africa* (New York: A Mariner Book, 1998).

43. From French: "Selective Immigration," as applied by the French and Canadian governments.

44.Nick Turse, "The US military's best kept secret." *The Nation.* Retrieved March 1, 2018. https://www.thenation.com/article/the-us-militarys-best-kept-secret/.

45. Degang Sun & Yahia H. Zoubir, "The Eagle's Nest in the Horn of Africa: US Military Strategic Deployment in Djibouti" in *Africa Spectrum* (January 2016), 111–124.

46. Chinweizu, *The West and the Rest of Us. White Predators, Black Slavers and the African Elite* (New York: Random House, 1975).

47. Tavis Smiley and Cornel West, *The Rich and the Rest of Us. A Poverty Manifesto* (New York: SmileyBooks, 2012).

48. Jacqueline Battalora, *Birth of a White Nation. The Invention of White People and its Relevance Today* (Houston TX: Strategic Book Publishing and Rights Co., 2013), 2.

49. Michel Foucault, *Discipline and Punish. The Birth of the Prison* (Trans. Alan Sheridan, New York: Vintage Books, 1995), 249.

50. *Ibid.*, 233.

51. *Ibid.*, 232.

52. *Ibid.*, 138.

53. *Ibid.*, 231.

54. Michel Foucault, *The Government of Self and Others* (Trans. Graham Burchell, New York: Palgrave Macmillan, 2011).

55. It is true that in his "What Are the Iranians Dreaming About?" written in October 1978, M. Foucault did optimistically address the Iranian revolution. See: Michel Foucault, "What Are the Iranians Dreaming About?" *Foucault and the Iranian Revolution.* Retrieved September 13, 2018. https://www.press.uchicago.edu/Misc/Chicago/007863.html.

56. My intention in this chapter is to analyze the concept of *aliénation* in CAD, who wrote in French, especially as it *(aliénation)* operates in the Afrikan literary neocolonial context.

57. The question mark (?) appended to 1945 suggests the idea that Adolf Hitler, a trope of exclusion and annihilation, is perhaps as alive today, at the dawn of the twenty-first century, as he was before his (presumed) death. The colonial ideology in which he partook is unabatedly carried out, masqueraded in the cosmetic gown of "liberal capitalism"; characterized by the alienation of human thought to the monoculture of material consumerism through a predatory global market of corporations. The German *Führer* might have survived World War II, as dubiously suggests the following link: Central Intelligence Agency (CIA), "Hitler." *CIA.* Retrieved January 11, 2018. https://www.cia.gov/library/readingroom/docs/HITLER%2C%20ADOLF_0003.pdf.

58. Adolf Hitler, the *Führer* bewitched Nazi Germany with the flawed idea that leadership and nationhood are exclusive and ethnic notions. He preached Aryan purity and invested himself with the mission to wipe out the Jew, whom he saw as parasitic. See: Adolf Hitler, *My Struggle* (London: The Gainsborough Press, 1988), 123–24.

59. Adolf Hitler declared war to the United States on December 11, 1941.

60. Alexandre Kum'a N'dumbe III, *Hitler Voulait l'Afrique. Les plans secrets pour une Afrique fasciste 1933–1945* (Paris: L'Harmattan, 1980).

61. *Ibid.*, 34–5.

62. *Ibid.*, 35.

63. *Ibid.*, 33–34.

64. Ibid., 34. From French: "When Hitler will rise to power in 1933, he will find a vast organized and dynamic colonial movement, where will be represented most of the political tendencies of Weimar and mainly those who will later be the most loyal political companions of the Führer."

65. *Ibid.*, 36. The Treaty of Versailles (June 28, 1919) split the Afrikan German colonies (Burundi, Kamerun, Namibia, Rwanda, Tanzania, and Togo) among the victorious allies.

66. In 2001, the enslavement of Afrikans by European nations was declared a "crime against humanity" by the Durban World Conference Against Racism, Racial Discrimination, Xenophobia and Related Intolerance.

67. The very invention of colonial-imperialism with its racist anthropology ("Black Codes," Apartheid, lynching, alienation, subjugation, cultural control and more) substantiates this point of view.

68. Arthur Comte de Gobineau, *The Inequalilty of Human Races* (Trans. by Adrian Collins, Burlington, IA: Ostara Publications 2011).

69. Georges Vacher de Lapouge, *L'Aryen. Son Rôle Social* (Paris: Albert Fontemoing [Ed.], 1899).

70. Siméon Basile Atangana Ondigui, *Le Dictionnaire Ewondo, op. cit.*, 31. One of such ideals is the knowledge, that is, the inner grasp of the *raison d'être* of things. It is a challenge for the inquisitive mind to produce an ontological account about the world.

71. David E. Stannard, *American Holocaust. The Conquest of the New World* (New York: Oxford University Press, 1992).

72. John Henrik Clarke, *Christopher Columbus and the Afrikan Holocaust. Slavery and the Rise of European Capitalism* (Buffalo, NY: EWorld Inc., 1998).

73. United Nations, *The United Nations Today* (New York: United Nations Publication, 2008), iii.

74. Basil Davidson, *The Black Man's Burden. Africa and the Curse of the Nation-State* (New York: Times Books, 1992); Edmund Dene Morel, *The Black Man's Burden* (Northbrook, IL: Metro Books, Inc., 1972).

75. From a Eurocentric standpoint, Charles de Gaulle would certainly not be viewed as a fascist, since he withstood Nazi Germany. However, when one considers his institutionalization of the neocolonial system, the Françafrique, operating till now in so-called "French-speaking" Afrikan countries, the personage appears in a different cloak; that of a venial colonialist. See: Thomas Deltombe et al., *La Guerre du Cameroun. L'invention de la Françafrique 1948–1971* (Paris: La Découverte, 2016).

76. Afrika is the cradle of the hominids, including the *Homo sapiens sapiens*, hence CAD's anthropological monogenetic theory. See: Cheikh Anta Diop, *Antériorité des Civilisations Nègres, op. cit.*

77. Perhaps the hope was fleeting, for if the armed inter-European and international pogroms were over, other types of warfare hovered over the world. First, emerged the so-called Cold War (1947–1991) between two competing ideological nuclear powers: The Soviet Union and the United States of America. But, with the collapse of Communism in the decade closing the 20th century until this second decennary in the 21st century, we have witnessed the surge of a limping geopolitical dispensation: the "Americanization of the world," to use Samir Amin's catchy phrase, through globalized liberal protectionism. The oxymoron is *à propos*, considering the current resurgence of micro nationalisms in the West and beyond. See: Samir Amin, *The Liberal Virus. Permanent War and the Americanization of the World* (New York: Monthly Review Press, 2004).

78. Emmanuel Chukwudi Eze, *Race and the Enlightenment. A Reader* (Malden, MA: Blackwell Publishers, 1997).

79. Cheikh Anta Diop, *Civilisation ou Barbarie, op. cit.*, 10. From French: "Thus imperialism, like the prehistoric hunter, begins by killing spiritually and culturally, before seeking to murder physically. The negation of the history and the intellectual achievements of black African peoples is the cultural, mental murder, which has already preceded and prepared genocide here and there in the world. To the extent that between the years 1946 and 1954—during which our project of restitution of the African authentic history took shape—the deforming perspective of the colonial blueprint had so profoundly altered the perceptions of intellectuals on the African past

that we were confronted to the greatest difficulties, even vis-à-vis Africans, to convey the ideas that today are almost becoming commonplace. One can hardly guess what the level of alienation of the Africans of that time was."

80. *Ibid.* From French: "project of restitution of the authentic African history, of reconciliation of African civilizations with history."

81. Jean Paul Mbelek, "*Le Déchiffrement de l'Os d'Ishango*" in *ANKH* (No. 12/13, 2003–2004), 118–137. A replica of the Ishango Bone is featured on the Munt Square in Brussels.

82. Figures in chapter 4.

83. Cheikh Anta Diop, *The African Origin of Civilization. Myth or Reality* (Ed. and trans. by Mercer Cook, Chicago, Illinois: Lawrence Hill Books, 1974), ii.

84. Cheikh Anta Diop, *Sciences et Philosophie. Textes de 1960–1986* (Dakar: IFAN Ch. A. Diop, Université Cheikh Anta Diop de Dakar, 2007).

85. Ama Mazama (Ed.*), The Afrocentric Paradigm* (Trenton, NJ: Africa World Press, Inc., 2003).

86. Plato, *Phaedrus*, 274c–275e.

87. Plato, *Apology*, 38a.

88. Thoth is the Kemetic god of calculation, measuring, and writing.

89. The problem with this Socratic view is that it seems to lean on "reproductive" or mimetic writing, such as done by secretaries or copyists. But it is doubtful whether creative writing, for example, is just reminiscent.

90. In his scholarship, CAD emphasizes the genetic kinship between the *Medu Neter* and other contemporary Afrikan languages, arguing that they all derive from a paleo Negro-Afrikan language. See: Cheikh Anta Diop, *Parenté Génétique de l'Égyptien Pharaonique et des Langues Négro-Africaines* (Dakar: Les Nouvelles Éditions Africaines, 1977), xxv. From this perspective then, I maintain from a morphological point of view that the Beti phrase "*Medzo me Nti,*" is a transliteration of the Kemetic "*Medu Neter*"; both meaning "Words from the divinity" or from the god. The notion of "god" here should not mislead us to understanding it as transcendent. It is striking that the concept "Beti" (of the Be-Ntu or Ba-Ntu [Bantu] larger Afrikan group) precisely means the "Gods," as I underscored earlier in chapter one. So, the Nti (singular of Beti) writing this text is an immanent "god" (being), a portion of God, yet striving to embody the eponymous divinity captured by his Nti-ness. In Beti, "*medzo*" is both a personal name (born by both females and males) and a common substantive. *Medzo* is the plural form of "*adzo,*" meaning discussion, debate, calumny, or trial. See: Siméon B. Atangana Ondigui, *Le Nouveau Dictionnaire Ewondo, op. cit.*, 20. The verb *dzo* means to say, such that "*Ma dzo na . . .* " means "I say . . . " or "I argue that. . . . "

91. Frantz Fanon, *The Wretched of the Earth* (Trans. Richard Philcox, New York: Grove Press, 2004).

92. Claude Lévi-Strauss, *Tristes Tropiques* (Trans. John and Doreen Weightman, New York: Penguin Books, 1992), 299.

93. *Ibid.*, 300.

94. Michel Foucault (Trans. Robert Hurley), *The History of Sexuality. Vol. I: An Introduction* (New York: Vintage Books, 1978), 60.

95. Cheikh Anta Diop, *Civilisation ou Barbarie, op. cit.*, 9. Bad faith scholarship serves destructive ideologies by consciously silencing, obscuring, or distorting the facts to be analyzed.

96. Malcolm X, *By Any Means Necessary* (New York: Pathfinder Press, 1992).

97. Cheikh Anta Diop, *Civilisation ou Barbarie, op. cit.,* 19–92. See also: Christopher Stringer and Robin Mckie, *African Exodus. The Origins of Modern Humanity* (New York: Henry Holt and Company, Inc., 1996).

98. Political struggles around the world seem to corroborate the view that human beings abhor protracted discrimination and exclusion, just as they resist, sooner or later, demagogy and exploitation.

99. W. E. B. Du Bois, *The Souls of Black Folk* (New York: Dover Publications, Inc., 1994), Du Bois diagnosed that "the problem of the Twentieth Century is the problem of the color-line."

100. Joel Augustus Rogers, *Nature Knows No Color-Line* (Middletown, CT: Wesleyan University Press, 2014 [1952]).

101. As we hear sounds day and night, as we write, speak, or interact with one another in society through gaze and gestures, we emit and receive positive or negative thoughts, feelings, energies, and impressions that arouse certain emotions (joy, love, compassion, surprise, pride, envy, etc.).

102. Paul Ricoeur (Trans. by Emerson Buchanan), *The Symbolism of Evil* (Boston: Beacon Press, 1967), 306.

103. From French: "For his eminent moral and professional qualities and for the exceptional services that he rendered to African research in the years during which he headed the administrative secretariat of the IFAN."

104. Présence Africaine is a telling name for a publishing company. It emphasizes the continuing Afrikan presence in world history, especially as different colonial ideologies have repeatedly been trying to maliciously vindicate their matricide by construing the cradle of sapient humanity and civilization (Afrika) as a-historical. See: Cheikh Anta Diop, *The African Origin of Civilization. Myth or Reality* (Trans. from the French by Mercer Cook, Chicago: Lawrence Hill Books, 1974); Makhily Gassama (Dir.), *L'Afrique répond à Sarkozy. Contre le discours de Dakar* (Paris: Philippe Rey, 2008). Présence Africaine is located at Rue des Écoles (Quartier Latin) and is a constituent of the documentary emulation of the neighboring Parisian Sorbonne.

105. V. I. Lenin, *Imperialism. The Highest Stage of Capitalism* (New York: International Publishers Co., Inc., 2011).

106. Cheikh Anta Diop, *Civilisation ou Barbarie, op. cit.*, 462 ff.

107. *Ibid.*, dedicatory page. From French: "Alioune, you knew what you came to do on earth: A life entirely consecrated to others, nothing for oneself, everything for others, a heart filled with goodness and of generosity, a soul kneaded with nobility, a mind always serene, simplicity personified! Did the demiurge want to propose us, as an example, an ideal of perfection, in calling you into existence?"

108. Caytu is the name of Cheikh Anta Diop's village, which I visited in December 2016. See Figure 2.1: The author in front of CAD's mausoleum in Caytu.

109. Cheikh Anta Diop, *Civilisation ou Barbarie, op. cit.*, 12, 16, 457–77.

110. *Ibid.,* 16. From French: "The African who has understood us is one who, after the reading of our works, would have felt burgeoning in him a different person, moved by a historical consciousness, a true creator, a Promethean bearer of a new civilization and perfectly conscious of what the whole world owes to his ancestral genius in all the domains of science, of culture and of religion."

111. The emphasis on Afrika is accounted by the scientific fact that *the Homo sapiens sapiens* is Afrikan in origin. In consequence, all subsequent humans must be conversant with the Afrikan facet of their particular histories.

112. Mary Lefkowitz, *Not Out of Africa. How Afrocentrism became an excuse to teach myth as history* (New York: BasicBooks, 1996), 135.

113. Cheikh Anta Diop, *Nations Nègres et Culture, op. cit*., 35–401.

114. The symposium was held in two stages: the first took place from 28 to 31 January 1974 and concerned 'The peopling of ancient Egypt,' the second dealt with 'The deciphering of the Meroitic script' and took place from 1 to 3 February 1974. The participants were as follows: Professor Abdelgadir M. Abdalla (Sudan); Professor Abu Bakr (Arab Republic of Egypt); Mrs N. Blanc (France); Professor F. Debono (Malta); Professor J. Dévisse (France); Professor Cheikh Anta Diop (Senegal); Professor Ghallab (Arab Republic of Egypt); Professor L. Habachi (Arab Republic of Egypt); Professor R. Holthoer (Finland); Mrs J. Gordon-Jaquet (United States of America); Professor S. Husein (Arab Republic of Egypt); Professor Kaiser (Federal Republic of Germany); Professor J. Leclant (France); Professor G. Mokhtar (Arab Republic of Egypt); Professor R. El Nadury (Arab Republic of Egypt); Professor Th. Obenga (People's Republic of the Congo); Professor S. Sauneron (France); Professor T. Säve-Söderbergh (Sweden); Professor P. L. Shinnie (Canada); Professor J. Vercoutter (France); Professor Hintze (German Democratic Republic); Professor Knorossov; Professor Piotrovski (Union of Soviet Socialist Republics) and Professor Ki-Zerbo (Upper Volta) were invited to the symposium but were unable to attend and sent their apologies. In accordance with the decisions of the International Scientific Committee, Professor J. Dévisse, the Committee's Rapporteur, was present and prepared the final report of the symposium. Unesco was represented by Mr Maurice Glélé, program specialist, Division of Cultural Studies, representing the Director-General, and Mrs Monique Melcer, Division of Cultural Studies.

115. G. Mokhtar (Ed.), *General History of Africa, Vol. II. Ancient Civilizations of Africa* (California: University of California Press, 1981), 76–77.

116. Pathé Diagne, *Cheikh Anta Diop et l'Afrique dans l'histoire du monde* (Paris: L'Harmattan, 2008), 102. From French: " . . . matriarchate the characteristic of European and Mediterranean societies."

117. Cheikh Anta Diop, *L'Unité Culturelle de L'Afrique Noire* (Paris: Présence Africaine, [1959] 1982), 33–38.

118. Cheikh Anta Diop, *Civilisation ou Barbarie, op. cit*., 12. In French: "*aucune pensée, aucune idéologie n'est, par essence, étrangère à l'Afrique, qui fut la terre de leur enfantement.*"

119. *Ibid.* In French: "*la plupart des idées que nous bâptisons étrangères ne sont souvent que les images, brouillées, renversées, modifiées, perfectionnées, des créations de nos ancêtres: judaisme, christianisme, islam, dialectique, théorie de l'être,*

sciences exactes, arithmétique, géométrie, mécanique, astronomie, médecine, littérature (roman, poésie, drame), architecture, arts, etc."

120. *Ibid.*, 16. In French: "*toutes les nations se donnent la main pour bâtir la civilisation planétaire au lieu de sombrer dans la barbarie.*"

Chapter 4

Zen

Afrosofia in the Antadiopian Mvettean and Scientific-Philosophic Méthode Directe

When shall we experience an era of lasting peace and shared prosperity among peoples and nations in this world? Prophetic, that is, liberatory voices, constantly address this crucial question, thus delineating the slippery redemptive path before us. While CAD, for example, warns that humanity should not be made by the erasure of some for the welfare of others,[1] Fanon summons our decision to re-member our humanity. He writes: "Let us decide not to imitate Europe and let us tense our muscles and our brains in a new direction. Let us endeavor to invent a man in full, something which Europe has been incapable of achieving."[2] But who is this "us" that Fanon repeatedly talks about? Well, his "us" seems to symbolize pan-Afrikan humanity, for Jean-Marc Ela, who considers that "*le cours de l'histoire peut changer si les peuples noirs renouent avec leur tradition scientifique et technique qui est à l'origine des civilisations antiques.*"[3]

The third chapter, dealing with the current global predicament of cultural alienation,[4] has led us, truth-seekers, to the crossroads of human history, with a decisive option and mission ahead of us: shape, through our lifestyles and writings, a more agential and accommodating civilization built on what CAD calls an openness toward the Other.[5] He uses other dynamic and visionary phrases like the general progress of humanity,[6] or the emergence of an era of universal concord,[7] to convey the same idea of humanity's reconciliation with itself. In listening to CAD, however, one wonders what he makes of the predatory geo-economic et geopolitical world we live in. Is he not an eschatological dreamer whose scholarship is tainted with gross reverie and sheer idealism? If so, why fantasize and summon a fictive ideal in a geopolitical world still all too hegemonic and predatory? If not, why would CAD defend some abstract humanism when, using his own terms, corporate "*charognards*"[8] (scavengers) and imperial "*pieuvres*"[9] (octopuses) still relentlessly peck and devour the masses worldwide?

If this Antadiopian diagnosis of our contemporary world is accurate, and if the Afrikan-Kenyan writer Ngũgĩ wa Thiong'o is right in his view that "there is no region, no culture, no nation today that has not been affected by colonialism and its aftermath,"[10] then the question to CAD's conciliatory philosophy of history could be formulated as follows: what is its epistemic foundation? In other words, what methodologies and procedures can enable present-day researchers to bring about the "Diopianization"[11] of human history in knowledge productions? In what ways can they transcend, in academia, the many cultural contradictions (ideological, economic, racial, etc.) inherent to contemporary societies? How can they produce informative, factual, inclusive, and comprehensive knowledges on us, humans, and on the world at large? What cognitive strategies can blend the various epistemic methods (empiricism, rationalism, pragmatism, authority, revelation, etc.)[12] and unite the compartmentalization of knowledges in contemporary academy? More prosaically, what organizing theoretical framework does CAD tool his readers with, to advance dialogical, conciliatory, and pluriversal epistemologies? These are a few interrogative imports from the third chapter.

My claim in this fourth chapter is that CAD, whose primary scientific terrain is globalized Afrika,[13] builds his unitive anthropological eschatology on a "*Mvettean*"[14] realistic utopia, using a scientific-philosophic direct methodology. It is my view that human cooperation around shared predicaments (at national and international levels) can indeed be fostered when reasoning reason, as I call it in this chapter, determinedly appraises reasoned reason as consigned in discourses and cultural artifacts. The Antadiopian suggested methodology functions with a complex, but workable circular historical blueprint, whereby the archeological (human oneness of origin) prefigures the eschatological (human reconciliation). For him, the scientific matrix of human civilizations, that is, precolonial *nations nègres* (black nations)[15] summons, in us, the seeker of the truth about our presence on earth.[16] What are we here on earth for? That is the key question confronting the potential "creator" of the Antadiopian projected humane civilization, who slumbers in each of us and must be awakened.

Let us then begin by raising a few objections to CAD's scientific-philosophic methodology, before examining its theoretical framework and contents relatively to the project at hand, namely the unfolding reconciliation of global humanity. Such an enlarged prospective outlook, I hope, will revitalize our epistemic practices in academia, and impact social and international relations among individuals, peoples, and nations.

CONTENTIONS AROUND THE ANTADIOPIAN METHODOLOGY

CAD's Af(i)ri-mediated[17] and Afrosofian[18] methodology, which proceeds from the view that no thought/philosophy can develop without a specific historical terrain,[19] has been differently appraised by his critics. But we must examine the facts in their validity and question the soundness of the arguments on both sides, beginning with CAD's view of human history. As we will see, the contention concerns both the latter and his intellectual posture vis-à-vis black Afrika's philosophic-scientific contributions to humanity.[20] But what triggers CAD's historiography and methodologies?

The Antadiopian interest in human history can be accounted for differently. First, he envisions history as sociological evidence: history, grandiose or mediocre, is consubstantial to each people,[21] and the latter can always consciously reconcile/reconnect to the former. But the history in question must be continuously investigated upon and thought into various social institutions with the best possible accuracy. Historical attributes, in this respect, do not really matter to CAD. The relevant point for a people is to know its origin, no matter how humble and modest it may be.

Second, CAD defines history as the key that opens the door to both the intelligence and the understanding of the Afrikan society,[22] and all others. Third, with a corrective intention, CAD denounces the intentional distortion of the Afrikan source in human history by Afrikanist historiography.[23] The latter purposely turns history into an imperial ideological weapon, thus feeding generations of students in Europe and beyond with a "cultural poison"[24] from their early childhood. Considering the above, it becomes necessary, for CAD, that more objective scholars in Afrika and beyond invest themselves in rewriting human history.[25]

One would agree, it seems to me, that CAD is right in denouncing deliberate historiographic distortions, the reason being that they cannot resist the test of time. Temporarily, they can regulate people's thoughts and actions, but their deceitful nature cannot be concealed in a perennial manner. Moreover, they betray their authors' lack of *franc-parler* (free-spokenness/veridicity), which Michel Foucault (1926–1984) analyzes in terms of *parrēsia*.[26] It may be objected that one's commitment to truth-telling in the academia and beyond can be perilous[27] and backlash[28] on the speaker. Agreed! But truth is stubborn and cannot be concealed *ad aeternum*. As such, it should remain the goal of inquiry. That is the sense in which Th. Obenga defends the demise of the Afrikanist lie when he writes: "*le mensonge africaniste doit mourir.*"[29]

Concerning the problem of sources, I credit Professors Jean-Marc Ela and Mary Lefkowitz for respectively gauging CAD's caution concerning the uncritical reliance on Afrikanist scholarship. In a decolonial tone, he warns of the danger, for Afrikans, to be uncritically instructed of their past, society, and thought through Western works.[30] The problem with this claim is that it seems to install an epistemic chasm between the West in general and the rest of the world. It gives the impression that the emphatic possessive pronoun "*notre*" (our) in CAD's text in French, apposed three times to different substantives (history/past, society, and thought) in the sentence, distances itself from the common Westerner's inquisitiveness in those different fields, instead of just certain types of Europe-centered epistemologies, namely those with actual hegemonic contents.

It means that all centric works need not necessarily be imperious, and this nuance is worth underscoring. But there remains a possible exclusive aperture in CAD's use of the possessive pronoun "*notre*" here. Yet, there is also an inclusive avenue in "*notre,*" more accommodating and pluriversal in scope. It is the communal receptive "our," hospitable[31] to all humans of good will interested in understanding their respective agential presences in space-time in the world.

Quite clearly, the preceding two paragraphs posit the problem of language in gestural, written, and oral communications, with their connotations and misapprehensions. Just as writers and interlocutors struggle to express themselves clearly, intelligibly, and unambiguously in order to be understood properly, so does CAD. Sometimes lexically eclectic, he exposes his readership to conflicting interpretations. But before examining his critical methodology, let us first consider Lefkowitz' and Ela's respective interpretations of the latter.

Mary Lefkowitz and The Critique of Afrocentric Methodologies

For M. Lefkowitz, who does not quote the Antadiopian excerpt that I referenced three paragraphs earlier, CAD's scholarship is tainted with a double methodological flaw, "because it requires its adherents to confine their thinking to rigid ethnic categories that have little demonstrable connection with practical reality."[32] Lefkowitz adds in the same vein: "we come now to the other flaw in Diop's methodology. As we saw in the last chapter, his mode of history writing allows him to disregard historical evidence, especially if it comes from European sources."[33]

One can surmise that the inflexible, stiff, or "rigid ethnic categories" that Lefkowitz decries here are "Afrocentric"[34] in character, even if she hesitatingly unfolds her views under the following interrogative caption: "Is Afrocentrism a new historical methodology?"[35] Her definitional caution vis-à-vis what she calls "Afrocentrism" is probably informed by her familiarity with Asante's following theorization of Afrocentricity as "the centerpiece of human regeneration":[36]

> *Afrocentricity is a mode of thought and action in which the centrality of African interests, values, and perspectives predominate. In regards to theory, it is the placing of African people in the center of any analysis of African phenomena. Thus, it is possible for anyone to master the discipline of seeking the location of Africans in a given phenomenon. In terms of action of behavior, it is a devotion to the idea that what is in the best interest of African consciousness is at the heart of ethical behavior. Finally, Afrocentricity seeks to enshrine the idea that blackness itself is a trope of ethics. Thus, to be black is to be against all forms of oppression, racism, classism, homophobia, patriarchy, child abuse, pedophilia, and white racial domination.*[37]

So, if the purpose of Afrocentricity is to bring about a renewed humanism, what is "rigid" and "ethnic" about such a project? Should oppression (in all its forms) be denounced euphemistically for one to sound more amenable? This question only holds because of the skeptical leap in Lefkowitzian Afrocentrism. The adjective "new," in her interrogation of Afrocentrism as a historical methodology seems suspicious and even menacing to her historiographic orientation, hence the injunction: "everyone should be aware that there are real dangers in allowing history to be rewritten."[38] The Lefkowitzian historiography would then be heuristically comprehensive, perennially capturing all possible interpretations of Afrikan agency in space-time. Else, Afrikanist historiography will often be challenged and revisited by Afrocentric perspectives, thereby undergoing the corrective process of updating (*aggiornamento)* and rewriting through research. Indeed, the discovery of new informative sources (archeological, botanic, chemical, iconographic, linguistic, mythological, oral, physical, written, zoological, etc.) can prompt such updating.

This said, I credit Lefkowitz for bringing the important issue of the "historical evidence" to the discussion table, because it falls within the scope of methodological approaches in scientific discourse. The phrase "historical evidence," however, begs the following semantic questions: what are we to understand by "history," "evidence," and their apposition? Is the evidence (a body of facts/information about someone or something) evident, obvious, and valid to all inquirers? What is this factual organism (evidence) made of? Can consensus easily be reached by scholars on the historical character of a given evidence? Can it be misrepresented and corrected?

These are controversial questions, which overtly yield conflicting epistemic and ideological postures between the "Afrocentrists"[39] and Lefkowitz herself, to the extent that she writes sarcastically: "I will suggest that arguing that Afrocentric writers offer a valid interpretation of ancient history is like being comfortable with the notion that the earth is flat."[40] This opinion is farfetched and Manichean: if CAD writes, it is precisely for the sake of debunking Afrikanist historio-mythography. He intends his scholarship to be examined with this key question in mind: "*mythe ou vérité historique?* ("myth or historical truth?"). We already heard the compelling pronouncement of the international community of Egyptologists[41] gathered in Cairo in 1974 on this daunting question:

> Although the preparatory working paper sent out by Unesco gave particulars of what was desired, not all participants had prepared communications comparable with the painstakingly researched contributions of Professors Cheikh Anta Diop and Obenga. There was consequently a real lack of balance in the discussions.[42]

Yet, as is apparent in Lefkowitz' preceding quotes, CAD, whom she groups among the Afrocentrists, is still charged with some discriminatory and ethnocentric obscurantism, which presumably misleads him to ignore the historical evidence, especially when Europe-centered. But is this claim true?

To answer this question, the least one can do is to consult the various bibliographical indexes of CAD's scholarship. This direct methodological confrontation of the inquirer with the Antadiopian works reveals the author's massive reference to Western sources (ancient, medieval, and contemporary alike), thus proving Professor Lefkowitz simply mistaken. CAD's alleged discriminatory methodology would be inconsistent with the dedication of his *L'Afrique Noire Précoloniale*[43] to his French lecturers of the Parisian Sorbonne Gaston Bachelard (1884–1962),[44] André Leroi-Gourhan (1911–1986),[45] and André Aymard (1900–1964).[46]

Furthermore, the author of *Civilisation ou Barbarie* is adamant that research should be anthropologically sound, that is, conducted without complacency;[47] authentically. Additionally, research should aim at comprehensiveness and inclusiveness. Afrikans must, therefore, freely fetch from the common intellectual heritage of humanity,[48] he writes. For CAD, all humans share in a reciprocal intellectual heritage, given that they can learn from one another under the guardianship of the veracity or the exactness of what one writes,[49] rather than ethnocentrism or chauvinism. These precisions are necessary when we keep in mind that the ultimate Antadiopian geopolitical project is precisely to witness, someday, the burgeoning of a genuine humanity and a new perception of the human being without ethnic factors.[50] How then could CAD be exposing and promoting ethnocentrism at the same time?

It would be contradictory for CAD to defend a humanity beyond ethnicism and, concomitantly, to champion "rigid ethnic categories" *à la* Lefkowitz. Accordingly, when CAD posits that modern technology and science come from Europe just as, in ancient times, universal knowledge flew from the Nile Valley to the rest of the world, and toward Greece (the intermediate link) in particular,[51] what he suggests to his audience is the need for a chronological and scientific restitution of the human historical thread, and not a factional defense of his insular Afrikan cultural heritage.[52] Yet, the latter disturbing tendency to culturally alienate ancient Greece from classical Afrika is apparent in Lefkowitz' revealing book title (*Not Out of Africa)* and in her methodology when she maintains: "it is from the Greeks, and not from any other ancient society, that we derive our interest in history and our belief that events in the past have relevance for the present."[53] It is my view that all human societies (ancient and contemporary), studied from endogenous perspectives, should all be given due attention in a "democratic" academe that values divers(e-un)ity.[54]

At this point, let us turn to Professor Ela who, through his book title *Cheikh Anta Diop ou l'honneur de penser*,[55] reveals his intention to assess CAD's thinking through his scholarly production. Ela perceives him as an honorer of critical thought and appraises his methodology as such. What then is the kernel of this "*honneur de penser*" ("honor to think") in CAD? How does he orient his reader toward the intellectual life? What is of value and worth of our attention in CAD's methodology? What fundamental problem does CAD address in revisiting the Afrikan segment of human History, and what enduring truth does he bequeath to contemporary humanity and future generations?

Jean-Marc Ela or the Afrikan Turn in Human Historiography

First and foremost, Ela defines CAD as "*ce travailleur intellectuel qui dit l'Afrique au monde des savants*,"[56] adding that he is "*l'un des grands maîtres du soupçon de l'histoire africaine*,"[57] because of his unabated scientific inquisitiveness. But why would CAD suspect the prevailing Afrikanist historiography of his time? Was it problematic? If so, what was the problem? These questions are clarified in the Antadiopian following concern: What were our ancestors doing on the continent since Prehistory? The question must be asked for, while the European can trace the course of his history up to the Graeco-Latin antiquity and the Eurasiatic steppes, the Afrikan who, through Western books, tries to trace her historical past stops at the foundation of Ghana. Beyond, those "works" are mute, seeing nothing but obscure darkness.[58]

In commenting upon these words, let us begin by observing that CAD's scholarship has immensely contributed to brightening the pleonastic "*nuit noire*" ("black night") that he evokes in his French text about classical Afrika in Afrikanist-Eurocentric historiography. However, when he writes *Nations*

Nègres et Culture in 1954 in a colonial context, Afrikan historiography is still predominantly Eurocentric. How did this hegemonic geo-political predicament impact the academe? CAD explains that the deforming perspective of colonial blinkers had so profoundly distorted the gazes of intellectuals on the Afrikan past.[59] In other words, as far as the Afrikan past was concerned, critical reason was emasculated and almost vanquished in most Afrikanist intellectuals, with the exception of some "good faith"[60] scholars like Volney (1757–1820),[61] Jean-Francois Champollion (1790–1832),[62] or Emile Amélineau (1850–1915),[63] etc. As CAD shows in the third chapter of *Nations Nègres et Culture* titled "*Falsification moderne de l'histoire*"[64] ("Modern falsification of history"), colonialism had become the ideological blinder from which Afrikanist historiography was constructed before and after the Euro-American Berlin Conference (1884–1885).

Classical Afrika was then wrapped in a quasi-incognoscibility. Beyond the third century BCE, there was utter silence or a pleonastic "*nuit noire,*" that is, the conundrum of the historiographic unknown, the "dark night." This is the epistemic context in which CAD engages in examining ways in which he could dissipate the thick obscurity that obstructed an intelligible access into Afrikan antiquities. The epistemic stakes of this search were high: human general history was in crisis and in need of renewal. Ultimately, as Ela contends, CAD had to take up the challenge to reconcile human history with itself by questioning the entirety of discourses which were constituted in Europe during the centuries of imperialism. Here, the real crisis in European sciences is not that which Husserl analyzes but that which is established when the natives of Afrika learn to study history.[65]

It is my view that these words preserve their cautionary freshness in the current decolonial context of our world. When "truth" becomes subservient to imperial designs as CAD denounces,[66] science (research) is jeopardized, waning in credibility and pertinence.

Thus, appraising CAD's methodology from a decolonial perspective, Ela emphasizes its thoughtful, critical, and corrective stance vis-à-vis Afrikanist scholarship. This intellectual posture is adopted from the backdrop of the Antadiopian constant warning against scientific crimes[67] respectively veiled under various deceptive cloaks: mythmaking,[68] "bad faith,"[69] "conscious falsification of human history,"[70] "intellectual and moral fraud,"[71] "imperial ideology,"[72] and "pseudo-science."[73]

In contrast to Lefkowitz' reading of CAD, Ela's is not that the researcher discards Western sources, but that she constantly resorts to her judgement as a good and reliable guide to scientific truth. The latter can be sieved out by a critical examination of data from the perspective of the inquirer's informed vision and values. This reform of one's understanding on the Afrikan past

- which is also the human past by virtue of the Antadiopian monogenetic theory - explains Ela's stand that the key to Afrika's mystery is uncovered when Afrikan women and men focus on their history/civilization and study the latter for a better understanding of themselves.[74]

Ela takes us to the opposite end of colonial truth, whose aim consists, according to CAD, in attempting to convince the Afrikan that she is not the author of the achievements found in her homeland.[75] Nothing is more erroneous: precolonial Afrika rather presents an instructive heritage of creative agency to contemporary humanity. Therefore, to restore this truth is not only an act of submission to the requirements of scientific rationality. It is also a violation of the ideological foundations of domination.[76] And "*cette vérité*" ("this truth") in the (re)making of Afrikan historiography, which Ela convokes, requires the active and enterprising presence of competent Afrikan scholars themselves in the sciences.[77]

So, for Ela, CAD's pursuit of researched truth about the meaning[78] of the human presence in the world serves scientific-philosophic purposes. It dis-alienates from the will to intellectual misguiding tutelage and stirs the mind toward critical thinking in view of a peaceful geopolitical coexistence: "*Tâchons d'inventer l'homme total que l'Europe a été incapable de faire triompher,*"[79] yells Fanon. Ela with Fanon, like a tree-hyrax in the dark night of human alienation. With truth-seeking pulling and stretching one's thought processes, it is the liberation of creative minds from alienating knowledges (institutional and informal) which is sought. The seeker of abiding truths thus reappraises the accuracy of historical discourses from the point of view of a cohesive paradigm. From this line of thought, the epistemic deepening of histories cannot but contribute toward the general grasping of humanity's cultural trajectories.

Consequently, the key elements that Ela underscores in CAD's methodology extend beyond those enumerated here, namely his unrelenting search for truth to advance science,[80] his methodical doubt (*soo*),[81] his intellectual autonomy, his trans-disciplinarity, and his courageous sense of agency. He considers these aspects decisive in bringing about firmer truths in human historiography.

At this juncture, the conclusive question about Ela's take on CAD's methodology may be formulated in the following manner: what novel truths does CAD drop into the world's epistemic basket about the human precolonial past in Afrika? Does CAD succeed in dissipating the historical "*nuit noire*" ("black night") we underlined earlier? If so, how? Ela's response to these questions is trenchant: reason was born among Black people. That is the scandalous truth shining forth from CAD's work. This explains why the latter raise(d) major scientific debates. CAD's message is the affirmation of a scandalous truth that could not be advertised.[82]

Ela, here, elucidates both the prevalent silence and obscurity ("*nuit noire*") on classical black Afrika in Afrikanist-Eurocentric scholarship: black Afrikans engendered and mobilized critical and creative reason. Ela depicts CAD as a defender of a "*scandaleuse vérité*" (scandalous truth), that could not be publicized within the context of Western hegemony over the rest of the world. Yet, though dimmed in imperial circles, this provocative and uncomfortable fact should, I think, be scrutinized through ongoing research, as CAD suggests with his historical methodologies.[83] That is how contemporary decolonial scholarship, I hope, can flesh out the rise of human civilization in black Afrika, investigating further the Antadiopian monogenetic theory explored earlier on, and building on his eclectic study of classical Afrika. What is at stake in such a perspective is simply the search for accuracy in Afrikan and world historiographies.

However, the argument that the use of cognitive powers for inquisitive and civilizational purposes was prompted by the ancient black Afrikans is not typically Antadiopian. It was already attested, as CAD evidences in the eleventh chapter of *Antériorité des Civilisations Nègres*,[84] by a few thought-provoking French scholars such as the Egyptologist Émile Amélineau (1850–1915) and the philosopher Paul Massson-Oursel (1882–1956), as well as the Belgian historian Jacques Pirenne (1891–1972). Another enthralling voice, in this regard, is that of the French philosopher Volney (Constantin-François de Chasseboeuf: 1757–1820).

This historical debate over the birth of civilization[85] in classical Afrika is interesting for many reasons. First, it helps the inquirer understand the chronological development of the human past on earth, especially how thinking helped our forebears, the *Femina/Homo sapiens sapiens*, survive and settle in nature. Second, it indicates that one's informed and creative good sense is a reliable guide to research, that is to science. Third, reasoning challenges the contemporary researcher to constantly (re)examine the ontological, ethical, and epistemic validity of its peer, namely reasoned reason, as it permeates academic, historical, institutional, and geopolitical[86] discourses. Reasoning reason is actively carried out by actual individuals, in the dynamic attempts to solve the philosophic, existential, and scientific problems of their time. Reasoned reason, on the contrary, concerns all cultural artifacts in any given society and beyond.

In questioning reasoned reason in its written, artistic, and symbolic forms, reasoning reason, without tutelage, can still reinvigorate the contemporary scientific-philosophic movement by advancing new insights and evidence in all fields of knowledge. That could be a decisive step toward the dissipation of any quandary of cultural alienation. It could equally constitute a path to scholarly emancipation and to the creative enlightenment that CAD earnestly aimed at in his scholarship.

We have now examined how Professors Lefkowitz and Ela respectively appraise CAD's methodology. While Ela extensively discusses many works of the Antadiopian corpus, rightly emphasizing his insistence on creativity, Lefkowitz' general outlook is unfairly[87] dismissive, not only of CAD's historiographic methodologies, but more generally of the works of those she sees as "extreme Afrocentrists"[88] (CAD himself, Molefi Kete Asante, Martin Bernal, etc.).

This said, the subsequent analysis examines the source itself, that is, CAD's conciliatory approach to knowledge. The key elements through which audacious inquiry is governed will be emphasized as we proceed, namely selfless critical reasoning and considerate truthfulness. Besides, it will be made plain that CAD propounds the idea of transversality in contemporary research. He defends the engaging view that various disciplines should intersect for inquiry to be both sound (flawless) and comprehensive. There must therefore be a necessary tie, he insists, between science and philosophy. Both are fruitless without this fellowship. Ongoing conversions must therefore occur in the inquirer, the philosopher becoming a scientist and conversely. Such a mutation constantly operates, for example, in Mbog Bassong's *La Méthode de la Philosophie Africaine*.[89] But then, can scientific philosophy pacify the ferocity of the present geopolitical world, which Plumelle-Uribe rightly denounces in *La Férocité Blanche*,[90] and Derrida in *Rogues*?[91]

THE ANTADIOPIAN SCIENTIFIC-PHILOSOPHIC METHODOLOGY

Since the French fabulist Jean de La Fontaine (1621–1695) reminds us that "the strong are always best at proving they're right,"[92] we should always assess our epistemic motives. Why do we engage in research? Why and for whom do we write? Is it to enforce the survival of the fittest in society, or to promote the natural law?[93] As we set out to examine the Antadiopian met(a)-hodology, this challenging question, even if dealt with in the previous chapter, nonetheless conserves its denseness and complexity. If the "why" and the "for whom" mobilized us toward the search for the ultimate motivations, goals, and intended recipients of the Antadiopian epistemology, the methodological question, for its part, challenges us to closely consider the raison d'être of the investigative process itself. It means that it is now the *zen*,[94] the searching path, the "how," that is, the mobilization or the movement toward a conciliatory anthropology without prejudice, which is our primary focus. Thus, addressing the Mvettean problematic raised at the beginning of this chapter, CAD announces his epistemological purpose on the humanity in becoming in the following manner:

> *Nous aspirons tous au triomphe de la notion d'espèce humaine dans les esprits et dans les consciences, de sorte que l'histoire particulière de telle ou telle race s'efface devant celle de l'homme tout court. On aura plus alors qu'à décrire, en termes généraux qui ne tiendront plus compte des singularités accidentelles devenues sans intérêt, les étapes significatives de la conquête de la civilisation par l'homme, par l'espèce humaine tout entière.*[95]

The Antadiopian project is clearly spelt out in this quote. It defends the idea that all humans, though nuanced through accidental singularities such as skin pigmentation, do share in the same species *("espèce humaine")*. Accordingly, their monographs (histories, philosophies, or cultures) are to be studied within the general framework of human improvement (quest for civilization) at all levels. In other words, if our writing, like CAD's, is understood as a contribution to the overall progress of humanity, to the emergence of an era of universal concord,[96] how are we to proceed? What epistemic path is likelier to orient the worldwide human consciousness toward the construction of an authentic anthropology, free from the scientific complacencies of "transparency"[97] and (pseudo-science)?[98]

The will to epistemic transparency in the inquirer's analyses can indeed slide into semantic enclosures, leaving no room for the abstruseness of things and their possible/inherent complexity. What psychological dispositions should we then mobilize in such a gigantic task? Does it require some sort of personal Maatic integrity and intellectual probity? Can we, like creators or geniuses, trust our own lightning intuitions,[99] vision, judgement, adaptability, and inventiveness on our inquisitive *hodos* (path/way)? To begin with, what are we to understand by the concept of methodology?

Of *Met(A)*-Hodology in Cheikh Anta Diop

The Greek prepositional adverb *meta,* to be sure, does not enclose the inquirer solely within what lies beyond her investigative path (*hodos)*.[100] Rather, just like with the old English *mid* (middle) or the German *mit* (with), the Greek preposition *meta* envelopes a whole complex of what is perceived, valued, forgotten, neglected, or ignored by the inquirer. Simply put, inquiry is traversed by documentary artifacts, which are either affirmed, and examined, or purposely/inadvertently avoided and consequently silenced. The onus, here, is put on the inquirer's attitude vis-à-vis data.

In terms of intellectual attitude, CAD calls the inquirer to practice without compromise the exercise of rationalism for the sake of discarding, once and for all, the darkness of obscurantism, in all its forms.[101] The uncompromising function of the tool of cognition/justification called reason, from this Antadiopian perspective, is to confidently make truth (ultimate meanings, values, and abiding explanations) epiphanic, that is, manifest. The intellect must be free from tutelage[102] or subservience to cultural ideologies such as imperialism,[103] for which truth is a tool for colonial subjugation.[104] And what is colonialism itself? It is de-civilization and barbarism. For Aimé Césaire, colonialism is a ferocious system which primarily "works to decivilize the colonizer, to brutalize him in the true sense of the word, to degrade him, to awaken him to buried instincts, to covetousness, violence, race hatred, and moral relativism."[105]

How then can abiding values and meanings (truth) yield to such a system (colonialism)? Not only should truth guide and shepherd the inquiring mind, but it should also rejuvenate and stir it toward right thinking and living. That is what makes it (truth) an ideal of the highest order and, more importantly, something worth owning and pursuing in life. I am therefore in tune with J. A. Rogers, when he declares through his character Dixon: "I have found truth the only thing worth living for."[106]

In CAD's methodology, this debate on truth undergoes an epistemic turn, focusing on the factual[107] accuracy of one's research. My goal here is not to discuss the various epistemic methods (empiricism, rationalism, pragmatism, authority, revelation, etc.),[108] but to underscore the idea that what matters in CAD's scientific-philosophy is the truthful exactness of what one writes.[109] This explains why, distancing himself from epistemic tutelage and paternalism,[110] CAD highlights that his philosophical met(a)-hodology is grounded but on scientific objectivity/truth;[111] which is achievable through comprehensive research and scholarly debates. In debating, however, the inquiring mind must constantly remain attuned to strange and unpleasant truths. In other words, the intellect must strive to infuse itself with new ideas for the sake of "*l'objectivité scientifique*" (scientific objectivity) or "*la vérité scientifique*" (scientific truth). Hence the epistemic posture to yield only to the evidence of facts,[112] using a trans-disciplinary[113] démarche nourished by ongoing field research and debates within and beyond the academe. Thus, could be understood the Antadiopian direct methodology, especially as epitomized in the 1974 Cairo symposium.

The 1974 Cairo Symposium: Honoring Scientific Truth through Debates

Why did CAD require that the Cairo symposium be held before he could contribute to the UNESCO[114] encyclopedic project of writing the general history of Afrika? Why did he engage in trans-disciplinary scholarship, trying to unify the various disjointed disciplines (anthropology, biology, physics, etc.)? We reckon that such an enterprise, in our own time, is a real challenge to the compartmentalized and specialized dispensation of science in the academy. Yet, it is CAD's view and mine that contemporary science should resist such mutilation and be rather given a diverse-unitive orientation. A hyphen should constantly be maintained between distinction-integration, conflict-consensus, and between the various methodological approaches (empiric-rational-intuitive-verified and more).[115]

That was the paradigm at work in CAD, when asked by UNESCO to contribute in the elaboration of the second volume of the general history of Africa.[116] He requested that a symposium be organized beforehand, so that his theses on ancient Egypt be challenged and debated by the acme of the world's Egyptologists of the time.[117] That is how the 1974 Cairo symposium (January 28–February 3, 1974) came about. Th. Obenga points out that, on their way to Cairo, CAD made it clear to him that they would endorse the verdict of the scientific community, whether in favor or against his theses after the symposium.[118] This epitomizes the Antadiopian will to scientific conviviality and truth in a world still marked, in the words of Edgar Morin, *by "une barbarie totale dans les relations entre races, entre cultures, entre ethnies, entre puissances, entre nations, entre superpuissances."*[119]

The symposium concerned itself with 'The Peopling of Ancient Egypt and the Deciphering of the Meroitic Script.' It intended clarifying, from a scientific point of view, the origin and identity of the ancient Egyptians for, as CAD observed alarmingly that nearly all Egyptologists posit, a priori, the falsity of the thesis of Black Egypt.[120] This a priori premise should be grasped against the backdrop of imperial distortions, which considered more and more "inadmissible" to continue accepting the thesis hitherto evident of a black Egypt.[121] At this juncture, we should perhaps pause for a while and turn to the Guyanese anthropologist Ivan Van Sertima (1935–2009). He provides an insightful explanation concerning the "inadmissibility" of a black Egypt in Afrikanist scholarship, arguing:

> This discovery by Europeans of ancient Egypt, and the disclosures of a powerful Negro-African element in the ancestry of a civilization to which Europe owed so much, came as an embarrassment. It came also at a most inopportune time. It threatened to explode a myth of innate black inferiority that was necessary to the peace of the Christian conscience in Europe that was then prospering from the massive exploitation of black slaves. Africa was being systematically depopulated. Its empires had disintegrated. Its history had been buried. Its movement in step with other world civilizations had been abruptly halted.[122]

What I. Van Sertima underscores here is the intrusion and ascendency of ideology over historico-scientific truth. Confronted with this awkward historical flaw in 1954, the question arose: "*Qu'étaient les Égyptiens?*" (Who were the Egyptians?), wondered CAD in the heading of the first chapter of *Nations Nègres et Culture*. Were they Afrikans as he evidenced in the latter chapter, or Europeans, or perhaps aliens from some cosmic star?

The answers came from many sources. Using a multi-faceted methodology (chemistry, ethnonymy *'Km,'*[123] anthropology, linguistics, iconography, ancient written sources, etc.), CAD and Th. Obenga evidenced that the ancient Egyptians were black Afrikans in origin, culture, and language, as endorsed by the following conclusive pronouncement from the symposium's final report itself:

> Although the preparatory working paper sent out by Unesco gave particulars of what was desired, not all participants had prepared communications comparable with the painstakingly researched contributions of Professors Cheikh Anta Diop and Obenga. There was consequently a real lack of balance in the discussions.[124]

It should be clear to the reader that this verdict constitutes a victory for scientific truth[125] alone and, consequently, the capitulation of obscurantism. Scientific truth is what the scholars gathered at the Cairo conference supposedly sought, valued, and live for. I use the adverb "supposedly" because the International Scientific Committee's Rapporteur, Professor Jean Devisse (1923–1996), highlights the presence, at the said symposium, "*des gens de très mauvaise foi qui refusent de prendre en considération, nous l'avons vu lors du Colloque du Caire, qui refusent de discuter, qui refusent d'ouvrir sérieusement le débat.*"[126] This presence of bad faith scholars in Cairo notwithstanding, the important achievement for global humanity is that its history, in its Afrikan facet, was restored and honored by good faith intellectuals, especially through the decisive scientific contributions of CAD and Th. Obenga.

The truth restored was not of a religious nature. It was not "revealed" by an extraterrestrial deity. Rather, it sprouted from human thinking, from research, and from the confrontation and exchange of ideas among inquirers. In this sense, ancient Egypt, through her contemporary descendants like CAD and Obenga, bore witness to the Afrikan ongoing contribution to the advancement of the entire human race. The implications of this assertion are epistemically far reaching. They reinstate the prevailing interest in Egyptology within its proper basin, which is Afrikology and conversely.

Thus, the Cairo symposium inaugurates a new era, a renewed interest in both Afrikological and Egyptological studies. Both disciplines can now mirror each other as the palm and the dorsal of the same hand. This line of thought leads CAD to the following conclusion:

Les études africaines ne sortiront du cercle vicieux où elles se meuvent, pour retrouver tout leur sens et toute leur fécondité, qu'en s'orientant vers la vallée du Nil. Réciproquement, l'égyptologie ne sortira de sa sclérose séculaire, de l'hermétisme des textes, que du jour où elle aura le courage de faire exploser la vanne qui l'isole, doctrinalement, de la source vivifiante que constitue, pour elle, le monde nègre.[127]

With Afrika re-emerging as a foundational center of inquiry worth the attention of the international academe, the Cairo symposium's deliberations spur us, above all, to reinvest our thinking in the question of Otherness; namely the Afrikan Other in global humanity. In daring to confront this question of Afrikan alterity worldwide, it is a new page in philosophy, science, and human relationships that is being rewritten. The question must be asked subjectively with the abruptness of the Harlem Renaissance figure Countee Cullen (1903–1946) in his poem 'Heritage': "What is Africa to me?" The same concern may be rephrased thus: what is Afrika, the birthplace of the arts and sciences[128] *in* me? How can the Afrikan scientific heritage inspire me/us?

At any rate, our Afrikan inward Otherness, if serenely addressed, can offer us an avenue to learn to think more creatively, originally, and humanely. That is the strenuous task undertaken in this Afrosofian text. It appears that such is also the perspective of the Afrocentric paradigm discussed earlier. Since we (humans) are all genetically siblings, because "Africans under the skin,"[129] the question about the meaning of our interconnected presence in this world raises a critical axiological concern. What are we here on earth for? What is the purpose of our endeavors within the "temple" of research? Is it not to awaken the creator who slumbers in us to mobilize her potential toward the shaping of a more considerate civilization? Knowledge for knowledge's sake is perhaps gratifying, but its acquisition for both the apprehension (understanding) and transformation of the world, alongside the growth of people's character for right living in societies within the cosmos seems to me even more valuable.

Now, coming back to our methodological concern, we should rightly ask what organ, in the individual, sieves truth or the "evidence" out of the opaque data spread along the spiraling[130] (winding) "creek" that one's meta-rational *hodos* supposedly represents? The answer to this question points to the human brain, that is, to the reflective stream/current which, in CAD's view, is certainly the most perfected emitting and receiving device which exist in nature.[131]

THE HUMAN BRAIN: THE FUTURE METHODOLOGICAL TOOL PAR EXCELLENCE?

CAD's opinion on the human brain in the preceding quote seems inflated assuming that, by "Nature" with capital N, he means the earthly environment, our universe, and those beyond the latter. If that is the case, it would be difficult to substantiate such a claim with scientific evidence. Even if our knowledge of planets and stars within our expanding universe gradually increases through ongoing research, it nevertheless remains quite shallow and fragmentary.

In this respect, Edgar Morin hits the mark when he considers that "*nous sommes toujours dans la préhistoire de l'esprit humain,*"[132] meaning that we are still at the threshold and dawn of knowledge. Our epistemic journey toward the truth about the potential powers of the mind and on the nature of be(com)ing is just beginning. Moreover, theories on extraterrestrial intelligence[133] give room for the postulation of more advanced beings in Nature with greater transmitting potential than the human brain. Of course, one can dismiss alienology (science of aliens) as mystical nonsense but, as the saying goes, absence of the evidence is not the evidence of absence. Who knows what more performed telescopes and spacecrafts will enable scientists to discover even by the end of the current century?

The point here is that, beyond the possible objections on the potential powers of the human brain, present-day "hard" science itself suggests the validity of CAD's claim. In neuroscience, for example, it is envisioned that future neuralnanorobotics "provide a technology at the appropriate scale, with a suitable level of complexity to robustly interface the human brain with the massive volume of data that is stored and processed in the cloud."[134] In fact, neuroscientists, through neuralnanorobotics, envisage mind-blowing capabilities of the brain in a nearer future, attesting:

> It is conceivable that within the next 20–30 years, neuralnanorobotics may be developed to enable a safe, secure, instantaneous, real-time interface between the human brain and biological and non-biological computing systems, empowering brain-to-brain interfaces (BTBI), brain-computer interfaces (BCI), and, in particular, sophisticated brain/cloud interfaces (B/CI). Such human B/CI systems may dramatically alter human/machine communications, carrying the promise of significant human cognitive enhancement.[135]

This is probable, but we are not yet in 2050 to assess the practical validity of the preceding prediction. What is more challenging, perhaps, is that inquiries on the brain also lead us into the slippery realm of psychic phenomena beyond "hard" scientific thought which, as the statistician Joel B. Greenhouse signals,

> are unexplainable by any current scientific theory and, furthermore, directly contradict the laws of physics. Acceptance of psi implies the rejection of a large body of accumulated evidence explaining the physical and biological world as we know it.[136]

Greenhouse raises the interesting point that it is not only parapsychic occurrences[137] which are problematic, but our knowledges thereon as well, which sometimes err, gloss over the complexity of the mind, or confuse illusions with certitudes.[138] However, if Greenhouse and Morin converge on the limitedness of our constituted knowledges, Morin, with his paradigm of complexity, would certainly transcend the chasm posited by Greenhouse between psi and current scientific theory. Accordingly, Morin's complex thought would be closer to CAD's conciliatory philosophy and inquiring openness to anomalous psycho-physical phenomena. This enigma of the human brain extends to the opacity and mysterious Otherness of Nature itself, as defends the French theoretical physicist and philosopher Bernard d'Espagnat (1921–2015):

> *C'est parce que je considère, sur la base d'arguments ancrés dans la physique, que la chose elle-même, le réel n'est pas connaissable par la science tel qu'il est. De l'espoir d'une telle connaissance nous devons, je l'ai dit, faire notre deuil.*[139]

Considering the above, what is the way forward if Nature, mind, and knowledge remain opaque? What should we do as inquirers attuned to our relative ignorance of things? We must, perhaps, adopt the cautiousness of Morin, who opines that true rationality is profoundly tolerant vis-à-vis mysteries and their residual opacity: "*je crois que la vraie rationalité est profondément tolérante à l'égard des mystères.*"[140] Thus, the breakthrough might reside, not only in our lenience in relation to the anomalous, but also in our creative agency, even if innovators are sometimes considered as fools[141] or threatening dissidents by the prevailing geo-academic, economic, and political establishment. Such was the case, in the Afrikan context, with CAD in Senegal, Ngũgĩ wa Thiong'o in Kenya, Mongo Beti in Cameroon, many of their contemporaries, and others before their era.[142] This said, how does CAD himself "*zen*"[143] the human brain and construe it as a methodological toolkit toward knowledge?

ZENNING THE BRAIN IN CHEIKH ANTA DIOP

As I explained earlier[144] the Beti term *zen* means track, route, path, passage, way, and other synonymous terms. *Zenning* connotes the ideas of pathing and mapping: one can follow or create paths. Beaten paths antedate their users, whereas pathfinders initiate theirs. Animals and humans (inquirers, scouts, travelers, foresters, hunters, and ordinary people) are familiar with these two types of paths which, however, can be delusive without proper self-guidance. For example, as we walk, jog, or ride around highways and rural/urban areas, road signs like "wrong way" help us securely navigate our itinerary toward our destination.

Following wrong ways, deliberately or mistakenly, certainly averts us from achieving our purposes. We make no progress and, getting nowhere, we U-turn and reorient ourselves. But there are also paths (*mezen*) that eventually bring errands and trips to successful ends. These experiences of being missing/retrieving and being of the right track) are constitutive of the *zenning* process of the human brain as it reflectively constructs knowledge on itself and the rest of Naure. From the Mvettean perspective in which matter (the human body and brain included) is at once furtive (because energetic), ductile, and unpredictable,[145] let us now address the *zenic* function of the mind in CAD.

In the philosophic poem *(poème philosophique)*[146] Mvett, the constitutive elements of the cosmos, like interwoven strings, vibrate (in phase/out of phase) with the human brain (*cerveau*) and with one another:

> *Le mvett permet à ceux qui l'écoutent de voyager dans le temps. Grâce aux sons des cordes de la harpe, des chants, le cerveau se met en interférence avec les autres points de l'univers. Avec les dieux, les ancêtres et les humains, l'environnement, etc.*[147]

This quote displays a scheme in which Mvettean meditators *(ceux qui l'écoutent),* echoing the cosmic interlacing *(interference avec les autres points de l'univers)* and spokenness of the harpist's sounds/vibrations,[148] modulate their consciousness to the *dieux* (enlivening principles), the ancestors, humans, and the natural environment. The voyage alluded to in the quote might consists in the mental nearing and meditative *écoute* (listening) of the Mvettophile to what is upliftingly principled in nature, society, and the ancestors' legacy.

The problem here is that listening is a thoughtful skill that everyone may not necessarily have. Moreover, listening does not shield us from not/non-understanding, misrepresentations, and misinterpretations. In these instances, the meaning of our object of attention is missed out and remains somehow concealed. But the epistemic impediment of mishearing does not foreclose the possibility of comprehension. This being the case, the Mvettean requisite of listening (*nvogolan*) resolves itself in the dialectical poles of knowledge and misapprehension.

The philosophic import of this idea is that the mind, in constructing knowledge, can either ascertain or misperceive the complex outlook of things (people, language, concepts, etc.), which the Mvett advocates. But the practice of dialogic attentiveness to both worldly (earthly) and abstract realities could guarantee, recursively, the mind's in-dwelling in its own mystery. Accordingly, the brain constitutes not only a promising avenue for scientific philosophy in the making, but also an enigma about its meta-psychological potential.

I might sound merely speculative here, but the opacity of what is to be known in the cosmos allows for openness to the Mvettean psychoacoustics that Alain Elloué-Engoune talks about, and to "queer" theories on the makeup of the mind and Nature itself.[149] These eccentric ideas find expression in Tsira Ndong Ndoutoume's viewpoint that "*l'Univers pluricosmique, l'existence des civilisations extra-terrestres technologiquement plus avancés ne constituent aucune surprise pour l'Initié Mvett.*"[150]

Of course, everyone is not a Mvett initiate *(initié Mvett),* even if research and the will to embody the Mvett can turn one into its neophyte: to be(come) Mvett is a process of self-reinvention. Since (meta)psychological processes such as languages,[151] thoughts, discourses,[152] drives,[153] beliefs, emotions, mental disorders,[154] post-traumatic syndromes,[155] dreams,[156] clairvoyance, dowsing, hypnotism, and more increasingly capture the attention of contemporary psychoanalytic theorists, we should not dodge, but rather examine the phenomenal and fabulous potential of the inner matter that the human brain is.

It is striking that the theory of an expanding universe defended by Edwin Hubble (1889–1953)[157] in the twentieth century validates the law of corporeal furtivity exhibited in Mvettean characters. Matter (conceptual/material), in both theories, is dynamic rather than static. In the Mvett in particular, the human body is so agile and subtle that it defies natural laws, moving at will in the air, underground, or on water as Angèle Christine Ondo underscores:

> *. . . les guerriers du Mvett se déplacent sous terre, sur l'eau, partout où leurs actions les entraînent, et généralement à grande vitesse. La matérialisation des objets ou des armes obéit aussi à cette logique de la "furtivité."*[158]

The question we are to confront, however, is whether the human body is capable of such actions. If so, how does it acquire them? It is difficult to envision any practical answer here, but the Mvett is adamant, in its archetypal thought, that bodily furtivity is acquired through the *akom*[159] (fashioning/regeneration) of one's *nyian* (will), *ngul* (power), *akeng* (intellect), and *nyëman* (knowledge).[160] Thus, to "furtivize" one's body or any other object/element in nature consists in enabling it to swerve, appear, disappear, and reappear at will, depending on its specific power of manifestation.[161]

Yet, beside the foregoing advocacy of the furtive (self-surpassing) human archetype, the Mvett,[162] and the ongoing scientific research from cognitive neuroscientists, experimental psychologists, and neurologists,[163] the notion of corporeal furtivity remains problematic in embodiment theories (epistemologies, praxeology, phenomenology, etc.), where subjective experiences such as human teleportation, bilocation, and multilocation still await the practical validation of concrete experiences beyond laboratory experiments.[164] But the scientific leap remains crucial here if the self-surpassing adventure of the human mind is to become a lived reality. This explains CAD's following view:

> *. . . on ne pourra peut-être apprécier sa perfection que lorsque la technologie atteindra le stade de la bioélectronique. Donc une communication physique par voie électromagnétique, entre deux cerveaux de deux sujets séparés par une grande distance n'est pas en soi un phénomène irrationnel, et le deviendra moins encore dans l'avenir: le support physique est évident.*[165]

This Antadiopian excerpt from his 1983 article titled "*Philosophie, science et religion. Les crises majeures de la philosophie contemporaine*"[166] defends the idea of a new rationality likely to further the knowledge of the Real.[167] This new rationality is actually a sort of complex meta-rationality grounded on the creative potential of the human brain to gradually decrypt the enigma that Nature is. Perhaps, with the contribution of undulatory mechanics in microphysics[168] and its theory of the complementarity wave-particle[169] the human brain could be proven capable of para-psychological "phenomena" such as telepathy, precognition, or premonition.[170] CAD, therefore, hopes that when technology reaches the stage of bioelectronics, parapsychology, still quite abstruse, complex, and opaque today, could considerably contribute to the renewal of scientific philosophy.

Provisionally, thought, as displayed in the Antadiopian met(a)-hodology, displays a critical-curative function, examining and surpassing its own possibilities as well as the realm of phenotypic appearances upon which the phenomenon of racial prejudice, for example, is still predicated today in the American society and beyond.

LIVED RACISM VERSUS THE ANTADIOPIAN RECONCILIATORY PHILOSOPHY

Having explored the *zenning* prospects of the brain in CAD's epistemology, we will now examine its curative dimension in relation to the systemic and learned prejudice[171] of racism today. In so doing, we, seekers of wisdom, want to find ways of promoting, subjectively, the expression of humanity as healing agency worldwide. The question confronting us, however, is to know whether contemporary humanity can concertedly challenge the discriminatory geopolitical and economic episteme of the epidermis? Put otherwise, can we, humans, be truer to ourselves and more authentic by promoting egalitarian and cooperative ways of social living that transcend systemic favoritism? What sort of anthropological chromatism[172] is likely to shield us from the prevailing ethnocentrism rightly denounced in Yancy's *Backlash,* Chinweizu's *The West and the Rest of Us*,[173] Smiley & West's *The Rich and the Rest of Us*,[174] or Agbohou's *Le Franc CFA et L'Euro Contre L'Afrique?*[175] Can humanity reconcile with itself, as CAD envisions, by learning to appreciate and value the beauty of harmony within itself? Can it decolonize and exorcize itself of its cannibalistic chauvinism, so maliciously keen of "strange fruits" à la Garner?[176]

We find more than enough of such "strange fruits" in Yancy's *Backlash*. Discourses, indeed, can be likened to fruits that reveal the ethical status and cognitive constitution of their producers. The following discursive venom, spat out by a white racist, instantiates my meaning as well as the urgent need for the Antadiopian advocacy of a reconciled humanity through scientific philosophy:

> Dear Nigger Professor. You are a fucking racist. You are a piece of shit destroying the youth of this country. You are neither African nor American. You are pure, 100 percent Nigger. You would never marry outside of your Nigger race. That's a fact. Your're a fucking smug Nigger. You are uneducated with education. You are a fucking animal. Just like all Black people in the United States of America. Including that Nigger Kenyan that was born in fucking Kenya that has usurped the white house. Yes. It is called the white house for a reason because white people made this country great you fucking Nigger.[177]

These demeaning words are symptomatic of the chaotic inwardness of their white racist author. His antipathic and aversive vocabulary seems to betray a deficit of self-contentment and appreciation. What then grows out of his ethical decaying humus, is a great deal of self-contempt, and phobia, exteriorized verbally as the "Nigger." This self-reification is repeatedly castigated and eventually projected upon Professor Yancy, President Barack Obama and, by amplifying induction, to "all Black people in the United States of America."

More explicitly, the white racist speaker expresses and addresses his objectified Nigger-ness in terms of "fucking racist," "piece of shit," "fucking animal," or "uneducated with education." These phrases lay bare, before the reader's eyes, the psychological tempestuousness in which their author wades. They apparently manifest a concealed longing for a less uncanny self; one which is more multicultural, thoughtful, and cultured. Yet, the exponent still seems overwhelmed by a depreciative bent for, while construing President Obama as a usurper of the White House, he outlaws Professor Yancy, charging him of Socrates' crime:[178] the destruction of the country's youth. As a result, the white racist speaker's inner bitterness turns into a scapegoating strategy of Black people, perhaps out of apprehensive jealousy, as the Jamaican American historian J. A. Rogers (1880–1966) suggests in his view that "in the United States we have color jealousy, and not color prejudice: not contempt, but fear."[179]

Presuming Rogers to be right in opining that jealousy and fear are disruptive tenets of the American unifying ideal captured by the toponym "United States," a question arises: why would one be dissatisfied or envious of accidental geographic endowments such as the epidermis? Why would the issue of desegregated marriage be brought up with angst in the above quote, and yet be quickly barred and redlined to G. Yancy? We are left with the wrong impression that matrimonial love is predicated upon a partner's epidermis.

A similar romance is constructed around the exclusivist equivalence between "greatness" and whiteness in America, with its author's racist belief that "white people made this country great." What about the multifarious contributions of other Americans in the building of the nation? The white author of the venom is strangulated in some metaphysics of silence thereupon. But we cannot but ask: what is greatness (glory) and how is it acquired? The Swiss philosopher Emer de Vattel (1714–1767) is incisive in his answer: "True glory consists in the favourable opinion of men of wisdom and discernment: it is acquired by the virtues or good qualities of the head and the heart, and by great actions which are the fruits of those virtues."[180]

Obviously, de Vattel's ethical understanding of greatness sharply contrasts with the content of the quote under analysis, which represents a telling discursive setback countering the Antadiopian project of a reconciled humanity today. Indeed, what meaning would one attach to white greatness, considering the sour bitterness and hostility spat out in the preceding two pages?

Does greatness not rather consist in a certain sense of rational/scientific, intersubjective, and existential contentment? If we respond in the affirmative, greatness would be constitutive of the daring task of meditatively "*in*-dwelling" the opacity of omnijective Otherness. What this means is that greatness arises from a more intimate acquaintance (knowledge) of beings (oneself included) and things. Greatness, as the word suggests, resides in a certain perspicacity of the beholding eye to expand its visual field. When sufficiently sharp, the latter can notice its own possible blurredness in comparison to the vastness and relative opacity of that which is investigated upon. This openness of the inquiring mind to the complex intricacy of things hopefully sets the mind toward the exploration of the interiority or within-ness of things. That is the genetic aspect of the Antadiopian methodology. From this perspective, greatness is neared through the building of affinitive relationships between the searching self and the nuanced morphological shades somewhat "willed" by nature.

So, what is missing in the quote under discussion is a sense of wonder, evidenced by an obvious dimness and aloofness of the inner gaze. Its foreign *out*-dwelling sees nothing within itself but the Nigger. In vain, does one await a word of self-appreciation in the quote. The outpoured despicable vitriol calls for a restless scientific inquiry beyond the negativity of the inner gaze. What seems to be expressed is the guilt of self-lovelessness and an anxious will to predation, which then mushroom in rogue speeches, antedating possible pogroms.

The Antadiopian project of human reconciliation with itself will therefore have to reckon with the predicament of self-hatred expressed in America and beyond in the systemic loveless-ness of one's Otherness, and the lack of self-contentment captured by J. A. Rogers through the category of "jealousy." Why? Because, out of such a malicious "tree" (jealousy), can grow but weird psychic-linguistic "fruits" such as the recurrent sour nut "Nigger" in the racist quote under analysis. And what/who is the Nigger? James Baldwin's contention is incisive. The Nigger is but its inventor,[181] agreed that the latter is revealed in his invention. In other words, the product reveals its producer. The Nigger, then, certainly knows the motives behind his abhorred self-creation as the Nigger in the United States of America.

The problematic invention and reality of the Nigger, in the Baldwinian sense, as witnessed in Yancy's *Backlash*, is indicative of the imperativeness of CAD's call for a global mobilization toward a conciliatory ontology within individuals and cultures alike. To be sure, the very idea of "*réconciliation,*" to use CAD's loaded parlance, suggests the reality of philosophic, social, and cultural ruptures, protracted in character, within humanity. The need for a culture (civilization) of forbearance and unity is thus felt. It is even a possibility that lies within our reach, provided we practice the demanding "religion"[182] of science, which the Haitian scholar Anténor Firmin (1850–1911) aptly construes as "the only true one, the only one worthy of the attention and infinite devotion of any man who is guided by reason."[183]

But then, questions about "scientific" contradictory views resurface. Does truth always guide and shape science? Is the sustained exertion of reason always shielded from the grip of ideologies and of market-oriented interests in the academy? If so, how can we "reconcile the conclusions some seem to draw on the basis of this same science?"[184] If not, should we despair? Should we tread down the tragic and pessimistic paths respectively unfolded before us by Friedrich Nietzsche (1844–1900)[185] and Oswald Spengler (1880–1936)?[186]

CAD suggests a hopeful answer to these questions. For him, who wraps his vision and voice in a humane blueprint, each human generation should *in*present (understand) itself retro-prospectively. In other words, the depth of one's struggle within the context of specific geo-economic, political, or cultural predicaments, and the active assumption (handling/management) of the latter, should be mediated by a buoyant inclusive project. He writes: "*Un optimisme africain atavique, mais vigilant, nous incline à souhaiter que toutes les nations se donnent la main pour bâtir la civilisation planétaire au lieu de sombrer dans la barbarie.*"[187]

It is indeed this atavistic Afrikan optimism that will distinguish CAD in the next chapter as a "Mvett," that is a subduer, overcomer, and surmounter of barbarism (predation, prejudice, racism, etc.). As we will see, the "Mvett," indeed, summons the tragic human to emulate the enlivening presence of Eyo (Life) when she experiences the tempestuousness of life. So, even if apparently all existential blinkers of one's individual, social, or cultural trajectory seem on the red; even if hopelessness seems to become a people's daily portion, that is the time for the "Mvett" to connect to her inner emboldening and tenacious voice that says "*Bikalik!,*"[188] meaning, "Let us not despair!" in Beti.

This chapter, as we have seen, has discussed CAD's methodology and epistemology with the important contributions of Jean-Marc Ela and Mary Lefkowitz. We then went on to examine how CAD, himself, articulates his intellectual démarche. We discussed his emphasis on the necessity to labor for the pacification of humanity through independent, tolerant, and deliberative thinking, under the guidance of the sunlight of truth in one's private life and scholarship. An interesting point for ongoing and future philosophical inquiry is the idea of the intimate relationship between science and philosophy in the constituting new rationality.

The Antadiopian "religion" of reason, though leading us into the "abyss" of quantum mechanics, genetics, and parapsychology, has the merit to stir the contemporary searching intellect to question the nature of things, as did the roman philosopher Lucretius[189] a century before our era. The meaning of "philosophy" itself remains one of these enigmatic things, because philosophy is not a Greek concept. The next chapter will then attempt its clarification in the light of CAD's scholarship and the Afrosofian Mvett.

NOTES

1. Cheikh Anta Diop, *Nations Nègres et Culture, op. cit.,* 17. In French: "*L'humanité ne doit pas se faire par l'effacement des uns au profit des autres.*"

2. Frantz Fanon, *The Wretched of the Earth* (Trans. from the French by Richard Philcox, New York: Grove Press, 2004), 236.

3. Jean-Marc Ela, *Cheikh Anta Diop ou l'honneur de penser* (Paris: L'Harmattan, 1989), 137. From French: "The course of history can change if black peoples reconnect with their scientific and technical tradition which is at the origin of ancient civilizations."

4. I used the term alienation in the Beti sense of *akud*, that is, one's experience of cognitive dislocation, de-centeredness, and lack of existential agency. The *akud* person lacks self-knowledge and would hardly think or act autonomously and creatively.

5. Cheikh Anta Diop, *Civilisation ou Barbarie, op. cit*., 477. In French: "*une ouverture vers autrui.*" CAD's geopolitical philosophy of human collaboration opposes the view that knowledge is about hegemony and exploitation or that human civilizations cannot coexist peacefully without bellicose clashes. Likewise, CAD dismisses the incorrect phenotypic opinion that humans emerged from different parts of the world (polycentrism). He corrects the latter blueprint by emphasizing the scientific monogenetic theory, which holds that all humans emerged from black Afrika. Accordingly, human otherness ("yellow," "red," and "white" phenotypes) are just climatic adaptations of melanated people. Accordingly, humans are somehow genetically interrelated and hence Afrikans under their skin color. In other words, there is a subtle unifying thread beneath human phenotypes, such that their genes are more homogeneous than distinct. Thus, to be opened to otherness is to mediate one's self-understanding by re-appropriating psychologically, not only the different hues of others as furtive shades of oneself, but more importantly, the cultural contributions of all humans toward civilization. Since humanity is one in origin, it can also unite in purpose, work toward peace and inclusive prosperity.

6. Cheikh Anta Diop, *Antériorité des Civilisations Nègres. Mythe ou Vérité Historique?* (Paris: Présence Africaine, [1967], 1993), 275. "*progrès général de l'humanité*"

7. *Ibid.* "*l'éclosion d'une ère d'entente universelle*"

8. *Ibid.*, 276.

9. *Ibid.*

10. Ngũgĩ wa Thiong'o, *Something Torn and New. An African Renaissance* (New York: Basic*Civitas* Books, 2009), xi.

11. Since CAD defends an honest, conciliatory, and cosmo-centric approach to knowledge, I phrase the concept "Diopianization" to imply an epistemic and geopolitical leap toward inclusion, unity, and order. The cosmo-centric orientation of the Antadiopian epistemology is particularly evidenced by his attempt to unravel the mystery of "matter." I will emphasize the latter point in the fifth chapter.

12. The "Religions of the book" (Islam, Christianity, and Judaism) believe that which is revealed by "God" to be true. Authority epistemology holds claims made by "experts" to be true. The pragmatic relies on what "works" in practical life

experiences. The rationalist believes in logical truths, and the empiricist verifies his logical constructions through his sensual "evidence."

13. The phrase globalized Afrika refers, from the monogenetic standpoint to the whole of humanity.

14. It will be shown in the fifth chapter that the Mvett is a kind of anti-tragic heroine, the joyful musician, or the overcomer of historical contradictions. Qualitative life is her ontological, cognitive, and ethical abode.

15. CAD's *Nègritude* is apparent in the titles of the following works: *Nations Nègres et Culture, op. cit.; L'Unité Culturelle de L'Afrique Noire* (Paris: Présence Africaine, 1982); *L'Afrique Noire Précoloniale* (Paris: Présence Africaine, 1987); *Antériorité des Civilisations Nègres* (Paris: Présence Africaine, 1993). The concept of *Nègritude* that I coin here should not be mistaken with the *Négritude* Movement of Aimé Césaire (1913–2008), Léon-Gontran Damas (1912–1978), and Léopold Sédar Senghor (1906–2001).

16. Cheikh Anta Diop, *Civilisation ou Barbarie, op. cit.*, dedication page; Prince Dika Akwa Nya Bonambela, *Hommage du Cameroun au Professeur Cheikh Anta Diop* (Dakar Fann. Sénégal: Presses Universitaires d'Afrique, 2006), 67.

17. I explained in chapter one that the Beti philosopheme *Afiri* is an anthroponym, which means "Hope." Accordingly, the Antadiopian Af(i)ri-mediated methodology can be construed as a hopeful path or a propaedeutic step toward the realization of the possible, namely the re-conciliation of global humanity through the constant quest for truth and peace. This third chapter examines how CAD theorizes this process.

18. We are now familiar with the Antadiopian theory that sapient humanity emerged from Africa. Thus, the prefix "Afro" (Afrika) can fittingly stand for modern humanity's attempt to reassess and reappraise itself discursively, the goal being the achievement of more cohesion and understanding among humans. This constant cultural quest for self-intelligibility, and revision of the human multifarious "self" is what I call in this methodological context "*sofia.*" We remember that earlier on in the first chapter, I defined the Beti concept *sofia* as an agricultural concept referring to a geographical space (territory, land) on which the toilsome activity of weeding [all that is considered undesired and worthless for a good harvest] is carried out by the laborer (the researcher). The Afrikan-Kameroonian Egyptologist Pierre Oum Ndigi, who taught me Egyptology at the Catholic University of Central Afrika, is more explicit on the origin and meaning of the telluric concept *sofia*. He argues that the substantive *sofia,* recurrent in many Bantu languages, is an ancient Afrikan term, which refers to each administrative subdivision of the Kemetic nation. Thus, the Kemetic *sofia* is what the Greeks later called *nomos*. See: Djasso Djasso, "L'Egyptologue Oum Ndigi nous explique l'oeuvre de Wêre Wêre Liking selon le paradigm Kamite" [Video]. *YouTube.* Retrieved March 10, 2018. https://www.youtube.com/watch?v=h-ZHnO_fNgI. Consequently, to labor on one's territorial *sofia* (epistemic, familial, political, economic, etc.) would mean to love it, own it, know it, protect it, and to shape it according to one's values and ideals. Sofia could be philosophically envisioned as a trope for a cosmopolitan realistic utopia, that is, a transcontinental federal state to come and which academics can help bring about through their cognitive endeavors and contributions.

19. Cheikh Anta Diop, *Civilisation ou Barbarie, op. cit.,* 12–13. In French: "*qu'aucune pensée, et en particulier aucune philosophie, ne peut se développer en dehors de son terrain historique.*"

20. *Ibid.,* 291–482.

21. Cheikh Anta Diop, *Nations Nègres et Culture, op. cit.,* 19. In French: "*chaque people a une histoire.*"

22. Cheikh Anta Diop, L'Afrique noire précoloniale, op. cit., 9. In French: "*la clef qui ouvre la porte de l'intelligence, de la compréhension de la société africaine.*"

23. The argument holds for all histories.

24. Cheikh Anta Diop, *Nations Nègres et Culture, op. cit.,* 15.

25. *Ibid.*, 30.

26. Michel Foucault, *The Government of Self and Others. Lectures at the Collège de France 1982–1983* (Trans. Graham Burchell, New York: Picador, 2011), 41–57.

27. Joseph Tchundjang Pouemi, *Monnaie, Servitude et Liberté. La répression monétaire de l'Afrique* (Yaoundé: MENAIBUC, 2000).

28. George Yancy, *Backlash. What Happens When We Talk Honestly about Racism in America* (Lanham, MA: Rowman & Littlefield, 2018).

29. Théophile Obenga, *Le sens de la lutte contre l'africanisme eurocentriste* (Paris: L'Harmattan, 2001), 108. From French: "The Africanist lie must die."

30. Cheikh Anta Diop, *Nations Nègres et Culture, op. cit.,* 14. In French: "*On saisit le danger qu'il y a à s'instruire de notre passé, de notre société, de notre pensée, sans esprit critique, à travers les ouvrages occidentaux.*"

31. Jacques Derrida, "Hospitality" in *Angelaki, Journal of the Theoretical Humanities* (No. 3, Vol. 5, 2000) 3–18; Emmanuel Lévinas, *Totalité et Infini. Essai sur l'Extériorité* (Paris: Brodard et Taupin, 1971).

32. Mary Lefkowitz, *Not Out of Africa. How Afrocentrism Became an Excuse to Teach Myth as History, op. cit.*, 159.

33. *Ibid.,* 160. In the last chapter of her book that Lefkowitz references here, she outlines her aim thus: "I shall discuss the work of the Afrocentrist writers, who, in the hope of promoting their own culture, disparage the ancient Greeks and encourage their readers to distrust those of us who believe that Greeks were the inventors of what has always been thought to be Greek philosophy." *Ibid.,* 124. What is at issue in this quote is the vindication of the originality of Greek philosophy by Lefkowitz. But, as I endeavor to show in this contribution, CAD always studies the particular in connection to the universal. In other words, his philosophic-scientific methodology consists in evidencing the "*apport de l'Afrique à l'humanité en sciences et en philosophie*" ("African contribution to humanity in sciences and in philosophy"). See the fourth part of *Civilisation ou Barbarie, op. cit.,* 291–482.

34. *Ibid.*, 158.

35. *Ibid.*, 158. The concept of Afrocentrism, as used by Professor Lefkowitz about CAD's methodology is tantamount to mythmaking, as suggests the subtitle of her book. It would mean that CAD is a sort of doxographer (writer of common opinions and beliefs). But CAD himself, as though anticipating on Lefkowitz' charge, seems to invite his reader to examine for herself the truth-centered quality of his scholarship

through the subtitle of *Antériorité.* See: Cheikh Anta Diop, *Antériorité des Civilisations Nègres. Mythe ou Vérité Historique?* (Paris: Présence Africaine, 1993).

36. Molefi Kete Asante, *Afrocentricity. The Theory of Social Change* (Chicago: African American Images, 2003), 2.

37. *Ibid.*

38. Mary Lefkowitz, *Not Out of Africa, op. cit.*, 8.

39. The term is from Lefkowitz and is repeatedly used in her book. See: Mary Lefkowitz, *Not Out of Africa, op. cit.*, 1, 2, 5, etc. Since she discusses CAD alongside Molefi Kete Asante in the book, I guess she equates her concept "Afrocentrism" used in the subtitle to Asante's Afrocentricity.

40. *Ibid.*, 8. Lefkowitz obliterates the fact that interpretations are inherently polysemic and often predicated upon one's integrity, intellectual courage, theoretical blueprint, rational imagination, perspicacity, interests, and experience of humans and things, etc.

41. To her credit, Professor Lefkowitz admits: "I know only a few words of Egyptian." See: *Ibid.*, 165.

42. G. Mokhtar (Ed.), *General History of Africa. II Ancient Civilizations of Africa, op. cit.*, 76–77.

43. Cheikh Anta Diop, *L'Afrique Noire Précoloniale* (Paris: Présence Africaine, 1987). I will critique both Lefkowitz' and CAD understanding of the notion of myth in the next chapter.

44. CAD expresses his indebtedness to Gaston Bachelard's rational methodology, writing: "*À mon Professeur Gaston Bachelard, dont l'enseignement rationaliste a nourri mon esprit*" ("To my Professeur Gaston Bachelard, whose rational teaching has nourished my mind").

45. André Leroi-Gourhan is repeatedly cited by CAD in *L'Afrique Noire Précoloniale, op. cit.*, 64, 87, 191, etc.

46. André Aymard is also quoted in *Civilisation ou Barbarie, op. cit.,* 268, 424, 479.

47. "*Anthropologie sans complaisance*" (authentic anthropology) is the subtile of CAD's *Civilisation ou Barbarie, op. cit.* In French: "*sans complaisance.*"

48. *Ibid.,* 12. In French: "*c'est en toute liberté que les Africains doivent puiser dans l'héritage intellectuel commun de l'humanité.*"

49. Cheikh Anta Diop, *Antériorité des Civilisations Nègres. Mythe ou Vérité Historique?* (Paris: Présence Africaine, 1993), 11. In French: "*la véracité ou l'exactitude de ce qu'on écrit.*"

50. Cheikh Anta Diop, *Civilisation ou Barbarie, op. cit.,* 477. In French: "*de voir éclore demain l'ère d'une humanité véritable, d'une nouvelle perception de l'homme sans coordonnées ethniques.*"

51. *Ibid.* In French: "*autant la technologie et la science modernes viennent d'Europe, autant, dans l'antiquité, le savoir universel coulait de la vallée du Nil vers le reste du monde, et en particulier vers la Grèce, qui servira de maillon intermédiaire.*"

52. After all, Afrika and the other continents co-belong to the world.

53. Mary Lefkowitz, *Not Out of Africa, op. cit.,* 6.

54. Mary Lefkowitz is also discussed by scholars such as Théophile Obenga, *Le sens de la lutte contre l'africanisme eurocentriste, op. cit.,* 49–66; Asa G. Hilliard, III, "Lefkowitz and the Myth of the Immaculate Conception of Western Civilization: The Myth is Not Out of Africa" in Molefi Kete Asante and Ama Mazama (Ed.), *Egypt vs. Greece and the American Academy. The debate over the birth of civilization* (Chicago: African American Images, 2002), 51–66; Charles Verharen, "In and Out of Africa: Misreading Afrocentricity" in *ibid.*, 67–90; Don Luke, "Preserving the Eurosupremacist Myth" in *ibid.*, 91–120.

55. Jean-Marc Ela, *Cheikh Anta Diop ou l'honneur de penser, op. cit.*

56. *Ibid.*, 31. From French: "this intellectual worker who expresses Afrika to the scientific world."

57. *Ibid.*, 112. From French: "one of the major masters of suspicion of African history."

58. Cheikh Anta Diop, *Nations Nègres et Culture, op. cit.,* 27. In French: "*Tandis que l'Européen peut remonter le cours de son histoire jusqu'à l'antiquité gréco-latine et les steppes eurasiatiques, l'Africain qui, à travers les ouvrages occidentaux, essaie de remonter dans son passé historique s'arrête à la fondation de Ghana (IIIe s. av. ou III e s. ap. J.C.). Au-delà, ces ouvrages lui enseignent que c'est la nuit noire. Que faisaient ses ancêtres sur le continent depuis la Préhistoire?*"

59. Cheikh Anta Diop, *Civilisation ou Barbarie, op. cit.*, 10. In French: "*l'optique déformante des œillères du colonialisme avait si profondément faussé les regards des intellectuels sur le passé africain.*"

60. That is, academics with sincere and inclusive minds, who value scientific evidence (truth) more than cultural ideologies.

61. *Ibid.*, 9.

62. Cheikh Anta Diop, *Nations Nègres et Culture, op. cit.* 63–5.

63. Cheikh Anta Diop, *Civilisation ou Barbarie, op. cit.*, 415.

64. Cheikh Anta Diop, *Nations Nègres et Culture, op. cit.* 49–203.

65. Jean-Marc Ela, *Cheikh Anta Diop ou l'honneur de penser, op. cit.*, 65–6. In French: "*l'ensemble des discours qui se sont constitués en Europe durant les siècles de l'impérialisme. Ici, la véritable crise des sciences européennes n'est pas celle qu'analyse Husserl mais celle qui s'instaure lorsque les indigènes d'Afrique apprennent à étudier l'histoire.*" Though my purpose is not to examine Husserl's analysis of the crisis in European sciences, Ela does well to establish a comparative parallel between Husserl's *Crisis* and the eruption of Afrikan scholars in the field of Afrikan historiography. The latter constitutes, for him, the truer crisis in European sciences: from CAD onward, silenced Afrika scientifically resurrects and can talks for herself to her progeny and to all humans worldwide. Nevertheless, what Ela seems to neglect is the fact that both Husserl and CAD do develop, with different emphases, the common theme of rational crisis (bankruptcy of the ultimate meaning of rational life) in contemporary philosophy, with its devastating consequences on the disjointed positive sciences. As we will see further in this contribution, it is within the context of CAD's treatment of the major crises of contemporary philosophy that he outlines his theoretical methodology toward the construction of his teleological dream, namely the reconciliation of humanity with itself. See: Edmund Husserl, *The Crisis*

of European Sciences and Transcendental Phenomenology (Trans. by David Carr, Evanston, IL: Northwestern University Press, 1970); Cheikh Anta Diop, *Sciences et Philosophie. Textes 1960–1986* (Dakar: IFAN Ch. A. Diop, Université Cheikh Anta Diop de Dakar, Sénégal, 2007), 163–190.

66. Cheikh Anta Diop, *Nations Nègres et Culture, op. cit.,* 14.

67. Cheikh Anta Diop, *Civilisation ou Barbarie, op. cit.*, 9. This page enumerates a series of scientific crimes.

68. Cheikh Anta Diop, *Nations Nègres et Culture, op. cit.,* 49–58.

69. Cheikh Anta Diop, *Civilisation ou Barbarie, op. cit.*

70. Cheikh Anta Diop, *Nations Nègres et Culture, op. cit.,* 59–203.

71. Cheikh Anta Diop, *Civilisation ou Barbarie, op. cit.*

72. *Ibid.*

73. *Ibid.*

74. Jean-Marc Ela, *Cheikh Anta Diop ou l'honneur de penser, op. cit.*, 107. In French: "*la vérité dont l'Afrique a besoin pour percer son mystère se trouve au bout d'un long chemin, lorsque 'les africains se penchent sur leur propre histoire et leur civilisation et étudient celles-ci pour mieux se connaître.'*"

75. *Ibid.*

76.*Ibid.*, 116. In French: "*rétablir cette vérité n'est pas seulement un acte de soumission aux exigences de la rationalité scientifique. C'est aussi une atteinte aux fondements idéologiques de la domination.*"

77. *Ibid.*, 123. These are Ela's words in this regard: "*Il serait anormal que 90% de la recherche sur l'Afrique se fassent en dehors de l'Afrique, au détriment des peuples de chez nous. Les pays du Sud ne sauraient rester éternellement des pays explorés, découverts et étudiés par les autres.*" From French: "It would be abnormal that 90% of the research on Africa be made outside of Africa, to the detriment of our own peoples. Southern countries should not eternally remain countries explored, discovered and studied by others."

78. It does matter for CAD that we know what we are here on earth for. See: Cheikh Anta Diop, *Civilisation ou Barbarie, op. cit.*, dedicatory page. See also: Prince Dika Akwa Nya Bonambela (Dir.), *Hommage du Cameroun au Professeur Cheikh Anta Diop, op. cit.*, 66–67.

79. Jean-Marc Ela, *Cheikh Anta Diop ou l'honneur de penser, op. cit.*, 126. From French: "Let us endeavor to invent a man in full, something which Europe has been incapable of achieving."

80. *Ibid.*, 124. J.-M. Ela writes about CAD: "*Si une exigence l'habitait, c'était celle de rechercher sans relâche la vérité. Ce qui oriente toute sa vie, c'est la volonté de mettre tout en œuvre pour qu'avance la science et triomphe la vérité, en approfondissant toujours davantage les questions traitées et en rejetant toute espèce de facilité.*" From French: "If a requirement was engraved in him, it was that of relentlessly looking for truth. What guides his entire life, is the will to do everything possible for the advancement of science and make truth triumph, by deepening always further the questions treated and by rejecting all kind of oversimplification."

81. The Beti verb *soo* means to doubt, to challenge the perception of something, and to investigate it further for a better understanding. See: Siméon Basile Atangana Ondigui, *Le Nouveau Dictionnaire Ewondo, op. cit.*, 192.

82. *Ibid.*, 57. In French: "*La raison est née chez les Noirs. Tel est le « scandale » qui est au centre de l'œuvre de l'historien africain. C'est pourquoi, cette œuvre a suscité l'un des grands débats de la science moderne. Le message de Ch. A. Diop est l'affirmation d'une scandaleuse vérité. Celle-ci ne pouvait connaître aucune publicité.*"

83. Cheikh Anta Diop, *Antériorité des Civilisations Nègres, op. cit.*, 195–214. In this tenth chapter of his work, CAD outlines different historical methodologies, including archeological ones (magnetic localization, prospection of soil resistivity, dendrochronology, etc.) likely to enable the researcher dig up the Afrikan past.

84. *Ibid.*, 215–28.

85. Molefi Kete Asante and Ama Mazama (Ed.), *Egypt vs. Greece and the American Academy. The debate over the birth of civilization, op. cit.*; Mary Lefkowitz, *Not Out of Africa, op. cit.;* Martin Bernal, *Black Athena: The Afroasiatic Roots of Classical Civilization; Volume I: The Fabrication of Ancient Greece 1785–1985* (New Brunswick, New Jersey: Rutgers University Press, 1989).

86. See: Makhily Gassama (Dir.), *L'Afrique Répond À Sarkozy. Contre le discours de Dakar* (Paris: Philippe Rey, 2008). This important contribution of twenty-three authors features philosophers like Mamoussé Diagne, Souleymane Bachir Diagne, or Théophile Obenga, who all deploy critical reasoning vis-à-vis and beyond Nicolas Sarkozy's arrogant 2007 Dakarian speech, to refresh the human contemporary consciousness on the past and continuing contributions of Afrika to the global civilization. President Sarkozy states ambiguously: "*Le drame de l'Afrique, c'est que l'homme africain n'est pas assez entré dans l'histoire*" ("The scourge of Africa, is that the Afrikan has not gone far enough into history"). More importantly, the authors invite global Afrika (continental and diasporic) to reconcile with the spirit of creativity to tackle their predicaments and shape, with a sense of duty and responsibility, a more humane civilization from Afrikan cultural traditions. This project, I think, can be brought to fruition through Af(i)ri-centric methodological paradigms. See the following link for Nicolas Sarkozy's speech at the Cheikh Anta Diop University in Dakar, Senegal. See: Le MondeAfrique, "Le Discours de Dakar de Nicolas Sarkozy." *Le Monde.* Retrieved December 11, 2018. https://www.lemonde.fr/afrique/article/2007/11/09/le-discours-de-dakar_976786_3212.html.

87. Lefkowitz imagines that the purpose of what she calls "Afrocentrism" in the subtitle of her book, is the worldwide promotion of the Afrikan culture. See: Mary Lefkowitz, *Not Out of Africa, op. cit.*, 124: "the Afrocentrist writers, who, in the hope of promoting their own culture. . . . " But the trained eye and ear, in reading CAD, for example, sees and hears his intersubjective and transcultural overtones, that is, the constant call to unity (without hegemony) within the human family, for "*l'humanité ne doit pas se faire par l'effacement des uns au profit des autres.*" From French: "humanity must not be achieved par the erasure of some in the benefit of others." See: Cheikh Anta Diop, *Nations Nègres et Culture, op. cit.*, 17.

88. Mary Lefkowitz, *Not Out of Africa, op. cit.*, 1, 2, 6, 155, etc.

89. Mbog Bassong is an Afrikan-Cameroonian planetologist who understands the necessity of philosophic inquiry in contemporary science. See: Mbog Bassong, *La Méthode de la Philosophie Africaine* (Paris: L'Harmattan, 2007).

90. The Colombian scholar Rosa Amelia Plumelle-Uribe thoroughly documents a series of overshadowed genocides performed by the ferocious West among non-Whites and non-Aryans in *La Férocité Blanche. Des non-Blancs aux non-Aryriens: génocides occultés de 1492 à nos jours* (Paris: Albin Michel, 2001).

91. Jacques Derrida, *Rogues Two Essays on Reason* (Trans. Pascale-Anne Brault, Stanford, CA: Stanford University Press, 2005).

92. See: *The Wolf and the Lamb* in lafontaine.mmlc.northwestern.edu/fables/loup_agneau_vv.html. Retrieved January 31, 2019. In the contemporary geopolitical arena, the so-called "strong" or chief "rogue state" is, in Derrida's view, the United States of America. He defines the latter as "the most perverse, most violent, most destructive of rogue states," because of its international cruelty, lawlessness, and imperial nature. See: Jacques Derrida, *Rogues, op. cit., 97.*

93. The natural/moral law constitutes a set of laws that can be derived from the general nature of the universe by the inquiring mind, without necessarily appealing to interests, feelings, or revelation, etc. *Maat*, in the Afrikan cultural tradition, is the embodiment of the said inward moral law. See: Théophile Obenga, *La Philosophie africaine de la période pharaonique. 2780–330 avant notre ère* (Paris: L'Harmattan, 1990).

94. *Zen* is the Beti word for the path, the way, or the track.

95. Cheikh Anta Diop, *Antériorité des Civilisations Nègres, op. cit.*, 275. From French: "We all aspire to the triumph of the notion of human species in the minds and in the consciences, such that the particular history of this or that race vanishes before that of the human tout court. One shall then be describing, in general terms which will no longer consider the accidental singularities henceforth futile, the significant steps of the conquest of civilization by the human being, by the entire human species."

96. Cheikh Anta Diop, *Antériorité des Civilisations Nègres, op. cit.*, 275. In French: "*au progrès général de l'humanité, à l'éclosion d'une ère d'entente universelle.*"

97. I use this word here in the sense of the Caribbean-French philosopher Édouard Glissant (1928–2011), who critiques a certain propensity to epistemic transparency in Western thought, and rather defends what he calls a "right to opacity for everyone." He writes: "If we examine the process of 'understanding' people and ideas from the perspective of Western thought, we discover that its basis is this requirement for transparency." See: Édouard Glissant, *Poetics of Relation* (Trans. Betsy Wing, Ann Arbor: The University of Michigan Press, 2010), 189–90.

98. Cheikh Anta Diop, "*L'unité d'origine de l'espèce humaine,*" Unesco Symposium on Racism, Science and Pseudo-Science: Proceedings of the Symposium to Examine Pseudo-Scientific Theories Invoked to Justify Racism and Racial Discrimination, Athens, 30 March to 3 April, in *Racisme, science et pseudo-science* (Paris: Presses Universitaires de France, 1982), 137–41.

99. The concept of intuition can be understood here both in the Kantian and Russellian senses. For Immanuel Kant, intuition -the receptive character of the mind as it is affected by external (spatial) objects- is the propaedeutic step toward the synthetic

a priori knowledge that he intends accounting for. He thus considers that, even if all cognition does not arise from experience, nonetheless, "no cognition in us precedes experience, and with experience every cognition begins." See: Immanuel Kant, *Critique of Pure Reason*, B1. Bertrand Russell, for his part, assimilates intuitive knowledge to self-evident truths, due to the vividness of experiences in the mind. Intuition is thus trustworthy, he argues, because it somehow brackets the elusiveness of past events, rather maintaining their freshness in one's memory. See: Bertrand Russell, *The Problems of Philosophy* (Oxford: Oxford University Press, 1976), 64–8.

100. With his concept of "hodological space," the social psychologist Kurt Lewin (1890–1947) offers an interesting analysis of how a person's spatiality (psychology and environment) weaves her behaviour. See: Kurt Lewin, "The Conceptual Representation and the Measurement of Psychological Forces" in *Contributions to Psychological Theory,* Vol. 4, (Durham, NC: Duke University Press, 1938). The Afrosofian and Antadiopian methodologies expand the notion of spatiality from the psychological to the linguistic, cultural (civilizational), and cosmic realms.

101. Cheikh Anta Diop, *Antériorité des Civilisations Nègres, op. cit.*, 278. In French: "*pratiquer sans compromis l'exercice du rationalisme pour chasser définitivement les ténèbres de l'obscurantisme, sous toutes ses formes.*"

102. Cheikh Anta Diop, *Nations Nègres et Culture, op. cit.*, 25.

103. Kwame Nkrumah, *Neo-colonialism. The Last Stage of Imperialism* (London: Panaf Books, 2004).

104. Cheikh Anta Diop, *Nations Nègres et Culture, op. cit.*, 14. In French: "*la vérité, c'est ce qui sert et, ici, ce qui sert le colonialisme.*"

105. Aimé Césaire, *Discourse on Colonialism* (Trans. Joan Pinkham, New York: Monthly Review Press, 2000), 35.

106. J. A. Rogers, *From Superman to Man* (Ocean Shores, WA: Watchmaker Publishing, 2015), 81.

107. The concept "fact" here refers to any documentary or informative source (written, oral, archeological, iconographic, linguistic, physical, chemical, botanical, zoological, mythological, etc.) likely to nourish inquiry.

108. The "Religions of the book" (Islam, Christianity and Judaism) believe that which is revealed by "God" to be true. Authority epistemology holds claims made by "experts" to be true. The pragmatic relies on what "works" in practical life experiences. The rationalist believes in logical truths, and the empiricist verifies his logical constructions through his sensual "evidence."

109. Cheikh Anta Diop, *Antériorité des Civilisations Nègres, op. cit.*, 11. In French: "*la véracité ou l'exactitude de ce qu'on écrit.*"

110. Cheikh Anta Diop, *Nations Nègres et Culture, op. cit.*, 18. CAD considers that truth alone should shepherd the inquiring mind.

111. Cheikh Anta Diop, *Antériorité des Civilisations Nègres, op. cit.*, 229.

112. *Ibid.* In French: "*nous ne demanderons qu'à nous rendre à l'évidence des faits.*"

113. *Ibid.*, 195–214.

114. UNESCO stands for the United Nations Educational, Scientific and Cultural Organization.

115. The problem, however, resides in the complexity of trans-disciplinarian scholarship and the tasking expertise that it requires. The solution seems to lie on the inquirer's intellectual blueprint and openness to ongoing research.

116. His contribution on the 'Origin of the ancient Egyptians' heads that volume. See: G. Mokhtar (Ed.), *General History of Africa, vol. II, op. cit.,* 27–82.

117. The list of participants in the symposium can be consulted in: G. Mokhtar (Ed.), *General History of Africa, vol. II, ibid.,* 58. The attendants were as follows: Professor Abdelgadir M. Abdalla (Sudan), Professor Abu Bakr (Arab Republic of Egypt), Mrs N. Blanc (France), Professor F. Debono (Malta), Professor J. Devisse (France), Professor Cheikh Anta Diop (Senegal), Professor Ghallab (Arab Republic of Egypt), Professor L. Habachi (Arab Republic of Egypt), Professor R. Holthoer (Finland), Mrs J. Gordon-Jacquet (United States of America), Professor S. Husein (Arab Republic of Egypt), Professor Kaiser (Federal Republic of Germany), Professor J. Leclant (France), Professor G. Mokhtar (Arab Republic of Egypt), Professor R. El Nadury (Arab Republic of Egypt), Professor Th. Obenga (People's Republic of the Congo), Professor S. Sauneron (France), Professor T. Säve-Söderbergh (Sweden), Professor P. L. Shinnie (Canada), Professor J. Vercoutter (France).

118. Kelvin Lu, "Kemtiyu Cheikh Anta Full Movie" [Video]. *YouTube.* Retrieved April 26, 2019. https://www.youtube.com/watch?v=tJ9573ExAvg. View the video in-between the following minutes: 47–50.

119. Edgar Morin, *Introduction à la pensée complexe* (Paris: Éditions du Seuil, 2005), 156. From French: "a total barbarism in the relationships between races, between cultures, between ethnic groups, between powers, between nations, between superpowers."

120. Cheikh Anta Diop, *Nations Nègres et Culture, op. cit.*, 62. In French: "*Presque tous les égyptologues posent, a priori, la fausseté de la thèse de l'Égypte nègre.*"

121. *Ibid.* In French: "*l'impérialisme aidant, il devenait de plus en plus 'inadmissible' de continuer à accepter la thèse jusqu'alors évidente d'une Égypte nègre.*"

122. Ivan Van Sertima, *They Came Before Columbus. The African Presence in Ancient America* (New York: Random House Trade Paperback Edition, 2003), 111.

123. CAD analyses the ethnonym *Km* under the heading 'The Egyptians as they saw themselves.' See: Cheikh Anta Diop, 'Origin of the ancient Egyptians' in G. Mokhtar (Ed.), *General History of Africa, vol. II, op. cit.,* 41–43.

124. *Ibid.*, 76–77.

125. The reader can fruitfully examine the scientific evidence behind this conclusive pronouncement of the Cairo symposium in G. Mokhtar (Ed.), *General History of Africa,* Vol. II, *Ibid.*, 27–82.

126. Prince Dika Akwa nya Bonambela (Dir.), *Hommage du Cameroun au Professeur Cheikh Anta Diop, op. cit.*, 55. From French: "people of really bad faith who refuse to take into account, we saw it at the Cairo Colloquium, who refuse to discuss, who refuse to open a serious debate."

127. Cheikh Anta Diop, *Antériorité des Civilisations Nègres. Mythe ou Vérité Historique?, op. cit.,* 12. From French: "African studies will break the vicious circle in which they spin, to retrieve all their meaning and all their fecundity, solely by orienting themselves to the Nile Valley. Reciprocally, Egyptology will break from its

secular sclerosis, from the hermeticism of texts, only when it will have the courage to dislodge the valve which alienates it, doctrinally, from the vivifying source that constitutes, for it, the black world."

128. C.-F. Volney, *History and Geography. Travels through Syria and Egypt, op. cit.,* 51.

129. This is the title of the seventh chapter of the following book: Christopher Stringer & Robin Mckie, *The Origins of Modern Humanity* (New York: Henry Holt and Company, Inc., 1996), 179–93.

130. The spiral, in the Mvettean gnosis, represents the initiatory totem (the tree-hyrax) with its nine voices, symbols of the nine cords of the Mvett (Life). The Mvett, as we will see in the next chapter, expresses the ideas of totality and perfection. It also conveys the musical idea of relationality implied in the c(h)ord. Research, itself, is like a cord, a string played with varying pitches and intensities on the fingerboard of fretted instruments like the guitar ("reality"). The spiral, thus understood, expresses vibratory (hermeneutical) possibilities. But research is also perhaps more like a chord, which is built with a set of notes played together, and yet heard in their choral singularity. Notes (inquiring possibilities) express both a chorus, that is, a collective symphony (a unity) in their uniqueness (diversity).

131. Cheikh Anta Diop, *Sciences et philosophie. Textes 1960–1960* (Dakar, Sénégal: IFAN Ch. A. Diop, 2007), 173. In French: "*est sans aucun doute l'appareil émetteur et récepteur le plus perfectionné qui existe dans la Nature.*"

132. Edgar Morin, *Introduction à la pensée complexe* (Paris: Éditions du Seuil, 2005), 24. From French: "we are still at the prehistory of the human mind."

133. Tsira Ndong Ndoutoume, *Le Mvett. L'Homme, la Mort et l'Immortalité, op. cit.*; David Lamb, *The Search for Extraterrestrial Intelligence. A Philosophical Inquiry* (New York: Routledge, 2005); Jeffrey Bennett, *Beyond UFOs: The Search for Extraterrestrial Life and Its Astonishing Implications for Our Future* (Princeton, NJ: Princeton University Press, 2008).

134. Nuno R. B. Martins et al., "Human Brain/Cloud Interface" in *Frontiers in Neuroscience* (March 2019, Vol. 13, Article 112), 18.

135. *Ibid.*, 2.

136. Joel B. Greenhouse, "[Replication and Meta-Analysis in Parapsychology]: Comment: Parapsychology—On the Margins of Science?" in *Statistical Science* (Vol. 6, No. 4, Nov. 1991), 387. In his three laws (orbits, areas, and periods) of planetary motion, the German mathematician and astronomer-astrologer Johannes Kepler (1571–1630) maintains: 1. All planets move in elliptical orbits, with the sun at one focus. 2. A line that connects a planet to the sun sweeps out equal areas in equal times. 3. The square of the period of any planet is proportional to the cube of the semimajor axis of its orbit. See: The Editors of Encyclopaedia Britannica, "Kepler's laws of planetary motion." *Encyclopaedia Britannica.* Retrieved January 30, 2020. https://www.britannica.com/science/Keplers-laws-of-planetary-motion.

137. Parapsychic occurrences include paragnosia/clairvoyance (extrasensory reception of information about objective events in the outer world), precognition/proscopy (extrasensory perception of future events), telepathy (transmission or

reading of other people's mental processes), psychokinesis/telekinesis (capacity to move objects through mental concentration alone), and more.

138. Edgar Morin, *Penser Global. L'humain et son univers* (Paris: Robert Laffont, 2015), 35.

139. Bernard d'Espagnat, *Penser la science ou les enjeux du savoir* (Paris: Bordas, 1990), 219. From French: "It is because I consider, based on arguments grounded on physics, that the thing itself, reality is not knowable by science as it is. Of the hope of such a knowledge we must, I said it, do our mourning."

140. Edgar Morin, *Introduction à la pensée complexe, op. cit.,* 156. From French: "I think that true rationality is profoundly tolerant vis-à-vis mysteries."

141. Edgar Morin, *Penser Global, op. cit.,* 62.

142. Nathan Reley Carpenter and Benjamin N. Lawrance (Ed.), *Africans in Exile. Mobility, Law, and Identity* (Bloomington, IN: Indiana University Press, 2018).

143. I will explain this term shortly.

144. See the first paragraph in section III.2. of this chapter on the Antadiopian scientific philosophic methodology.

145. Daniel Assoumou Ndoutoume, *Du Mvett, op. cit.,* 153; Alain Elloué-Engoune, *Du Sphinx au Mvett, op. cit.*, 79–86; Grégoire Biyogo, *Encyclopédie du Mvett, op. cit.,* 77. Put in Einsteinian terms, matter and energy are interchangeable forms of reality, hence the equation: $E = mc^2$ (energy equals mass times the speed of light squared).

146. In his preface to Assoumou Ndoutoume's work, Grégoire Biyogo writes: "*le Mvett est indissolublement musique et poème philosophique . . .* " (the Mvett is indissolubly music and philosophic poem). See: Daniel Assoumou Ndoutoume, *Du Mvett, op. cit.,* 8. This said, let us bear in mind the extreme complexity of the Mvett, since it is construed by Mvettologists as "*d'abord une harpe et une institution musicales, ensuite, il désigne l'artiste conteur lui-même. Enfin, la culture qui s'en degage*" (first a harp and a musical institution, then, it disignates the narrating artist. Finally, the ensuing culture). See: Grégoire Biyogo, *Adieu à Tsira Ndong Ndoutoume. Hommage à l'inventeur de la raison graphique du Mvett* (Paris: L'Harmattan, 2006), 121–122.

147. Alain Elloué-Engoune, *Du Sphinx au Mvett, op. cit.*, 81. From French: "The mvett enables those who listen to it to navigate temporality. Assisted with the sounds of the harp strings, of songs, the brain interacts with the other points of the universe. With the gods, ancestors and humans, the environment, etc." In the Mvettean interactive model, the notions of immanence and transcendence no longer hold. The Mvett asserts the presence of the generative *Atò(u)m* Eyo in all things. See: *Tsira Ndong Ndoutoume, Le Mvett. L'Homme, la Mort et l'Immortalité, op. cit.,* 22.

148. Namely her/his performance, body language, regalia, voice, message, music, and choreography, etc.

149. Bernard d'Espagnat, *Penser la science ou les enjeux du savoir, op. cit.*; Michio Kaku, *Quantum Field Theory. A Modern Introduction* (New York: Oxford University Press, Inc., 1993); *Hyperspace. A Scientific Odyssey Through Parallel Universes, Time Warps, and the Tenth Dimension* (New York: Doubleday, 1995).

150. Tsira Ndong Ndoutoume, *Le Mvett, op. cit.*, 28. From French: The pluricosmic Universe, the existence of extra-terrestrial civilizations technologically more advanced are not of any surprise to the Mvettean Initiate."

151. Cheikh Anta Diop, *Parenté Génétique de l'Egyptien Pharaonique et des Langues Négro-Africaines, op.*; Théophile Obenga, *Origine Commune de l'Egyptien Ancien, du Copte et des Langues Négro-Africaines Moderne. Introduction à la Linguistique Historique Africaine, op. cit.*; Umberto Eco, *Semiotics and the Philosophy of Language* (London: The Macmillan Press Ltd, 1984).

152. Michel Foucault, *The Archaeology of Knowledge and the Discourse on Language* (Trans. A. M. Sheridan Smith, New York: Pantheon Books, 1972).

153. Michel Foucault, *The History of Sexuality. An Introduction, Vol. I.* (Trans. Robert Hurley, New York: Random House, Inc., 1978).

154. Psychoses, hallucinations, nightmares, insomnia, depression, depersonalization, etc. are examples of mental disorders ensuing from the (neo)colonial dispensation in Fanon. See: Frantz Fanon, *The Wretched of the Earth, op. cit.*, 181–233.

155. Joy DeGruy, *Post Traumatic Slave Syndrome. America's Legacy of Enduring Injury and Healing* (Portland, OR: Joy DeGruy Publications Inc., 2017); Frances Cress Welsing, *The Isis Papers. The Keys to the Colors* (Washington, DC: C.W. Publishing, 2004).

156. Carl Gustav Jung, *Dreams* (Trans. R.F.C. Hull, Princeton, NJ: Princeton University Press, 1974); Sigmund Freud, *The Basic Writings of Sigmund Freud* (Trans. A. A. Brill, New York: Random House, Inc., 1995).

157. In his 1929 theory of cosmological recession, the American astronomer Edwin Hubble argues for the speedy outward motion of interstellar matter from the earth. For him, the further a galaxy, the faster it recedes from the earth.

158. Angèle Christine Ondo, *Mvett Ekang: Forme et Sens. L'épique dévoile le sens* (Paris: L'Harmattan, 2014), 176. From French: "Mvett warriors move underground, on water, wherever their actions lead them, and generally at great speed. The materialization of objects or weapons equally follows this logic of 'furtivity.'"

159. *Ibid.*, 180; Tsira Ndong Ndoutoume, *Le Mvett, op. cit.,* 22–29.

160. Tsira Ndong Ndoutoume, *Le Mvett, Ibid.,* 23.

161. Angèle Christine Ondo, *Mvett Ekang: Forme et Sens., op. cit.,* 176.

162. Angèle Chritine Ondo rightly observes after Grégoire Biyogo: "*Mvett nomme celui qui travaille à s'élever par la pensée en vue de recueillir la parole qui contient la sagesse de la combinaision du juste et du vrai.*" From French: "Mvett designates one who strives toward self-overcoming through thought in view of garnering the word that contains the wisdom combining the just and the true." See: Angèle Christine Ondo, *Ibid.,* 186.

163. Tiziano et al., "The bilocated mind: new perspectives on self-localization and self-identification" in *Frontiers in Human Neuroscience* (March 2013, Vol. 7, Article 71).

164. Corey S. Powell, "Will Human Teleportation Ever Be Possible?" *The Sciences*. Retrieved February 13, 2020. https://www.discovermagazine.com/the-sciences/will-human-teleportation-ever-be-possible. If the human brain unlocks its ability to project the human body in concrete and virtual spaces, what will become of the whole industry of aircrafts, trains, cars, bikes and more? What will we make of the internet and computers if the brain could download information directly from the cosmos and store it in its cells? If intersubjective communication became effective

through telepathic actual thinking, what would happen to cell-phones, television, and print media? These hypothetical questions, though seemingly conjectural, do diagnose some complex but crucial investigative avenues for contemporary and future researchers.

165. *Ibid.*, From French: "One would perhaps prize its perfection only when technology will reach the stage of bioelectronics. So, a physical communication by electromagnetic means, between two brains of two individuals separated by a huge distance is not in itself an irrational phenomenon and will lessen still in the future: the physical medium is obvious."

166. "Philosophy, science and religion. The major crises of contemporary philosophy." *Ibid.,* 163–90.

167. *Ibid.*, 180. In French: "*nouvelle rationalité qui permettra d'avancer dans la connaissance du réel.*"

168. I do not discuss microphysics in the current analysis but do mention it cursorily as a promising avenue for future research on the brain and parapsychological phenomena.

169. *Ibid.*, 179. Similar types of interdependence are expressed in the field of quantum mechanics in terms of space-time, immanence-transcendence, body-mind, etc.

170. *Ibid.*, 171.

171. George Yancy, *Backlash. What happens when we talk honestly about racism in America* (Lanham, MD: Rowman & Littlefield, 2018), 108.

172. The concept of anthropological chromatism is inspired by the ternary epidermal theorization of the various components of global humanity, which the Beti generally group in the following manner: the *Firi* people who are charcoal-like in color; the *Fem* people with a lime-like complexion; and the *Ba* people whose skin pigmentation is red-like. See: Grégoire Biyogo, *Adieu à Tsira Ndong Ndoutoume. Hommage à l'inventeur de la raison graphique du Mvett* (Paris: L'Harmattan, 2006), 122. This threefold chromatism will be used from now onward.

173. Chinweizu, *The West and the Rest of Us, op. cit.*

174. Tavis Smiley and Cornel West, *The Rich and the Rest of Us, op. cit.*

175. Nicolas Agbohou, *Le Franc CFA et L'Euro Contre L'Afrique, op. cit.*

176. François Kodena, "'I Can't Breathe!': Eric Garner's Salutary Verdict to the Racist Euro-American World and Its Implications for the African Worldwide" in *APA Newsletter on Philosophy and the Black Experience* (Vol. 14, No. 2, Spring 2015), 12–17.

177. George Yancy, *Backlash, op. cit.*, 36–37.

178. Plato, *Apology,* 23c.

179. Joel Augustus Rogers, *From Superman to Man* (2nd Edition, Ocean Shores, WA: Watchmaker Publishing, 2015), 61.

180. Emer de Vattel, *The Law of Nations* (Ed. Knud Haakonssen, Carmel, IN: Liberty Fund, Inc., 2008), 203.

181. James Baldwin, "Who is the Nigger?" [Video]. *YoutTube.* Retrieved January 9, 2020. https://www.youtube.com/watch?v=L0L5fciA6AU.

182. Religion is here understood as an insatiable quest for truth.

183. Anténor Firmin, *The Equality of the Human Races* (Trans. Asselin Charles, Chicago: University of Illinois Press, 2002), lv.

184. *Ibid.* In asking this question, A. Firmin certainly had in mind Gobineau and his idea of racial inequality. See: Arthur Comte de Gobineau, *The Inequality of Human Races* (Burlington, IA: Ostara Publications, 2011). In today's America for example, the instructive book of M. Alexander on the prison system is indicative of the "scientific" discrepancies one is faced with when it comes to racial profiling. See: Michelle Alexander, *The New Jim Crow. Mass Incarceration in the Age of Colorblindness* (New York: The New Press, 2012).

185. Friedrich Nietzsche, *The Birth of Tragedy or Hellenism and Pessimism*, 16–18. In these sections of his work, Nietzsche denounces Western science (knowledge) as an optimistic theoretical culture firmly founded on the *aeternae veritates* (eternal truths) of space, time, and causality. Yet, for him, this optimism was victoriously challenged by both Immanuel Kant (1724–1804) and Arthur Schopenhauer (1788–1860). Both reinstated the Attic pessimistic and tragic culture, whose main goal consists in replacing science (optimism, clarity, and transparency) by the wisdom (love) found in the dissonant, ugly, and redemptive art of Dionysian music. Here is where life, that is, the embodied will in "the eternal abundance of its joy" is found.

186. Oswald Spengler, *The Decline of the West. Vol. 1. Form and Actuality* (New York: Charles Francis Atkinson, 1927).

187. Cheikh Anta Diop, *Civilisation ou Barbarie, op. cit.*, 16. From French: "An African atavistic optimism, but vigilant, inclines us to wish that all nations join hands to build a planetary civilization instead of crumbling into barbarism."

188. Steve Elvis Ella, *Mvett ékang et le projet bikalik. Essai sur la condition humaine* (Paris: L'Harmattan, 2011), 232.

189. Lucretius, *The Nature of Things* (Trans. A. E. Stallings, New York: Penguin Books, 2007).

Chapter 5

Sofia

From Philosophia to Afrosofia

The archeology of Being/Matter constantly haunts deep thinkers. This fact is evidenced, for example, in both CAD and Molefi Kete Asante. The first observes that energy is the source of all things ("*au commencement est l'énergie, tout le reste en découle*,")[1] while the second suggests: "If people could see that they have similar histories and origins, then they would more easily see the unity of their cultures."[2] In a similar fashion, I am existentially preoccupied with the enigmatic concept of "philosophy."

What is its meaning, content, and purpose in Cheikh Anta Diop (CAD)? Is it just a scholarly study of a canonical corpus qua "*ensemble des conceptions d'une quarantaine d'individus 'divinisés?'*"[3] If so, what is the thematic breadth and semantic depth of those academics marking out philosophic curricula? What personal and social ideals inform their philosophizing? Could philosophy be about the boundless discursive examination of the question of be(com)ing? What is this be(com)ing and how does it occur? If philosophy transcends authorial confinements to address the quality of human lived experiences within their scientific, socio-historical, economic, ethical, geopolitical, cosmological, and theological[4] dispensations, what is its apex? Could it be the devoted pursuit of wisdom as the Greek concept *philosophia* suggests, even if its etymology remains unknown?[5] What is the genealogical status of *sophia* (wisdom) and how is it acquired? Is it through experiential science? Is wisdom innate, that is, inherent to the human self,[6] or does it require training and time? When does one become sapient (wise)? Is there any philosophic age? In a word, what is CAD's take on wisdom and how can the latter impact present and future generations of philosophers the world over?

This introductory paragraph is purposively interrogative. It questions the notion of philosophy from the lived perspective of agential centeredness[7] as evidenced, for example, in CAD's following philosophy, and in Afrocentric scholars such as Ama Mazama,[8] Maulana Karenga[9] or Molefi K. Asante.[10]

Fanon's embodied will to knowledge is equally telling in this regard, since he entreats his body in demiurgic terms thus: "*o mon corps, fais de moi toujours un homme qui interroge!*"[11] Inquiry is thus the means through which conceptual obscurities can be clarified and resolved.

That is the purpose of the unfolding chapter. It holds, as we will witness, that *Afrosofia* fittingly unravels the puzzling etymology, meaning, and purpose of *philosophia*. Moreover, my *Afrosofian* blueprint examines CAD's analysis of the concept of philosophy from the cosmological standpoint. His notion of *kheper/sopi* shall be discussed from the perspective of his synthetic vision. The crucial question confronting us in the Antadiopian dispensation is the following: is philosophy a barbaric or civilizational enterprise? His Afrosofian[12] views, though contentious among Afrikan scholars, as the text will evidence, nevertheless stand, unambiguously, on the side of rational optimism and civilization. He holds that an Afrikan atavistic, but vigilant optimism, inclines us to wish that all nations join hands to build a planetary civilization instead of crumbling into barbarism.[13]

I will substantiate that this hopeful coming into enlightenment or civilization is what *sofia* is all about. *Sofia,* as ethical trope, invites present-day humanity not to straddle between "barbarism" and "civilization," but rather ascend, resolutely and collaboratively, toward a planetary civilization, more humane in outlook, through watchful thinking and living; hence its *Mvettean*[14] character. Ultimately, it will be shown that CAD's re-membering with philosophy as a civilizational endeavor will prove to be a crucial contribution to present-day geopolitical and ethical philosophy. The challenging task awaiting us now is to articulate this Afrosofian *ebug*[15] (word/discourse) in the tempestuous geopolitical dispensation of our own time.

PHILOSOPHY AS *KHEPER*/BE(COM) ING IN CHEIKH ANTA DIOP

In previous chapters, rationality or *sapientia* (wisdom/intelligence) has been pinpointed as the genealogical trait/seat[16] of contemporary humanity in the *Femina/Homo sapiens sapiens*.[17] It was also underscored that sapient humanity is not polycentric, meaning that humans, despite their numerous phenotypes, do not have natural origins other than the Afrikan one: "*la nature a créé l'homme une seule fois et l'homme se différencie, évolue, s'adapte ou disparaît; mais la nature ne crée pas deux fois l'espèce humaine. Elle n'a pas créé deux fois le cheval,*"[18] explains CAD in his irreversibility theory of natural processes. This view holds that nature does not repeat itself in its production of species, hence the monogenetic origin of humanity. This scientific find is of a deep philosophic import. It could generate a more cordial consciousness within global humanity, under the impulse of committed individuals who think, write, and live from sororal and fraternal perspectives.

Since nature produced an intelligent human being, twice wise (*sapiens sapiens*), the question becomes: what is this "nature" itself? Why this factorization of be(com)ing? Why repeat our sapient nature? Why are we not just sapient, but twice sapient? An interesting clue to these questions would be not only that nature and intelligence are adjacent, but also that the human being epitomizes the said intelligence. Having produced the human species once, just as the horse or any other being, nature seems to express itself, in the former, as a dynamic intelligence, hence its factorization. Accordingly, the development and embodiment of wisdom would be a key component of the human worldly presence.

CAD's monocentric theory of human genesis, we should remember, corrects the erroneous polycentric ideology and its attendant racial hierarchization,[19] based on the genetic, chronological and paleontological evidence.[20] But what interests us here more, is to know the nature of the generative fount behind *sapientia*, and what that first principle respectively means.

The foregoing thoughts give us the epistemic motivations of my quest for *sofia.* We inspect its affinity with *sophia* in view of bettering our lives and the world we live in. We want to understand who we are, whence we come, why we are here on earth, what life is all about, how the cosmos came/comes about, how it functions, and what its purpose(s) is/are.

These thoughts provide us with the rational backdrop against which CAD and I elaborate on the self-conscious intellectual activity called philosophy[21] or wisdom (*sagesse*).[22] It thus appears, in Antadiopian terms, that the uncompromising practice and exercise of rationalism that dispels all forms of darkened obscurantism,[23] is a key that possibly elucidates the preceding concerns. Without reason qua *zenning* (methodological) faculty to inquiry, things remain enigmatic and the human being a sheer stranger to herself. But we must know the being that we are in relation to the whole realm of cosmic be(com)ing, under the auspices of *sofia*[24] in CAD. I explain.

It is within the paradigm of the Afrikan renaissance[25] and cultural unity[26] at the historic, linguistic, and psychological[27] levels that CAD attempts to explain *sofia.* He leads us into the complex and challenging field of comparative linguistics in Afrikology, to examine the concepts for the law of material transformation, using the Walaf, Coptic, and Medu Neter languages respectively.[28] Thus, CAD establishes the following three correspondences of the concept of be(com)ing: *sopi* (Walaf) → *šopi* (Coptic) → *kheper* (Medu Neter).[29] "*'Sopi' en walaf, signifie 'transformer,' 'devenir,' tout comme dans les deux premières langues,*"[30] he argues revertively.

I add that *kheper*, *šopi, and sopi* are principles of transience in the universe. They express the metamorphoses (transmission and concretion) of life in be(com)ings. As such, they provide a higher intelligence of things, raising the mind to its inner ethereal spheres, in search of the primordial matter.

For CAD,[31] Théophile Obenga,[32] or Jean-Claude Mboli,[33] beside the Walaf and the Coptic, other Afrikan languages, ramifications of the Ntil (Medu Neter), are equally equipped to help us account for the meaning of wisdom, provided we, inquirers, undertake the painstaking task of conversing interrogatively with them. Between the Ntil and present-day Afrikan languages,[34] there is a psychological and cultural reciprocity, contentiously defended by CAD in the following terms:

> *Aujourd'hui encore, de tous les peuples de la terre, le Nègre d'Afrique noire, seul, peut démontrer de façon exhaustive, l'identité d'essence de sa culture avec celle de l'Égypte pharaonique, à telle enseigne que les deux cultures peuvent servir de systèmes de référence réciproques. Il est le seul, à pouvoir se reconnaître encore de façon indubitable dans l'univers culturel égyptien; il s'y sent chez lui; il n'y est point dépaysé comme le serait tout autre homme, qu'il soit indo-européen ou sémite. . . . la psychologie et la culture révélées par les textes égyptiens s'identifient à la personnalité nègre. Et les études africaines ne sortiront du cercle vicieux où elles se meuvent, pour retrouver tout leur sens et toute leur fécondité, qu'en s'orientant vers la vallée du Nil. Réciproquement, l'égyptologie ne sortira de sa sclérose séculaire, de l'hermétisme des textes, que du jour où elle aura le courage de faire exploser la vanne qui l'isole, doctrinalement, de la source vivifiante que constitue, pour elle, le monde nègre.*[35]

Though this contention is scientifically vindicated by the 1974 Cairo Egyptological Symposium,[36] for example, some critics such as the historian Maghan Keita or the philosopher Valentin-Yves Mudimbe still construe CAD as a diffusionist. M. Keita writes: "the diffusionist aspect of Diop's work is one of the areas in which he has received the greatest criticism."[37] What could this notion of diffusionism mean in CAD? Let us examine the facts by focusing on Mudimbe's take on CAD's diffusionism.

VALENTIN-YVES MUDIMBE: ADVERSUS CHEIKH ANTA DIOP'S "DIFFUSIONISM"

As we proceed with our inquiry on the mysterious foreignness of *sophia*, let us present once again, CAD's geopolitical dream and epistemic intent. The polymath argues with verve that contemporary humans interact based on their retrieved/reinforced cultural identity. Hence his Afrikan atavistic, optimistic, but vigilant call to all nations to concertedly carve an inclusive planetary civilization, instead of stubbornly sinking into the current barbarism of Western geo-cultural predation.[38]

The Antadiopian vision that world nations mobilize to build a planetary civilization is both communitarian and Afrikan. It highlights the interdependence of the world in this technological-atomic age, especially in the face of nihilistic threads such as the thoughtlessness of the human mission in the universe and the various predicaments of our time ("democracy," corporate capitalism, global warming, terrorism, etc.).[39] But, if the humanistic focus of the Antadiopian epistemology is underscored by Théophile Obenga,[40] Pathé Diagne,[41] or Jean Devisse,[42] it remains obscured by other scholars like Valentin-Yves Mudimbe,[43] Alain Froment,[44] or Mary Lefkowitz.[45] The subsequent analysis focuses on Mudimbe's assessment of CAD's "diffusionism."

In his work just referenced, Mudimbe writes that CAD is the "most extreme example" in the appraisal of "good" and "bad" works on Afrika, and the "best and probably excessive" illustration of the Africanization of diffusionism. I credit Mudimbe for his courage to make such loaded claims, and we cannot know whether he is right or wrong, unless we ourselves shoulder the laborious task of examining CAD's works.

So, a sympathetic reading of Mudimbe resides in the necessity, for the inquirer, to delve deeper into CAD's scholarship and be precise about his terminology and appraisal of other scholars' works on Afrika. The outcome of this tasking process is revealing. CAD often critiques his contemporaries like Léopold Sédar Senghor or Aimé Césaire,[46] despite his deep consideration for both, for the blatant *aliénation culturelle* (cultural alienation) in some of their respective writings.[47]

Furthermore, CAD operates a dichotomic distinction of Western scholars on Afrika, distinguishing those *de bonne foi* (of good faith) from those *de mauvaise foi* (of bad faith).[48] The former are scientific truth seekers, while the latter deliberately surrender to intellectual and moral fraud.[49] Thus could be understood the Mudimbean classificatory terms of "good" and "bad" works on Afrika in CAD's scholarship.

This distinction is critical because it underscores a crucial nuance in Western scholarship on Afrika. It can be truth-centric as evidenced in Volney (1757–1820),[50] Jean-François Champollion (1790–1832),[51] or Emile Amélineau (1850–1915),[52] etc. Its flip side, however, is that it can also be imperial[53] and pseudo-scientific.[54]

This said, I now focus on Mudimbe's controversial claim that CAD actualizes the "best and probably excessive" illustration of the "Africanization of diffusionism," and his further Otherization of Afrikological scholarship. To begin with, what is diffusionism? It is the transmission of cultural traits between kindred societies or from a society to other ones. And when Mudimbe speaks of CAD's Africanization of diffusionism, what he means is primarily his expansion of the archival datum deep beyond the Islamic-Christian-Judaic library. In other words, for Mudimbe, the Kemetic civilization diffused or gradually spread around the rest of Afrika. Put differently, Ta-Merry (Kemet) cultured the rest of Afrika in a unilateral manner.

For unknown reasons, Mudimbe omits the fact that the Kemetic culture itself sprang from the South in Ta-Netcher (Central Afrika) and Ta-Seti (Nubia); a point strongly highlighted by CAD for whom the circulation of information within Afrika is rather bidirectional/spiral as the following conclusive argument shows. Afrikan studies, he maintains, will free themselves from the vicious circle in which they are entangled, to retrieve all their meaning and fecundity, only through their decisive orientation to the Nile Valley. Conversely, Egyptology will liberate itself from its secular sclerosis, from the hermeticism of texts, only if it courageously explodes the valve that insulates it, doctrinally, from its vivifying Black Afrikan Source.[55] Consequently, no thought/ideology is, by nature, foreign to its Afrikan native land. Therefore, Afrikans must freely draw from the common human intellectual heritage, guided only by the notions of utility and efficiency.[56]

It follows that the flow, transmission, and dissemination of information in Afrika and beyond constitute what CAD calls "*l'héritage intellectuel commun de l'humanité*" (common intellectual heritage of humanity) in the quotes just referenced. It means that all civilizations, like different tonalities of a musical key, form a large, interconnected network, enriching one another, and contributing to the overall enlightenment of humanity. They are products of the human heart-mind in its confrontation with specific predicaments.

Therefore, one wonders what makes CAD "extreme" and "excessive" in Mudimbe, since for him, all humans contribute and feed from a shared intellectual heritage. Is such a view extreme and excessive? I do not think so. What must be said is that if CAD castigates certain types of literature, it is because of their blatant historical distortions,[57] hence the importance of "direct knowledge," as argued in the fourth chapter. The academe does not fare any better if misguided by a scholar.

Thus, the Mudimbean claim about the Africanization of diffusionism by/under the influence of CAD is faulty because it construes CAD's epistemology from the perspectives of geographic insulation (seclusion), abstraction, and mythology. Mudimbe writes disturbingly: "This struggle for scientific responsibility rapidly led to myths and theories of the 'Africanization of sciences.' For several years, Cheikh Anta Diop's influence for example, allowed the hypostasis of African civilizations."[58]

It would be interesting, in some further research, to examine Mudimbe's understanding of myth. Is it to be construed, as in Wole Soyinka, as our attempt, as humans, to externalize and communicate our inner intuitions?[59] Could it be that he rather equates myth to pseudo-science? For now, these queries remain unanswered.

As we turn to the phrase "hypostasis of African civilizations" I am puzzled by its semantic haziness. What does Mudimbe mean by "hypostasis?" If he intends to say the essence/quintessence of Afrikan civilizations, what could it mean for a civilization to be essentialized? Who essentializes it, why, and what is the content of the said essentialization? Could it mean a summative apprehension of its key features? If so, what are they? What defines a specific civilization in space-time? Could such a hypostatization be constant/perennial, factual, and tangible? A positive response to these questions is uncertain. So, it seems to me that the essentialization of Afrikan civilizations is rather an artistry and invention of the author of *The Invention of Africa*. It is Mudimbe's mental construct.

A more accurate view of civilizations is dynamic. In their material life/lives, civilizations evolve and are subject to the waving process(es) of (re) birth (renaissance) after their optimal development and subsequent demise. So, a civilizational renaissance (Afrikan, Asian, European, etc.) cannot mean a mere repetition without creative difference or a copy/imitation of foundational traits or "hypostases" (be they symbolic, linguistic, or psychological) by historical subjects.

Perhaps, what is essential (hypostatic) in civilizations is precisely their cultural project with its underlying ideals and their inspirational potential for present and future generations. I understand hypostases as "punctual" perceptions, that is, lightning flashes and revelatory epiphanies of facets of things (concrete or abstract) by the inquiring unfathomable and mysterious heart-mind.[60]

In writing "*Quand pourra-t-on parler d'une renaissance africaine?*"[61] in 1948 and his subsequent works, CAD's goal is neither self-glorification in some more or less grandiose and "hypostatized" Afrikan civilizations,[62] nor the promotion of pseudo-science ("myth"). His purpose is rather to express a basic fact: every people is historical, and its history is retrievable through adequate and methodological inquiry.[63] As it were, CAD responds, anticipatively, to the Mudimbean charge of mythmaking and pseudo-science, arguing:

> *On a tendance à croire que toute pensée, toute activité intellectuelle devant contribuer à l'éveil de la conscience culturelle d'un peuple, doivent, forcément, pécher sur le terrain scientifique. . . . Il suffisait d'admettre que chaque peuple a un passé, si modeste soit-t-il, qu'il est relativement possible de le découvrir par une investigation appropriée. . . . Si nos historiens, ethnologues, sociologues traditionnels avaient réalisé pleinement, comme on est en droit de s'y attendre, que l'essentiel pour un peuple c'est moins de pouvoir se glorifier d'un passé plus ou moins grandiose que de découvrir et de prendre conscience de la continuité de ce passé quel qu'il fût, ils ne se seraient pas livrés à une fausse interprétation. Ce facteur seul est déterminant pour la vivification de la*

> *conscience nationale. Or, pour atteindre un pareil objectif point n'est besoin d'altérer sciemment les faits.*[64]

I would then argue that civilizations, just like philosophies and other knowledges, are essentially diffusive because they are reflective of the synthetic potential of the human heart-mind. The latter can metaphorically breathe the mysterious universe, find meaning ("see" the shining sun) in opaque concepts, "hear" conversations held years before, sing inwardly in the loudest possible way without uttering a word outwardly, etc. If we think contemporarily, it would be rhetorical to ask whether different cultures diffuse their ideas, gastronomies, languages, technologies, musical genres, spiritualities, and more in today's world.

Now, since the sub-Saharan origin of modern humanity from the *Femina/Homo sapiens sapiens* (the Greeks included)[65] is evidenced by the scientific community,[66] the contention over the spread of civilization within Afrika and beyond should wane and leave room for a reconciliation of cultural heritages for the advancement of humanity. A close reading of CAD reveals this conciliatory approach displayed before him by the French philosopher Volney[67] (1757–1820), the Egyptologist Jean-François Champollion[68] (1790–1832), and many others.

It is against the backdrop of cultural contributions[69] (*apports*) of cultures to a shared world's civilization that CAD thinks that since modern technology and science come from Europe, so too, in antiquity, did universal knowledge flow from the Nile Valley to the rest of the world, and particularly to Greece, which will serve as intermediate link.[70]

Mudimbe does not seem aware or fails to grasp these bonding dimensions of CAD's epistemology and the inclusiveness of his scientific terminology. This might explain why he Otherizes Afrikan intellectuals in terms of "their conception of the value of their own civilization."[71] Mudimbe insulates Afrika, giving the wrong impression that the latter is alienated from the rest of the world. It is my view that geographic distinctions should not obliterate their synthetic unity, since humans have always interacted through diplomacy, education, matrimony, trade, or travels, and equally confronted one another through scientific achievements, sports, or warfare . . .

Additionally, what escapes Mudimbe's perception is that Afrika is a polysemic toponym in CAD scholarship. CAD primarily uses the concept Afrika in a generative and matrixial sense: it refers to sapient humanity in becoming. For CAD, the raison d'être of Afrika is to birth humans who, collaboratively, can labor to build a planetary civilization instead of sinking into barbarism.[72] The Antadiopian planetary civilization in the making, which this contribution hopefully advances, will make us wiser, more humane, and worthy of our generative "Mother" Afrika. Like other beings in nature, namely plants and animals, humans are also to undergo a maturing process for their mental and ethical full-grownness. CAD's scholarship embodies this endeavor toward progress (civilization), and this surely explains why Molefi K. Asante rightly defines him as "a humanist of the highest order."[73] The inclusive name Afrika(n) is thus an ethical trope, which points to the inner pinnacle toward which humans must ascend: wisdom.

The second connotation of the concept Afrika(n) in CAD is precolonial and relative to the rise of the Afrikan classical philosophy around 2,780 BCE,[74] that is, at a time when the Greeks themselves did not yet exist in history, and when the notions of Chinese or Hindu philosophy were meaningless.[75] My purpose, however, is not to discuss the philosophic anteriority of black civilizations[76] in comparison to those of India, China, or Greece, but to try to explain the enigmatic foreignness of the Greek *sophia.*

The third Antadiopian use of the term Afrika(n) is renascent. It results from the successive conquests of Ta-Merry (Kemet) by the Persians with Cambyses II in 525 BCE, the Macedonians with Alexander in 332 BCE, the Romans with Julius Cesar in 31BCE, etc. The loss of Ta-Merry's political sovereignty led to the gradual dissemination of her population across the continent.[77] How does this dispersion within Afrika relate to *sopi (kheper*)?

We might answer this question by resorting to two types of arguments, one linguistic, and the other cultural. The linguistic argument relates to the dynamic interaction between the inquirer and the mutative concepts *kheper*, *šopi, sopi, sofia,* and more. The question here would consist in knowing whether there is a semantic continuity between these concepts despite their phonetic and graphic differences. To be sure, such a dialogical relation requires a listening and meditative attitude from the researcher vis-à-vis concepts and language(s) in general. Jay Lampert seems therefore apropos when he writes: "you cannot speak a language if you will not let it speak to you"[78] and impact your thinking, hence the relevance of polyglottery. But I add that the researcher should attend to both language(s) and culture(s) for in-depth meaning. This is where the cultural argument comes into play and enriches our understanding of scarab *kheper.*

Th. Obenga provides us with the following valuable information about *kheper*: "*ce scarabée sacré égyptien se rencontre ailleurs sur le continent, avec la même valeur symbolique, dans un contexte culturel et métaphysique identique.*"[79] Obenga is right. The scarab *kheper* called *kpwâma* in Beti, which I photographed[80] during my field research in Cameroon, is indeed the symbol of formal mutations in beings. *Kpwâma* is a metamorphosis of an edible caterpillar called *fos*. This word is read reversely as *sof*, which is the linguistic radical (root) of *sofia*. Thus, through languages and textual corpuses, we can retrieve the possible archeology of *sofia*[81] (motion and mutation) by *in*presenting (indwelling) and navigating its cultural breadth and semantic depth.

THE *SO*: CIPHER OF WISDOM (*SOPHIA*)

Language in its units (signs, symbols, letters, syllables, phonemes, words, etc.) whispers and speaks,[82] provided we allow ourselves to be moved by its speaking. It encodes the life of a people's culture (science, education, cosmology, metaphysics, anthropology, ethics, social organization, medicine, spirituality, and more) and institutions. Language or rather certain concepts, as the *so(fia)* stem will instantiate, can reflect a people's worldview. Language, being an evolving production of the human mind, could be said to be active reasoning. It addresses what is autochthonic to the thinker's cultural and cognitive spaces. A thinker thinks what she/he beholds, imagines, or envisions. Words appear to her/him in their furtive elusiveness. They conceal more than they reveal. They inaudibly whisper their meanings.

In a dialogue, for example, whispered words require more attention for the interlocutors. Without heed, what is uttered quickly vanishes like lightnings' errands, leaving the auditor perplexed and unable to respond adequately to the speaker. This sometimes happens when we converse with people, prompting phrases like "pardon me?" or "come again?" from us. Similarly, we cannot respond to language if we do not understand its ciphers. Applied to the stem *so*, the problem grows in complexity today as we lose our capacity to track down concepts, rationally and culturally, until they possibly lead us to some uplifting information.

What then does the shortened monosyllabic stem of *so-fia* mean? Could the *so* particle constitute an epistemic key to the intelligibility of the worldwide philosophic culture, just as the Antadiopian *sopi* accounts for the coming into being of things (ideas and beings in the natural and cosmic orders) from a matrix which is yet to be identified? *Sopi,* as we have seen, is the realm of metamorphoses, of (per)mutations, and of flux in space-time. *Sopi* is the gradual actualization of pure potentialities (truth, justice, integrity, beauty, and more) in the natural realm. Its extension, in the human sphere, instills the notion of perfectibility and progress in personal and socio-political events.

I will now attempt a contentious graphic reading of the *so*. I explain. To begin with, *so* is an alphabetic pack of the letters (*bikang)*[83] "s" and "o." "S" is a fricative consonant and could be construed as a symbol of the energetic constitution of things. The diphthong "o" could be read as a circle and a representation of the sun[84]/be(com)ing and its enlivening power. Beyond this symbology, the verbs *sò* (to come/acclaim/welcome) and *sô* (to doubt/challenge) respectively open a broader semantic horizon to the concept of *sofia*. Thinking does not occur without doubt and an ongoing appraisal of that which is thought. As a noun, the *so* refers to the antelope, which is a totemic swift animal, not just for the Beti in Central Afrika, but also for the Kurumba and Bambara of Mali in West Afrika.[85] Becoming *so-fia* from this perspective, precisely means becoming speedy like the antelope and energetic like lightning. The verb *fia,* indeed, means to radiate/shine.

This is where the *So* becomes an educative institution, modeling society after its starry Tara ("Father"), the (in)visible Sun.[86] The lengthy process of the Sofian education is to achieve individual and social solarization (enlightenment). Becoming sun-like, resourceful, life-giving, and energizing is the point here. One is trained to undergo a comprehensive enhancement of one's mental, spiritual, emotional, and physical selves. One who underwent this formative and developmental process was qualified in Kemet as *śesa* (to be wise).[87] The person embodying this ideal of self-solarization is called *soso mod* by the Beti, meaning that she/he is a truthful, accomplished, and impeccable person. She/he is the person who acts above passions and self-interest according to the sole reason of equity.[88]

The *So* is theorized in the institution Mvett Ekang, the dwelling place of blazing letters. The Mvett defends an upward fall of the thinker toward the dazzling symphonic Chorus Eyo [Be(com)ing]. From a Sofian perspective, to write is to reverberate and manifest Eyo, for "*il s'agit dans le So d'un engendrement du même par le même.*"[89] The logic of self-causality in the Mvett makes all things surge from within Eyo. They are Its ontological spits. The Mvettographer, then, continuously rises (*a vet*) toward Eyo. Tsira Ndong Ndoutoume expresses this ongoing ascent, albeit infinite, toward the generative Atòm Eyo by doubling ts (tt) on the substantive Mvett.[90]

It is worth underscoring the striking graphic and semantic convergences between the *so* and 5O[91] (fifty), the Platonic age for philosophic elevation and solarization. Plato argues:

> At the age of fitty, those who've survived the tests and been successful both in practical matters and in the sciences must be led to the goal and compelled to lift up the radiant light of their souls to what itself provides light for everything. And once they've seen the good itself, they must each in turn put the city, its citizens, and themselves in order, using it as their model. Each of them will spend most of his time with philosophy.[92]

Alternative etymologies to wisdom, drawn from the Kemetic concepts *ser(t), sebayit,* and *seba* are respectively suggested by Raymond Faulkner[93] Th. Obenga,[94] Molefi Kete Asante, and Ama Mazama.[95] Coincidentally (?), *sat, sebayit,* and *seba* brood the same prefixal energy *so(fia)* -the shining *so-,* which is recurrent in some Indo-European languages referring to the English word sun, like *soleil* in French, *Sonne* in German, *sole* in Italian, or *sol* in Spanish.

From the foregoing examination, I argue that *sofia* is but a cultural process of civilization, which is tantamount to self and social solarization (creativity, enlightenment, and progress). Civilization being the purpose of CAD's epistemology, I construe the latter as Sofian-Mvettean: it is Mvettean because it heightens toward a planetary civilization as a corrective to planetary barbarism, and it is Sofian because of its generative and creative underpinning.

Indeed, CAD considers creativity as the requisite for genuine academicity: "*l'intellectuel digne de ce nom c'est le créateur, moi je ne connais que le créateur,*"[96] he observes, defining the specificity of the intellectual. Moreover, the concept of *sofia* helps us decode the etymological and semantic conundrums of the Greek *sophia*, which CAD indirectly examines through the interesting notion of becoming (*kheper/sopi);* the epiphany *in actu* of some foundational reality. As it were, *sopi* is an enabler of transient metamorphoses within an anterior be(com)ing called *Noun*. That is the Matter in which *sopi* [be(com)ing] occurs.

SOPI: NOUN'S EXTENSION

So far, the concept of *sopi* has helped us account, downstream, for the dynamic genealogy of cosmic diversity. We shall now also attempt to provide an upstream explanation of the said Antadiopian *sopi*. This methodology would dissipate, I hope, Plato's dubiousness about the linguistic and etymological origin and meaning of wisdom when he writes: "As for 'wisdom' ('*sophia*'), it signifies the grasp of motion. But it is rather obscure and non-Attic. . . . 'Wisdom' signifies the grasping (*epaphē*) of this motion, on the assumption that the things that are are moving."[97]

If Plato concurs that wisdom consists in understanding and cognizing how things proceed, he does not, in the above quote, explain what motion itself is, how it occurs, and what its cause in nature is.[98] The same haziness lingers in the moral order: in what direction do our mind and character move? Is it from ignorance to knowledge, from vice to virtue, or in some other course? Is wisdom motional because inquiry stirs the mind into action instead of keeping it at rest? Is the presumed "wise" person always restless even when metaphorically asleep, that is, ignorant? If so, what do we mean by restlessness, and what happens when understanding and virtue are achieved? Do aha moments not soothe the mind for a while, even as it continually quests for wisdom?

These questions are indicative of the need to elucidate the semantic obscurities surrounding the non-Atticness of wisdom.[99] We must attempt to decipher the contiguity between wisdom and motion in the cosmic realm and in the sapient be(com)ings that humans are. But do we have the scientific evidence to do so? The answer is positive, and can be substantiated historically at, genetic, linguistic, and cultural levels.

Beginning with genetics, in their 2001 article titled "HLA genes in Macedonians and the sub-Saharan origin of the Greeks," the Spanish immunologist Antonio Arnaiz-Villena and nine other medical scientists write:

> Greeks are found to have a substantial relatedness to sub-Saharan (Ethiopian) people, which separate them from other Mediterranean groups. Both Greeks and Ethiopians share quasi-specific DRB1 alleles, such as *0305, *0307, *0411, *0413, *0416, *0417, *0420, *1110, *1112, *1304 and *1310. Genetic distances are closer between Greeks and Ethiopians/sub-Saharan groups than to any other Mediterranean group and finally Greeks cluster with Ethiopians/sub-Saharans in both neighbour joining dendrograms and correspondence analyses. The time period when these relationships might have occurred was ancient but uncertain and might be related to the displacement of Egyptian-Ethiopian people living in pharaonic Egypt.[100]

This quote says nothing about wisdom but stresses the Afrikan pronounced presence in Greek genes without explaining its historical occurrence. How do we justify the genetic relatedness of populations that seem phenotypically alien to each other? This is where Afrikological studies, whether in CAD,[101] Théophile Obenga, Jean-François Champollion (1790-1832[102]–), the founder of scientific Egyptology, and many others, provide resourceful monumental hieroglyphic texts and papyri for our purpose. As is apparent from Plato[103] and Aristotle[104] his alumnus, Kemet (ancient Egypt) seems to be a fertile ground for further research on the meaning, practice, and purpose of philosophy. And what is Pharaonic philosophy, if not a thoughtful experience of the world by sub-Saharan Afrikans in Antiquity?[105] The archeological linguist Pathé Diagne emphasizes this view, arguing that the Ntil[106] (Pharaonic language),

> *. . . celle qui inspire les premiers hiéroghyphes, appartient au groupe mennfarite ou lébu-bantu. Elle relève du même ensemble qui compte le lingala, le kiswahili, le Kongo, le serer, le pulaar, le joola de Casamance, le sara tchadien, le dwala, le miele, le ngola ou le zulu.*[107]

Pathé Diagne understands the Pharaonic Ntil (Medu Neter) to be a synthesis from the "lébu-bantu" linguistic substratum, which still covers the entire spectrum of sub-Saharan Africa today. It is these Meridional Lebu-Bantu who, from 4,000 to 2,000 BCE, spread their Tara[108] mono-substantial ontology and culture beyond Afrika (Tabari Kas) to Tarana (the Americas) and Taraba (Europe).[109] Toponyms like Tanamarakus (Danemark), Taramenna (Germania), or Marasila (Marseille), in P. Diagne's perspective, vindicate this view.[110]

Diagne's linguistic argument partly throws some light on Antonio Arnaiz-Villena and his colleagues' enigma concerning the genetic consanguinity between present-day sub-Saharan Afrikans and the Greeks. His evidence is the trans-continental cultural continuum, developed by Lebu-Bantu populations two millennia before the settlement in Hellas (Greece) of the first Greeks among the Sicels, Scythes, and Pelasgians from -2,200 onwards.[111] But Diagne's chronology seems deliberately shallow, because he silences the archeological evidence[112] documented by CAD on the Afrikan Grimaldi's exclusive presence in Europe before her differentiation into the Cro-Magnon around 20,000 BCE.

Besides CAD, Champollion supplements Diagne's cultural and linguistic argumentation by inviting us to examine, like Volney in *The Ruins*,[113] Kemetic monuments in our quest for *sofia.* In his "*Discours d'ouverture du cours d'archéologie au Collège Royal de France,*" Champollion observes:

> *L'interprétation des monuments de l'Egypte mettra encore mieux en évidence l'origine égyptienne des sciences et des principales doctrines philosophiques de la Grèce; l'école platonicienne n'est que l'égyptianisme, sorti des sanctuaires de Sais.*[114]

It means that we are invited to trans-disciplinary thinking and expertise as we question the meaning of *sophia* in the contemporary geo-epistemic context. If we are to interpret Kemetic monuments and the numerous texts engraved in them in Ntil (Medu Neter), do we have the cultural and linguistic expertise to "see,"[115] that is, to understand them? We must surely know what *tekhenu* (obelisks), *meru* (pyramids),[116] or the Hor-em-Akhet (Sphinx) of the Giza Plateau, for example, stand for. Without some curious interest and attentive communication with those artworks and their authors, our inquiry might be fruitless. The forward path resides, I suggest, in our ability to trialogue with both the disguised *betil* (writers/artists) and their artistic *mintil* (scripts/works). What do they convey to/ conceal from us today?

Why are they hewn in stone instead of any other material? It is hard to find convincing answers to this question. However, we might conjecture that it is perhaps because rocks are intense energy condensers and the most suitable tropes of divine (beauteous) steadiness in nature?[117] What is it that the artists and their megalithic works signal to us about human life? How do artworks and their authors energize our minds and make them more resourceful? As already observed, beneath the ontological concepts of *sopi*, *šopi*, and *Kheper*, lies the Antadiopian theory of the cultural unity[118] between ancient and contemporary Afrikans at historical-linguistic[119] and psychological (spiritual) levels.[120] For this reason, the three Antadiopian linguistic terms *Kheper*, *šopi,* and *sopi* are interchangeable, because they express the same dynamic ontological idea of be(com)ing as energetic tension[121] within the first fluidic Ato(u)m called *Noun*.

So, *Kheper,* regressively, accounts for the origin of the universe in the first material principal *Noun* and the generation, therefrom, of all that is. In other words, *Kheper* is the dynamic nature and inherent process of the eternal self-transforming Matter, which the Kemtiyu,[122] in their Ienuan (Heliopolitan) cosmogony,[123] called *Noun/Toum*[124] (Primordial Waters). *Noun* is be(com)ing and answers the ontological question about what "is," even if this "be(com)ing" or *Noun* requires, as will be shown further down, a more scientific examination.

In postulating a single principle (the *Noun*) as cause of things, classical Afrikan (Kemetic) thinkers construed wisdom as a quest for the generative Energy, which the Bantu Kuba and Beti respectively call Bumba[125] and Eyo.[126] What characterizes both Bumba and Eyo is that they are, like the *Noun*, unconditioned conditions of time, motion, and change [be(com)ing]. They lift our minds to the highest realm of philosophical inquiry, namely ontology. The universe is their verbal emission; it is a vomit that comes from their entrails. Bumba "*vomit d'abord le soleil, puis la lune et ensuite les étoiles; c'est ainsi que naquit la lumière,*"[127] reveals Th. Obenga. Eyo, reports the Mvettographer[128] Tsira Ndong Ndoutoume, performs the same outpouring activity in the following fashion:

> *Eyô e nye ang'ayo*: it is Eyo who vomited all things.
> *Eyô âng'ayô a ne viô*: Eyo then multiplied like mushrooms.
> *Eyô â ng'ayô biom bise biyola*: Eyo named all things.
> *Eyô a ne dzom'ase été*: Eyo is in each thing.
> *Dzom'ase éne Eyô été*: Each thing is in Eyo.[129]

I am struck by the foundational status and self-reproductive dynamism of *Noun*, Bumba, and Eyo. As unconditioned principles of all existence, they engender all things and maintain their be(com)ing in co-existing harmony. Philosopher Alain Elloué-Engoune is therefore sagacious when he specifically writes about Eyo: "*Eyo seul est immortel et puissant, et la relation avec lui est la seule possibilité pour devenir immortel, libre, intelligent: l'intelligence de la nécessité.*"[130]

In the *Coffin Texts*[131] or in the *Bremner Rhind Papyrus*[132] commented by Th. Obenga,[133] the resting, inorganized, and archetypal *Noun* of the Heliopolitan cosmogony contains a transformative energy called *Kheper*, which actualizes its essence through an ongoing multiplication of beings: stars, planets, air, fire, water, minerals, plants, animals, humans, etc. Additionally, the self-unfolding (evolutionary) *Noun* also contains *Ra* (the demiurgic consciousness) and its creative word, the *Ka* (immanent word/reason in each being in the universe),[134] which carries out the self-mushrooming activity initiated by its originator *Noun.*

Ra, energized and anthropomorphized, that is, speaking in human terms in the Heliopolitan cosmogony, describes his activity in *Noun* saying: "*je me dilatai en lui. Je nouai ma propre main, tout seul.*"[135] *Noun* here takes up the attributes of agency, thought, and speech, which CAD complements with those of sight (understanding)[136] and filiation under the auspices of *Kheper ("dieu du devenir")*:

> *En effet, le noun primordial, sous l'action du dieu du devenir, engendre Ra, qui est le premier "œil," la première conscience qui observe le monde, et qui prend conscience de sa propre existence. Le noun est le père de Ra, et de fait, Ra l'appelle ainsi dans la cosmogonie héliopolitaine. C'est donc le fils du noun, Ra, qui une fois apparu, achève la création en tant que démiurge, tandis que son père, le noun, retourne dans son repos initial et n'intervient plus dans la création.*[137]

Now that our inquiry on the origin and meaning of the concept of *sophia* has led us to the Afrikan ontological fundaments *Noun,* Bumba, and Eyo, what could their epistemic imports be?

NOUN, BUMBA, AND EYO: DRIFTS OF S*OPHIA*

In questioning ways in which the foregoing Afrikan ontology could impact our quest for wisdom (*sophia)* and inform our epistemic practices, we could be inspired by its intertwined materialist-idealist (spiritualist) trend. Positing *Noun* comes down to professing a metaphysical gestational principle which, however, is enunciated in the material form of bottomless water with an inherent potential for metamorphosis in *Kheper*. Now, if we construe the *Noun-Kheper-Ra* imbrication as a metaphor for thought, it appears that reasoning (*Ra)* occurs only insofar as agential subjects experience the universe interrogatively. In this way the mind is enlightened by the radiance of knowledge and wisdom (self-understanding as historical subject) achieved.

What is wisdom (*sophia*), if not a wrestle with the conundrum of subjective existence? Who am I if my writing, for example, conceals Eyo [Be(com) ing] more than it discloses Her? What is this material shade (particle) of the universe that my body is? This is a shared conundrum for philosophers.[138] When addressed concretely, philosophy reconciles speculation with peoples' cultural life at every stage of their historical trajectory. That is the sense in which CAD contends:

> *Aucune philosophie ne peut se développer en dehors de son terrain historique.*[139] *Nos jeunes philosophes doivent comprendre cela et se doter rapidement des moyens intellectuels nécessaires pour renouer avec le foyer de la philosophie en Afrique . . . Il faut donc rompre avec l'étude structurale atemporelle des cosmogonies africaines.*[140]

CAD recommends that contemporary thinkers reconnect with the Afrikan philosophical locus because wisdom, as reveals the archeological analysis of the concept of change (*Kheper*), is a trans-millennial effort upheld by thoughtful humans to better their socio-cultural fabric.[141] It is this cultural life, this experiential "given," this active matter which, like the generative *Noun*, is pregnant with "archetypes" (ideals/ideas) likely to be brought to fruition by thinkers as they exercise their demiurgic power of reason (*Ra*). *Ptah (Ta*?)[142] and *Thoth (Tot?)*[143] are the Memphite and Hermopolitan counterparts of Ra. In the cosmogony of Iunu[144] (Heliopolis), through *Kheper*, *Ra* (the autogenous consciousness, the Good, ordering, and beautifying Principle of the world)[145] rises in *Noun* and creates the first syzygy *Schou* (air/space) and *Tefnut* (humidity/water), declaring: "I was one, I became three" ("*J'étais un, je devins trois*").[146]

It should be observed that the hypostatic epiphanies of *Ra* as Beauty-Good-Order are not just a priori attributes, since we do experience them in ourselves and in nature. Our corporeal body, for example, is an ordered and harmonious unit when healthy. In this state, we feel apt for intellectual and physical endeavors. Thus, the enlivening reason *Ra,* for CAD, is truly an inner dormant demiurgic energy/consciousness that each human being can awaken in herself.[147] How?

Becoming *Ra*, for us conscious and sapient beings, could mean at least two things. First, understand ourselves as life-improvers and endeavor to behave accordingly at both familial and societal spaces. Second, face the complex conundrum of matter in scientific terms.

MATTER, ENERGY, AND UNIVERSOLOGY IN CHEIKH ANTA DIOP

This section of the book will express CAD's views (not mine)[148] on the complex field of microphysics. In his 1983 contribution to the colloquium organized in Dakar (Senegal) from June 7–8 by the *Revue Sénéglaise de Philosophie*, CAD addresses the question of philosophy within the context of a rational crisis. He underscores the continuing scientific, philosophic, and spiritual uncertainties on the ontological status of "reality," and reappraises the rationalistic explanation of the world in its expansion. For him, the question of what "is" and how it comes/came into being is the conundrum with which contemporary thought still wrestles.

If the mathematical or exact sciences such as (astro)physics, chemistry, or molecular biology etc. construe "matter" as a given, the nature of the latter, however, remains enigmatic and far beyond the three reductive principles of determinism, objectivity, and completeness[149] propounded by classical mechanics. This view validates the quantum theory, which rather interprets microscopic matter as energetic. In his own terms, CAD observes:

> *Comme nous allons le voir, c'est le rationalisme scientifique dans sa forme classique qui est remis en question: on parle souvent d'une crise de la raison dans la mesure où le principe de causalité, le déterminisme, la séparabilité des phénomènes et leur objectivité qui règnent en macrophysique sont fondamentalement mis en cause en microphysique . . . De la sorte, observateur, instrument d'observation et corpuscule ou phénomène observé forment un tout indissoluble, qu'il est impossible de séparer. C'est pour cette raison que la réalité physique observée cesse d'être indépendante de l'observateur, comme le postule la physique classique . . . D'autre part, la complémentarité onde-corpuscule montre qu'on ne peut pas embrasser d'un seul 'regard' à la fois, tous les aspects de cet univers: on observe ou l'aspect ondulatoire ou l'aspect corpusculaire, jamais les deux à la fois.*[150]

This quote underscores, from a microphysical standpoint, the undulatory and interwoven nature of cosmic matter. This simply means that phenomena (psychic and microphysical) interact for better or worse, because intertwined at the (sub)atomic level; hence CAD's philosophical universology, which is repeatedly translated in his epistemology through the bridging concepts of reconciliation,[151] unity,[152] federation,[153] and more.

Universology is the *logos* (science) of the entire celestial whole called the universe/pluriverse. It is a rational inquiry on the essence and functioning of the universe. Universology seeks to examine the mystery of being (what is) from both micro and macroscopic dimensions. This view confronts us with the gigantic scope of scientific philosophy in CAD, who writes that the description of Nature/of the structure of the pluriverse goes from the sub-quantic to the galactic and hyper-galactic levels.[154]

But can reason fully account for what the universe is? The answer is uncertain. But there is hope, since the uncompromising exercise of speculative-scientific rationalism is predicated upon an openness to all possible knowledges (cosmogonies, parapsychology, psychotronics, physics, astrophysics, astronomy, biology, anthropology, and more). *sofia*, the torch for self-enlightenment and knowledge must become, I suggest, a sort of universonomy which endeavors to shine forth what is of the universe or what its regulative law is. And the engendering Atom Tara,[155] our sun, would be a suitable locus of scientific focus.

According to CAD, scientists consider that our sun will remain alive in the next fifteen billion years[156] unless its demise occurs earlier than expected. The eventuality raises disturbing questions: what would become of sapient humanity on earth? Would it be destroyed by blaze or cold? In either case, what preventive measures can we envision to keep the sun in combustion? Can we tame it through applied science and how? CAD is as concerned as we all presumably are and, as a nuclear physicist, expounds the challenges ahead of global scientific think-tanks and inquiring communities thus:

> *. . . l'homme se rendra compte que sa tâche ne fait que commencer. Il découvrira alors qu'il est absolument dans ses possibilités bien avant 15 milliards d'années de réflexion, de domestiquer le système solaire et d'y régner jusqu'à la planète périphérique de Pluton, d'une façon pratiquement éternelle. Y arrivera-t-il peut-être en nourrissant le soleil par des satellites précaires formés avec la matière sidérale qui finissent par tomber dans sa masse, ou peut-être en restituant au soleil l'énergie rayonnée en l'accélération des noyaux d'hydrogène à partir d'immenses champs électro-magnétiques artificiels? Refuser la mort thermodynamique, stabiliser le système solaire, le protéger des météorites dangereux, solidifier les planètes gazeuses, réchauffer celles de la périphérie pour les rendre habitables, empêcher l'apparition et la prolifération de monstres biologiques, contrôler les climats et l'évolution des planètes, découvrir et entretenir toutes les routes praticables du système, communiquer avec les étoiles proches de la galaxie, créer un surhomme à vie plus longue, telles seront peut-être les préoccupations enthousiastes du savant de demain. La vie aurait ainsi à sa manière triomphé de la mort, l'homme aurait réalisé un paradis terrestre pratiquement éternel, il aurait triomphé par la même occasion de tous les systèmes métaphysiques et philosophiques pessimistes, de toutes les visions apocalyptiques du destin de l'espèce. Une étape grandiose de l'évolution de la conscience humaine serait franchie. L'homme apparaitrait comme un Dieu en devenir . . .*[157]

For CAD, the raison d'être of scientific rationality consists in gradually raising humanity toward a quasi-demiurgic status. With her critical thought, this "*Dieu en devenir*" (God in becoming), in the face of the predicament of natural death and the possibility of cosmic annihilation, is challenged to mobilize her creative potential and thus rise above all agnosticism, pessimism, or nihilism. CAD's rationalism leads him to the propitious view that humans can tame the sun and its energy. They can even explore the entire Milky Way, stimulating life where it seems wanting and moving further and further into the universe by creating a bondless interstellar communicative network. The task ahead is immense but performable by demiurgic minds probing their own safeguarding potentialities on earth, within the solar system, and in the expanding cosmos at large.

What is worth our meditative attention is the Antadiopian view that the "*civilisation planétaire*" (planetary civilization) in prospect requires the concerted effort of teams of researchers in various fields.[158] Their unique and synthetic perspectives could result in a better grasp of the universe, as it continuously mushrooms (expands) in various shades and volumes, and as it holds itself in harmony without an annihilation of expanding and gravitational forces. Indeed, the concept of universe connotes this relational turning into unity of multifarious celestial bodies under a conciliatory dispensation.

Following this reasoning, CAD adopts and advocates a unitive (trans-disciplinarian) epistemic blueprint. He is of the view that scientific specialization, though important for analytic purposes, be however trans-disciplinary and synthesized in view of a comprehensive science of the totality of being. This scientific outlook is crucial for our philosophic and spiritual purposes. Not only does it transcend claims to epistemic "neutrality" or "objectivity,"[159] but more broadly because it brings to light the dynamic interwovenness (non-separability) of phenomena within the complex cosmic web:

> *Compte tenu du principe de non-séparabilité, l'existence d'entités, d'objets indépendants possédant des propriétés est niée, et l'univers apparaît dans les nouvelles théories comme une pièce d'un seul tenant dont toutes les parties peuvent vibrer en phase.*[160]

This microphysical argument on the interwovenness of phenomena is valid in contemporary cultural, ecological, energetic, and geo-economic matters. Though intricate, there is however a close connection between critical issues of our time such as corporate imperialism, migrations, terrorism, etc. Even if there is an apparent synchronicity within systems as they seem to withstand internal rifts, these do sometimes happen, engendering a disharmonious internal functioning, with some elements vibrating out of phase with others and jeopardizing the coherence of the entire system. But more positively construed, microphysical thinking, notwithstanding the interferences (disruptions) inherent to systems, tunes us up to the idea of possible equilibrium within the latter. But such a rapprochement or reconciliation, to use CAD's parlance, does not happen haphazardly in the macro-physical realm of human affairs, where agency propels culture and civilization through sofian (renascent) thinkers.

SOFIANIZING PHILOSOPHY

This title is purposely repetitive. It calls for a mutation in the practice of philosophy, considering the foregoing appraisal of *sophia* ("wisdom") as *sofia* (enlightening/enlivening process). Sofian thinking is a civilizational "sickle" that psychologically transforms the inquirer, in Antadiopian terms, into a renascent Af(i)rikan, that is, one who is moved by a historical consciousness, a true creator, a Prometheus bearer of a new civilization and perfectly conscious of what the entire world owes to her ancestral genius in all the realms of science, culture, and religion.[161]

The first chapter provided us with different etymologies of the toponym Afrika. It also underscored that the eponym Afrika is a diminutive of the anthroponym Af(i)ri Kara.[162] As an ethical and purposive trope, the Afrikan is the Promethean latent consciousness that CAD speaks about. It is a demiurgic potentiality attuned to the ancestral achievements of sapient humanity in science, culture, spirituality and more. Such a historical consciousness, for CAD, is the springboard toward the planetary "*nouvelle civilisation*" (new civilization) in the making.

One would observe that the interesting point about the Antadiopian renaissance is its boundless outlook. It is not caged within the boxes of colors, creeds, or ideologies. It even transcends the "*terre entire*" (the whole world) to venture into the starry cosmos. Here lies the open horizon of scientific philosophy, the field of the "*nouveau philosophe*"[163] (new philosopher). The novelty of this renascent philosopher will consist in her perception and commitment to this grandiose cosmic vision that requires the mutation of speculative philosophers into philosophic scientists and conversely. Here is CAD, the philosopher-scientist (mathematician, chemist, and nuclear physicist), defending transdisciplinary scholarship.[164]

However, what is contentious in the above quote is his argument that history, a social science –or more specifically historical knowledge/consciousness *("conscience historique")-* is consubstantial with an inventive (Promethean) and renascent consciousness.

If Fanon, for example, concurs with him, CAD, that creativity and self-surpassing are correlates of be(com)ing,[165] he sometimes underrates the role of history in his praxeology, construing it (history) in broad strokes as passéist in the following manner: "*Je ne suis pas prisonnier de l'Histoire. Je ne dois pas y chercher le sens de ma destinée . . . La densité de l'Histoire ne détermine aucun de mes actes.*"[166] But Fanon, the psychoanalytic thinker and decolonial militant, who struggles to disentangle himself from the socio-historical grip, is not consistent with this foregoing view. He emends his opinion, declaring that "*tout problème humain demande à être considéré à partir du temps,*"[167] that is, from a historical perspective, before adding with verve:

> The colonist makes history and he knows it. And because he refers constantly to the history of the metropolis, he plainly indicates that here he is the extension of this metropolis. The history he writes is therefore not the history of the country he is despoiling, but the history of his own nation's looting, raping, and starving to death. The immobility to which the colonized subject is condemned can be challenged only if he decides to put an end to the history of colonization and the history of despoliation in order to bring to life the history of the nation, the history of decolonization.[168]

Fanon injects a dialectical dimension into history that swings the latter between not-being (colonial barbarism: "looting, raping, starving to death") and be(com)ing (decolonial struggle for independence), with the crucial actional category of decision.

A resolution (decision) is the outcome of a deliberative process. It is reached when the pros and cons of a predicament have been carefully weighed up. But, in Fanon, just like in CAD, it is the informed disposition of the mind within specific conundrums which stirs individuals/communities to militant action for a qualitative socio-economic/(geo)political change. When brains are ablaze (tuned up) with the will to harmonies (psychological, social, geopolitical, and cosmic), then human agency (history) can be mobilized in the direction of progress. If not, barbarism is likely to ensue.

Other renaissance theorists like Kwame Nkrumah offer further invigorating insights on the role of history in the renascent process within societies. Nkrumah considers that history is assimilable to matter, which is prone to self-motion[169] and undulatory cohesiveness, even if its inner tension does yield discordant social forces. He contends:

> In the new African renaissance, we place great emphasis on the presentation of history. Our history needs to be written as the history of our society, not as the story of European adventures . . . and from the point of view of the harmony of progress of this society . . . In this way, African history can come to guide and direct African action. African history can thus become a pointer at the ideology which should guide and direct African reconstruction.[170]

Nkrumah's "African reconstruction" requires, among other things, that historiography (the writing of history) be socially mediated and serve the cause of unity, given that "the people are the reality of national greatness."[171] Though the notion of "people"[172] remains ambiguous in contemporary geopolitical philosophy and constitutional forms of governance where money, class, race, gender and more seem to determine who counts and belongs to that slippery social category, it might be argued with Nkrumah that a people is a cohesive and self-productive social power. This assertion must be understood within the framework of the liberation of the acme of inventiveness by a specific people. Greatness is the unrelenting pursuit of the realistic ideal of mental and national independence; construed by a people as achievable. This resoluteness frees the mind from the shackles (boxes) of imitation, pessimism, ignorance, fear, superstition, and possibly arises from one's auto-didactic immersion in the genealogy of ideas.

Nations, as it were, prosper when people awake to a sense of historical cohesiveness and shared purpose. Thus, in our contemporary world, Nkrumah's renascence of the idea of unity among humans could be experientially lived if popularized through educational conversations at different social spheres and gradually appropriated as such by the elite as well. It becomes an *adzo-bod*,[173] that is, a people's prerogative and event. Nkrumah's anthropology sprouts from what he calls "the traditional face of Africa,"[174] which presents the *mod*[175] as "primarily a spiritual being, a being endowed originally with a certain inward dignity, integrity and value,"[176] and which makes human welfare a supreme social ideal.

I find this ethical orientation of Nkrumah's historiography compelling for educational purposes. If history is purposively resourceful, it must indeed be engagedly articulated around cohesive socio-ethical signposts for present and future generations. In other words, humans are historical beings in the sense that they can constantly reshuffle the global predicaments that confront them through critical thought and active resistance. By mediating their prospective gaze on humanity via an accurate apprehension of their common past, they can labor collaboratively toward a better understanding of themselves and of the universe. Here lies, for me, the Antadiopian "*optimisme atavique*" (atavistic optimism) or the possibility of the human renaissance. History, qua rational (fact-based) quest[177] for a better world via a retro-prospective methodology becomes both revolutionary and redemptive for global humanity in its wrestle against planetary barbarism.

SOFIA: PLANETARY CIVILIZATION VERSUS PLANETARY DEMISE (BARBARISM)

The following questions are worth pondering as we step into this last section of the chapter. What triggers, moves, and motivates philosophic thinking? Why do we engage in research or write papers and books? More crucially, what do we live for? Do our *nsisim*[178] ("shadow"/life principle/soul) and *nnem*[179] ("heart"/rational faculty) constantly seek wisdom, human progress, and happiness? If so, how? How do we envision our post-mortem condition and destination, death being an important dialectical category in my thinking, just like in both CAD and Plato?[180]

Death, a be(com)ing event, a mutation in form from sameness to otherness, would explain life and conversely. Death raises metaphysical questions on the atomic constitution of matter and human embodiment. What is this body that we are? Do our atoms, like hard or soft drives, store our cognitive and emotional lives for the hereafter? If so, what becomes of those atoms once they disaggregate in our bodily breath, fluids (sweat and urine), wastes, and after death? Do they duplicate their data in our immaterial principle; the shadowy *nsisim* ("soul"), and spread them the world over? What would individuality mean in this case? Who are we in the atomic conglomeration of the cosmos? These are concerns beyond the scope of this reflection.

However, as we proceed with the conclusion of our inquiry on the purpose of *sofia* (wisdom/enlightenment), the category of death awakens us to our ephemerality, possibly triggering questions about the goal of our transient presence on earth. Assuredly, human bodies change and grow stronger if healthy or weaker if sickened. The Antadiopian *sopi* [be(com)ing] confronts us with a natural challenge: the certainty of our physical demise, until we find its medical remedy. In the meantime, our gradual journey toward death might make us more mindful about our contribution to the quality of life in this world.

For CAD, people's philosophical eschatology, cultural achievements, and history are connected to the way they tackle the problem of death.[181]

Plato's Socrates, on his side, considers that death is the whole purpose of philosophy: "I am afraid that other people do not realize that the one aim of those who practice philosophy in the proper manner is to practice for dying and death."[182] Socrates further expatiates on this opinion in the *Phaedo*, arguing that self-care, piety, and philosophy are life's ultimate goals,[183] and that they can be acquired by education and upbringing.[184] For him, it is toward the axiological trinity of philosophy, piety, and self-care that one's soul, adorned with "moderation, righteousness, courage, freedom and truth"[185] should ascend. "You will please me and mine and yourselves by taking good care of your own selves in whatever you do,"[186] confides Socrates to Crito after explaining to Simmias:

> Those who are deemed to have lived an extremely pious life are freed and released from the regions of the earth as from a prison; they make their way up to a pure dwelling place and live on the surface of the earth. Those who have purified themselves sufficiently by philosophy live in the future altogether without a body; they make their way to even more beautiful dwelling places which it is hard to describe clearly, nor do we now have the time to do so. Because of the things we have enunciated, Simmias, one must make every effort to share

> in virtue and wisdom in one's life, for the reward is beautiful and the hope is great.[187]

Thus, nothing flows from inertia and certainly not virtue and wisdom. It is the soul's ascent to philosophic purgation, which leads to felicity (through death to vice and ignorance) both here on earth and in the underworld. At the cosmic level, the active power, *sopi*, dilates the primordial Atò(u)m *Noun* revealed via spiral, rotatory and revolutionary swerves, and in the antithetic tension between harmonic and chaotic energies. At the human and animal planes, similar sporadic strains do occur. Human psychology and axiology vindicate this view, since they are not always restorative. Experience shows that humans often change to become more civilized, but sometimes barbaric too at workplaces, for example, and beyond. This gives us a clue as to why CAD dialectically polarizes his epistemology between civilization and barbarism.

Within this conflicting interstice, *sofia* rises as a transcending tide toward progress. It is not contented with human waddling into ignorance, vice, chaos, conflict, or exploitation. Rather, *sofia,* like *kheper*, duplicates and conveys the creative power of the initial principle (*Noun/Eyo)* to subsequent ones. This raises some optimism about the possibility for humans to rationally attune themselves to the rejuvenating archeological and teleological circle of sapient life. Again, thought is indeed what, ideally, defines the *Femina/Homo sapiens sapiens*, the be(com)ing that is twice wise (*sapiens sapiens*).

The Sofian ontology factorizes wisdom in a similar fashion, and speaks of the *soso mod*: "*sǒsǒ correspond au français 'droiture'*; *sǒsǒ mod est l'homme 'juste,' . . . , l'homme qui agit au-dessus des passions et de l'intérêt propre selon la seule raison de l'équité.*"[188] In other words, *sǒsǒ mod* is a reasonable, skilled, "accomplished," and "impeccable" person.[189] She can circularly think her origin and identity in a future mediated by the past and conversely.

Accordingly, *so-fia* (radiance of wisdom), far from being a fixed feature of the human character, rather illumines, defers itself, rising or crumbling in *fia-s(c)o*, depending on the intensity of care that individuals invest in their intellectual and moral endeavors. The intransitive Beti verb *sòbi*[190] means to work hard, to endure, or to toil. It also expresses the subjective action of making one's way through/over/under some concrete predicament. In both cases, *sòbi* conveys the active ideas of personal effort and labor. Now, as we break down the composite verb *sòbi*, we get two additional verbs, namely *sò* (to come/to welcome/to acclaim)[191] and *bi* (to grasp/to catch/to arrest someone).

In a philosophical sense, the concept *sòbi* would refer to a sapient process, whereby knowledge and enlightenment are achieved through doubt *(bisò)*. To be *bisò* is to be dubious about thoughts, concepts, opinions, ideologies, discursive formations, and the appearance of things in general. The *bisò* person rationally probes her own discourses and life, as well as their nature before reaching any conclusion about them. A practical example of the *sòbian* process would be the lived experiences of our embodiment in a world still politically divided along ethnic, racial, and economic lines. The current text itself is constitutive of a similar movement since it goes through the cultural life of contemporary humanity and hands itself over to an ongoing intersubjective appraisal. It can no longer be reduced to the realm of its author's reflective privacy.

Sofia requires (fore)sight,[192] intelligence, and understanding. It demands that tho(ugh)t[193] deepen and expand its understanding of the genealogy and teleology of the human life in the universe. How do we know this as seekers of wisdom? We know it because of our unquenchable thirst to be-come humane and not barbaric. Ongoing inquiry at personal and institutional levels is a sign of our will to progressive, unprejudiced, and liberal knowledge. We have been asking all sorts of questions from childhood to this age. Children and adults around us continue to do so as well.

Research (questioning), as it were, seems to be the path to our cognitive solarization, that is, our harmonious incorporation into Nature (our solar system and the cosmos at large). Ideally, we know what is good and desirable for us, humans, as witness the constitutions, laws, and regulations in our families, institutions, societies, and countries. Some of us are people of their word, seeking coherence between what we think, say, and do. Others endeavor to achieve polyglottery as means to more comprehensive, direct, and trans-disciplinarian inquiry. As we reflect daily on how to solve problems and improve the quality of life on earth, we exercise our sapient nature and will to knowledge.

This intelligent quest is actively carried out when we write or teach. In these linguistic and cognitive activities, we want to make sure that things are clearer to us and to others. We strive to lessen the ambiguities of our thought processes. We create concepts, examine existing ones like that of "philosophy," and explore their possible semantic thickness and meanders in the realms of mental and practical lives.

Because we harbor the seed of sapient life in us, we confront unsettling questions on human relationships, "*lesquelles sont barbares non seulement entre les peuples, entre les religions, mais souvent dans un même bureau, dans une même université,*" as E. Morin strikingly observes.[194] Confronted with these worrying facts, the crucial question put before us by CAD remains: *civilisation ou barbarie* (Civilization or barbarism)? What do we opt for? My Afrosofian analysis, in this chapter, has sided with civilization.

As I bring it to a close, I hope to have tested, even partially, my hypothesis that the Beti *sofia* can elucidate and clarify its Greek homophone *sophia*, whose archeology still remains unknown to etymologists, as witnesses Pierre Chantraine's *Dictionnaire étymologique de la langue grecque.*[195] As we have seen, Plato concurs with Chantraine and argues for the non-Atticness of the concept of philosophy.[196]

As was underscored, what is instructive in both Plato[197] and Aristotle[198] on the origin, semantic thickness, and socio-political relevance of wisdom is their Af(i)ri-centric orientation. This motional reterritorialization of wisdom (*sophia*) has prompted me to investigate *sofia* after a historical and hermeneutic detour on the Kemetic notion of *Kheper* in CAD's philosophic corpus. A common semantic ground was thus found between *sophia, kheper, sopi* (Walaf), and *sofia.* They all connote the ideas of be(com)ing, transformation, change, and motion.

A find worth our epistemic and geo-economic attention is the energetic foundation of the tautological enlightenment process *so-fia*. It seems to me that this conative sense of wisdom, which wraps and transforms the investigator from within, has been the most concealed and puzzling aspect of philosophy in the academy. *Sofia,* that is, wisdom factorized by the infinite number of the sun's rays, is the metaphor of the potential shining forth of sapient energy in people's concrete lives.

The sun, omnipresent in many philosophic and even literary works, surely summons humanity's upward fall (transcendence) and fundamental cosmicity. This is the case, for example, in the Kemetic Heliopolitan cosmogony,[199] in Plato's *Republic*,[200] CAD's *L'unité Culturelle de l'Afrique Noire*,[201] Grégoire Biyogo's *Encyclopédie du Mvett*,[202] Mbog Bassong's *La Méthode de la Philosophie Africaine,*[203] or Mongo Beti's *Mission to Kala*.[204] Obviously, the challenge, for us academics in particular and other humans in general, consists in reterritorializing our lives and epistemic practices in *sofia,* the sun-like and civilizing dimension of our sapient nature.

Figure 5.1. Akoa Mfula: Sapient Vision. Photo taken by François Ngoa Kodena.

Figure 5.2. Inner view of the left eye of Akoa Mfula (Cameroon): Regeneration. Photo taken by François Ngoa Kodena.

Figure 5.3. ***Kheper*** **or** ***Kpwâma*** **in Beti.** Photo taken by François Ngoa Kodena.

Figure 5.4. A geometrical representation of a pyramid through the linking of five holes found engraved on the peak of Akoa Fotna (Mvog-Okom, Cameroon). Photo taken by François Ngoa Kodena.

Figure 5.5. Inner view of the right eye (the sun) of Akoa Mfula (Cameroon). Photo taken by François Ngoa Kodena.

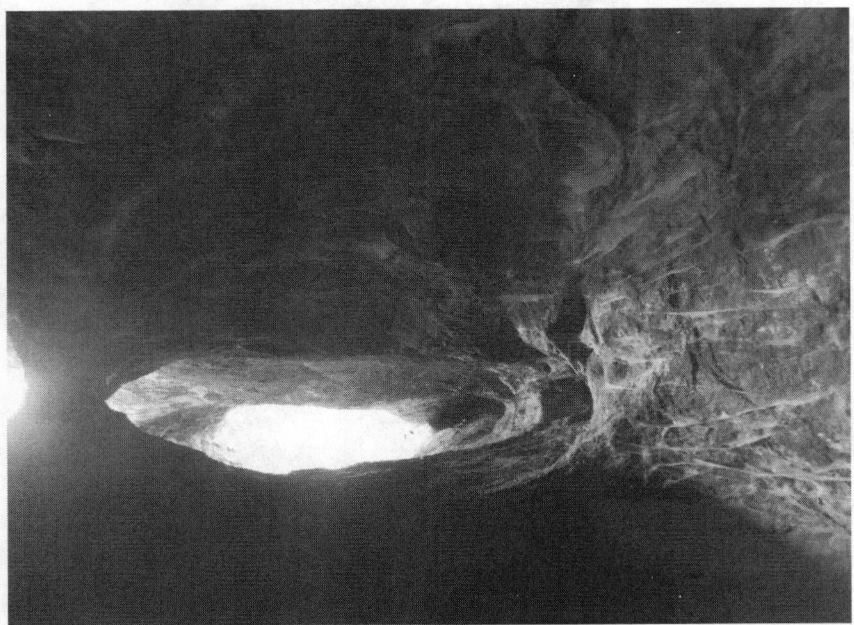

Figure 5.6. A further inner view of the right eye of Akoa Mfula (Cameroon). Photo taken by François Ngoa Kodena.

Figure 5.7. ***Sofia*: The Seat of Wisdom (Akoa Fotna, Cameroon).** Photo taken by François Ngoa Kodena.

Figure 5.8. Eyo, the Dome and sun-like Generative Atòm (Akoa Mfula, Cameroon). Photo taken by François Ngoa Kodena.

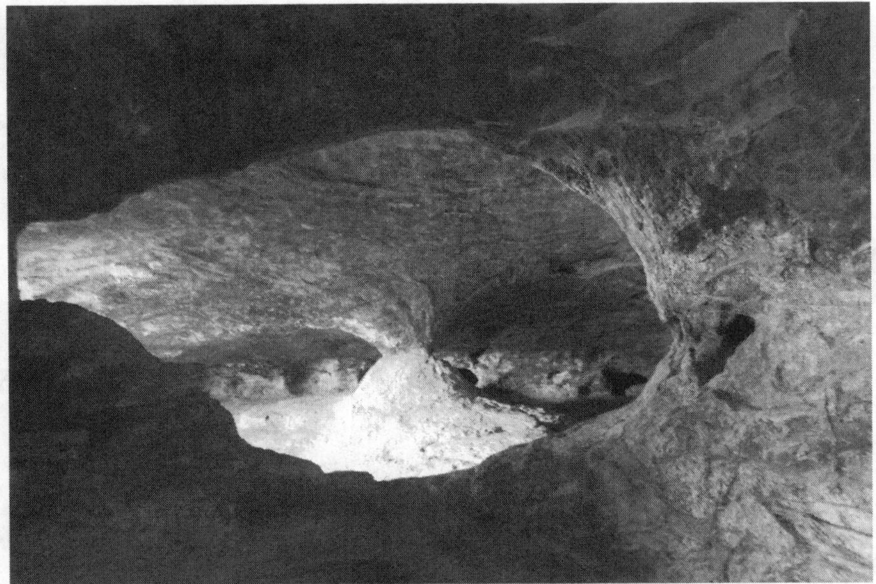

Figure 5.9. Tara: The divine Eye/Intelligence in the beholder (Akoa Mfula, Cameroon). Photo taken by François Ngoa Kodena.

Figure 5.10. Inner view left eye of Akoa Mfula (Cameroon). Photo taken by François Ngoa Kodena.

Figure 5.11. Field research with ZENN at Akono (Cameroon). Photo taken by François Ngoa Kodena.

NOTES

1. Cheikh Anta Diop, *Les Fondements Économiques et Culturels d'un État fédéral d'Afrique Noire* (Paris: Présence Africaine, 1960), 7. From French: " . . . at the beginning is energy, all the rest proceeds from it."

2. Molefi Kete Asante, *Cheikh Anta Diop. An Intellectual Portrait* (Los Angeles: University of Sankore Press, 2007), 21.

3. Mubabinge Bilolo, *Les Cosmo-Théologies philosophiques de l'Égypte Antique. Problématiques-Prémisses herméneutiques-et-problèmes majeurs* (Kinshasa: Publications Universitaires Africaines, 1986), 14. From French: "series of conceptions from about forty 'deified' individuals."

4. Aristotle, *Metaphysics* A, 2, 983a 6–10: " . . . and this science alone has both these qualities; for God is thought to be among the causes of all things and to be a first principle, and such a science either God alone can have, or God above all others."

5. Pierre Chantraine, *Dictionnaire Étymologique de la Langue Grecque* (Paris: Librairie Klincksieck, 2009), 1162; Plato, *Cratylus,* 412b.

6. I identify this "self," this human "soil" (essence) or ground upon which human unification can sprout with the human sapient nature.

7. For me, the inquiring agent thinks in space-time and orients her/his work and cultural life in a certain ethical direction.

8. Ama Mazama, "An Afrocentric Approach to Language Planning" in Ama Mazama (Ed.), *The Afrocentric Paradigm* (Trenton, NJ: Africa World Press, Inc., 2003), 201–14.

9. Maulana Karenga, "Afrocentricity and Multicultural Education: Concept, Challenge and Contribution" in Ama Mazama (Ed.), *Ibid.*, 79–81.

10. Molefi Kete Asante, *Afrocentricity. The Theory for Social Change* (Chicago, Illinois: African American Images, 2003), 63.

11. Frantz Fanon, *Peau noire, masques blancs, op. cit.*, 188. From French: "O my body, make of me always a man who questions!"

12. Though the concept is mine, it will be shown that its constituents, namely Afrika and *sofia* are inherently Antadiopian.

13. Cheikh Anta Diop, *Civilisation ou Barbarie, op. cit.*, 16. In French: "*un optimisme africain atavique, mais vigilant, nous incline à souhaiter que toutes les nations se donnent la main pour bâtir la civilisation planétaire au lieu de sombrer dans la barbarie.*"

14. The Beti verb *a vet* precisely means to lift or upraise oneself.

15. The discursive word in Beti, which dismantles (*a bug*) and restructures concepts, discourses, and the world itself.

16. Annex 8.

17. We examined the monogenetic theory through the *Femina/Homo sapiens sapiens*, who migrated from Afrika to other parts of the world through her Grimaldi branch. See: Cheikh Anta Diop, *Civilisation ou Barbarie, op. cit.,* 17–132; Christopher Stringer and Robin McKie, *African Exodus, op. cit.*

18. Prince Dika Akwa Nya Bonambela, *Hommage du Cameroun au Professeur Cheikh Anta Diop, op. cit.*, 26. From French: "nature in its evolution never creates

he same being twice. Nature created the human being once and the human being differentiates, evolves, adapts or disappears; but nature does not create twice the human species. It did not create the horse twice."

19. *Ibid.*, 26–27.

20. Cheikh Anta Diop, *Civilisation ou Barbarie, op. cit.*, 17–132.

21. *Ibid.*, 387.

22. Edmund Husserl, *Cartesian Meditations. An Introduction to Phenomenology* (Trans. Dorion Cairns, Hingham, MA: Kluwer Boston. Inc., 1982), 2.

23. Cheikh Anta Diop, *Antériorité des Civilisations Nègres, op. cit.*, 278. In French: "*pratiquer l'exercice sans compromis du rationalisme pour chasser définitivement les ténèbres de l'obscurantisme, sous toutes ses formes.*"

24. It was argued in the first chapter that *sofia,* in the literal sense, is an economic (agronomic) concept which accounts for the material transformative betterment (coming into being) of the natural order through human thoughtful labor. The present chapter will emphasize its philosophical underpinnings.

25. Cheikh Anta Diop, "Quand pourra-t-on parler d'une renaissance africaine" in *Alerte sous les Tropiques, op. cit.*, 33–44.

26. Cheikh Anta Diop, *L'Unité Culturelle de l'Afrique Noire, op. cit.*

27. CAD considers optimism to be a distinctive mark of the Afrikan psychology. He writes: "*l'univers mental égyptien—et méridional, en général—est bien optimiste, et d'un optimisme conscient et raisonné.*" From French: "the Egyptian mental universe—and meridional, in general—is indeed optimistic, and of a conscious and reasoned optimism." See: Cheikh Anta Diop, *L'Unité Culturelle de l'Afrique Noire, Ibid.*, 169.

28. The Walaf/Wolof was CAD's maternal language, whereas the Coptic is a later version of the Kemetic Medu Neter. See: Théophile Obenga, *Origine Commune de l'Égyptien Ancien, du Copte et des Langues Négro-Africaines. Introduction à la Linguistique Africaine* (Paris: L'Harmattan, 1993), 16.

29.Cheikh Anta Diop, *Civilisation ou Barbarie, op. cit.*, 414, 431, 450. I will be calling the Medu Neter (Divine Words) Ntil. This Beti concept is more convenient in conveying the ideas of both transcendence (divine words) and writing than *Medzo me Nti* (Medu Neter). The substantive Ntil, composed of the theonym Nti (God) and the verb *til* (to write), literally means the demiurgic writer/writing/script. See: Siméon Basile Atangana Ondigui, *Le Nouveau Dictionnaire Ewondo, op. cit.*, 164.

30. *Ibid.*, 431. From French: "and sopi in walaf, means 'to transform,' 'to become,' just as in the first two languages."

31. Cheikh Anta Diop, *Parenté Génétique de l'Egyptien Pharaonique et des Langues Négro-Africaines, op. cit.*

32. Théophile Obenga, *Origine Commune de l'Egyptien Ancien, du Copte et des Langues Négro-Africaines Modernes, op. cit.*

33. Jean-Claude Mboli, *Origine des Langues Africaines, op. cit.*

34. Languages, writes Th. Obenga after Volney (1757–1820), are nations' genealogies and encyclopedias, since they contain their knowledges, ideas, and histories. See: Théophile Obenga, *Cheikh Anta Diop, Volney et le Sphinx, op. cit.*, 60.

35. Cheikh Anta Diop, *Antériorité des Civilisations Nègres, op. cit.,* 12. From French: "Today still, of all the peoples of the world, the Black African Negro, alone, can show in a comprehensive manner, the identity of essence of his culture with that of Pharaonic Egypt, to the extent that both cultures can serve as systems of reciprocal reference. He is the only one, to still be able to recognize himself in an indubitable fashion in the Egyptian cultural universe; he is at home there; he is not disoriented in the latter as would any other human being, be he Indo-European or Semite. . . . the psychology and the culture revealed by the Egyptian texts identify themselves to the Negro personality. And African studies will free themselves from the vicious circle in which they move, to retrieve all their meaning and all their fecundity, only by orienting themselves to the Nile Valley. Reciprocally, Egyptology will disentangle itself from its secular sclerosis, from the hermeticism of texts, only the day when it will have the courage to explode the valve that insulates it, doctrinally, from the vivifying source that constitutes, for her, the Negro world." This does not, however, mean that only contemporary Afrikan languages understand/derive from the Ntil (Medu Neter) or account for the cosmos. The idea put across here is that of linguistic reciprocity of languages pertaining to the same cultural backdrop.

36. G. Mokhtar (Ed.), *General History of Africa, Vol. II, op. cit*., 76–77.

37. Maghan Keita, *Race and the Writing of History. Riddling the Sphinx* (New York: Oxford University Press, Inc., 2000), 172.

38. Cheikh Anta Diop, *Civilisation ou barbarie, op. cit.,* 16. In French: "*Aujourd'hui, chaque peuple, armé de son identité culturelle retrouvée ou renforcée, arrive au seuil de l'ère post-industrielle. Un optimisme africain atavique, mais vigilant, nous incline à souhaiter que toutes les nations se donnent la main pour bâtir la civilisation planétaire au lieu de sombrer dans la barbarie*."

39. William Blum, *America's Deadliest Export: Democracy—The Truth About US Foreign Policy and Everything Else* (London: Zed Books Ltd, 2014); Richard Peet, *Unholy Trinity, The IMF, World Band and WTO* (New York: Zed Books Ltd, 2010); Michel Parenti, *Profit Pathology and Other Indecencies* (Boulder, CO: Paradigm Publishers, 2015).

40. Théophile Obenga, *Le sens de la lutte contre l'africanisme eurocentriste* (Paris: L'Harmattan, 2001), 112.

41. Pathé Diagne, *Cheikh Anta Diop et l'Afrique dans l'histoire du monde* (Paris: L'Harmattan, 2008), 131.

42. Prince Dika Akwa Nya Bonambela (Dir.), *Hommage du Cameroun au Professeur Cheikh Anta Diop, op. cit*., 53.

43. Valentin-Yves Mudimbe, *The Invention of Africa* (Bloomington and Indianapolis: Indiana University Press, 1988), 78, 181.

44. Pathé Diagne, *Cheikh Anta Diop et l'Afrique dans l'histoire du monde, op. cit.,* 129. Froment defines CAD as a "defender of Africa," without defining what he means by that toponym, and without connecting the latter to the rest of the world as CAD does.

45. Mary Lefkowitz, *Not Out of Africa, op. cit.,* 16. Like Froment, Lefkowitz makes an ambiguous claim when she writes about CAD: "the Senegalese humanist and scientist Cheikh Anta Diop undertook to construct a usable past for African

people." How do we reconcile the adjective "humanist" with the construction of a usable past for African people? What is that past and what does it consist of? Is the African past not primarily the human past, considering the prevalent monogenetic theory of humanity?

46. Teodros Kiros critically alludes to Senghor, Césaire, and Damas as "the theorists of negritude." See: Teodros Kiros, *Zara Yacob: Rationality of the Human Heart* (Trenton, NJ: Africa World Press, 2005), 132. I observe that the concept used by the aforementioned theorists was Négritude rather than negritude as Kiros writes.

47. Cheikh Anta Diop, *Nations Nègres et Culture, op. cit.,* 54–57.

48. Cheikh Anta Diop, *Civilisation ou Barbarie, op. cit.,* 9.

49. Cheikh Anta Diop, *Nations Nègres et Culture, op. cit.,* 59–203.

50. Cheikh Anta Diop, *Civilisation ou Barbarie, op. cit.,* 9.

51. Cheikh Anta Diop, *Nations Nègres et Culture, op. cit.* 63–5.

52. Cheikh Anta Diop, *Civilisation ou Barbarie, op. cit.*, 415.

53. *Ibid,* 9.

54. *Ibid.*

55. Cheikh Anta Diop, *Antériorité des Civilisations Nègres, op. cit.,* 12. In French: "*Les études africaines ne sortiront du cercle vicieux où elles se meuvent, pour retrouver tout leur sens et toute leur fécondité, qu'en s'orientant vers la vallée du Nil. Réciproquement, l'égyptologie ne sortira de sa sclérose séculaire, de l'hermétisme des textes, que du jour où elle aura le courage de faire exploser la vanne qui l'isole, doctrinalement, de la source vivifiante que constitue, pour elle, le monde nègre.*"

56. Cheikh Anta Diop, *Civilisation ou Barbarie, op. cit.,* 12. In French: "*Par conséquent, aucune pensée, aucune idéologie n'est, par essence, étrangère à l'Afrique, qui fut la terre de leur enfantement. C'est donc en toute liberté que les Africains doivent puiser dans l'héritage intellectuel commun de l'humanité, en ne se laissant guider que par les notions d'utilité, d'efficience.*"

57. Cheikh Anta Diop, *Nations Nègres et Culture, op. cit.*, 59–203.

58. Valentin-Yves Mudimbe, *The Invention of Africa, op. cit.,* 169.

59. Wole Soyinka, *Myth, Literature and the African World* (Cambridge: Cambridge University Press, 2006), 3.

60. Teodros Kiros, *Zara Yacob: Rationality of the Human Heart* (Trenton, NJ: Africa World Press, 2005), 145.

61. Cheikh Anta Diop, "*Quand pourra-t-on parler d'une renaissance africaine?* " ("When shall we be able to talk of an African Renaissance" in *Alerte sous les Tropiques, op. cit.,* 33–44.

62. Cheikh Anta Diop, *Civilisation ou Barbarie, op. cit.,* 27.

63. This theme of agency in the Antadiopian epistemology converges with Mudimbe and Foucault's respective methodologies. See: Mantha Diawara, Reading Africa Through Foucault: V. Y. Mudimbe's Reaffirmation of the Subject" in *The MIT Press* (October, Vol. 55, Winter 1990), 79–92.

64. Cheikh Anta Diop, *Nations Nègres et Culture, op. cit.,* 25. From French: "There is a tendency to think that every intellectual thought, every activity that must contribute to the awakening of the cultural consciousness of a people, must, necessarily, falter on the scientific field. . . . It was enough to concede that every people have a

past, however modest it be, which was relatively possible to discover by an appropriate investigation. . . . If our traditional historians; ethnologists, sociologists, had fully realized, as one would rightly expect, that what is essential for a people is less to glorify itself of a more or less grandiose past than to discover and be conscious of the continuity of that past regardless of what it was, they would not have given in to wrong interpretation. This factor alone is determinant for the vivification of national consciousness. But, to reach such a goal there is no need to deliberately distort the facts."

65.A. Arnaiz-Villena et al., "HLA genses in Macedonians and the sub-Saharan origin of the Greeks" (in *Tissue Antigens,* 2001, No. 57), 118–127.

66. Cheikh Anta Diop, *Civilisation ou Barbarie, op. cit.,* 19–138; G. Mokhtar, *General History of Africa, Vol. II. Ancient Civilizations of Africa, op. cit.*; Christopher Stringer and Robin McKie, *African Exodus, op. cit.*; Yosef A. A. ben-Jochannan, *Africa. Mother of Western Civilization* (Baltimore, MD: Black Classic Press, 1988).

67. Constantin-François Volney, *Volney's Ruins* (Trans. Count Daru, Boston: Josiah P. Mendum, 1869), 3 titled "Invocation."

68. Champollion le Jeune, *Grammaire Égyptienne, ou Principes généraux de l'écriture sacrée égyptienne* (Paris: Imprimeurs de l'Institut de France, 1836), xxij–xxiij. Champollion is the founder of modern Egyptology in the sense that he deciphered the Ntil (Medu Neter) called Hieroglyphs by the Greeks.

69. Cheikh Anta Diop, "Apport de l'Afrique à l'humanité en sciences et en philosophie" in *Civilisation ou Barbarie, op. cit.,* 291–482; Théophile Obenga, *La Géométrie Égyptienne. Contribution de l'Afrique antique à la Mathématique mondiale* (Paris: L'Harmattan, 1995).

70. Cheikh Anta Diop, *Civilisation ou Barbarie, op. cit.* In French: "*autant la technologie et la science modernes viennent d'Europe, autant, dans l'antiquité, le savoir universel coulait de la vallée du Nil vers le reste du monde, et en particulier vers la Grèce, qui servira de maillon intermédiaire.*"

71. Valentin-Yves Mudimbe, *The Invention of Africa, op. cit.*, 78.

72. Cheikh Anta Diop, *Civilisation ou Barbarie, op. cit.*, 16. In French: "*pour bâtir la civilisation planétaire au lieu de sombrer dans la barbarie.*"

73. Molefi Kete Asante, *Cheikh Anta Diop. An Intellectual Portrait, op. cit.,* 20.

74. Théophile Obenga, *La Philosophie Africaine de la Période Pharaonique. 2780–330 avant notre ère* (Paris: L'Harmattan, 1990). Contrary to Obenga, CAD situates the factual (that is, on the basis on written texts) beginning of Afrikan classical philosophy around 2600 BCE.

75. Cheikh Anta Diop, *Civilisation ou Barbarie, op. cit.*, 388. In French: "*à une époque où les Grecs mêmes n'existaient pas encore dans l'histoire, et où les notions de philosophie chinoise ou hindoue étaient des non-sens.*"

76. Cheikh Anta Diop, *Antériorité des Civilisations Nègres. Mythe ou Vérité Historique? op. cit.*

77. Cheikh Anta Diop, *L'Afrique Noire Précoloniale* (Paris: Présence Africaine, 1987), 201–22; Grégoire Biyogo, *Encyclopédie du Mvett. Tome I—Du Haut Nil en Afrique Centrale* (Paris: Menaibuc, 1997). Kemet, as contemporary scholarship evidences, was gradually peopled from sub-Saharan Afrika. See: Pathé Diagne, *Bakari II*

(1312) et Christophe Colomb (1492). À la rencontre de Tarana ou l'Amérique (Paris: L'Harmatten, 2014).

78. Jay Lampert, "Hegel and Ancient Egypt: History and Becoming" in *International Philosophical Quarterly* (Vol. XXXV, No. 1, Issue No. 137, March 1995), 55–56.

79. Théophile Obenga, *La Philosophie Africaine de la Période Pharaonique, op. cit.,* 62. From French: this Egyptian sacred scarab is found elsewhere on the African continent, with the same symbolic value, in an identical cultural and metaphysical context."

80. Figure 5.3.

81. In the Eton alphabet for example, which is a phonological variant of the Beti language, the consonant "f" does not exist. So, the Eton speaker often compensates this phonetic lack with the use of the letter "p," such that she/he would vocalize *sofia* as *sopia*.

82. Martin Heidegger, *Poetry, Language, Thought* (Trans. Albert Hofstadter, New York: Harper Colophon Books, 1975), 191.

83. *Bikang* is the plural of *ekang* (letter). But Ekang is also another ethnonym of the Beti people. The verb *Kang* means to paint, tattoo, to be grateful, or to sculp. See: Steeve Elvis Ella, *Mvett ékang et le projet bikalik. Essai sur la condition humaine, op. cit.*; Angèle Christine Ondo, *Mvett Ekang. Forme et Sens, op. cit.*

84. Kimbwandende Kia Bunseki Fu-Kiau, *Self-Healing Power and Therapy. Old Teachings from Africa* (Baltimore, MD: Inprint Editions, 2003), 9. Here the author offers a graphic representation of the Bantu view according to which "a human being is a rising and setting sun around the world."

85. Jean Mazel, *Présence du Monde Noir* (Paris: Éditions Robert Laffont, 1975), 29.

86. Philippe Laburthe-Tolra, *Initiations et Sociétés Secrètes au Cameroun. Essai sur la religion beti, op. cit.,* 37, 318–9.

87. E. A. Wallis Budge, *Easy Lessons in Egyptian Hieroglyphics* (New York: Dover Publications, Inc., 1983), 62.

88. Philippe Laburthe-Tolra, *Initiations et Sociétés Secrètes au Cameroun. Essai sur la religion beti, op. cit.,* 324. In French: "*l'homme qui agit au-dessus des passions et de l'intérêt propre selon la seule raison de l'équité.*"

89. Philippe Laburthe-Tolra, *Initiations et Sociétés Secrètes au Cameroun. Essai sur la religion beti, op. cit.,* 322. From French: "What is at play in the So is the engendering of the same by sameness."

90. Tsira Ndong Ndoutoume, *Le Mvett. L'Homme, la Mort et L'Immortalité* (Paris: L'Harmattan, 1993); Grégoire Biyogo, *Adieu à Tsira Ndong Ndoutoume. Homme à l'inventeur de la raison graphique du Mvett* (Paris: L'Harmattan, 2006).

91. This is not to say that the Greeks used Arabic numerals, since they represented fifty as ΠΔ. See: Wikipedia, "Greek Numerals." *Wikipedia, The Free Encyclopedia.* Retrieved February 22, 2020. https://simple.wikipedia.org/wiki/Greek_numerals.

92. Plato, *Republic*, VII, 540a–b. If we agree with CAD that Plato was trained at Heliopolis, then this passage and that of the previous book on the allegory of the sun (Plato, *Republic,* VI, 508a–e) become clearer. See: Prince Dika Akwa Nya Bonambela (Dir.), *Hommage du Cameroun au Professeur Cheikh Anta Diop, op. cit.*, 30.

93. Raymond O. Faulkner, *A Concise Dictionary of Middle Egyptian* (Oxford: Griffith Institute, 1991), 210.

94. Kwasi Wiredu (Ed.), *A Companion to African Philosophy* (Malden, MA: Blackwell Publishing Ltd, 2004), 34.

95. Molefi Kete Asante & Ama Mazama (Ed.), *Encyclopedia of African Religion* (Thousand Oaks, CA: Sage Publications, Inc., 2009), 596.

96. Prince Dika Akwa Nya Bonambela (Dir.), *Hommage du Cameroun au Professeur Cheikh Anta Diop, op. cit.*, 77.

97. Plato, *Cratylus,* 412b. What is of interest in this quote is not so much the definition of wisdom, but rather Plato's claim that *sophia* is non-Attic, that is, non-Greek.

98. Plato's *Timeaus*, however, provides an insightful account of becoming.

99. Pierre Chantraine, *Dictionnaire Étymologique de la Langue Grecque* (Paris: Librairie Klincksieck, 2009), 1162; Plato, *Cratylus,* 412b.

100. Antonio Arnaiz-Villena et al., "HLA genes in Macedonians and the sub-Saharan origin of the Greeks" in *Tissue Antigens* (Feb. 2001: Vol. 57, Issue 2), 118. My intention here is not to suggest that wisdom is genetic, but rather to provide a scientific and coherent account of vindicates an Afrosofian perspective on the question of wisdom.

101. Cheikh Anta Diop, *Antériorité des Civilisations Nègres, op. cit.*; *Civilisation ou Barbarie, op. cit.,* 291–482.

102. Théophile Obenga, *La Philosophie Africaine de la Période Pharaonique, op. cit.*

103. Plato, *Phaedrus*, 274c-d; *Timaeus,* 24b-c; *Laws*, 799a, 819a–e.

104. Aristotle, *Metaphysics* I, 981b.20; *Politics* VII, 1329b, 30–35.

105. Cheikh Anta Diop, *Civilisation ou Barbarie, op. cit.,* 132–38.

106. The concept is mine.

107. Pathé Diagne, *Bakari II (1312) Christophe Colomb (1492) à la rencontre de Tarana ou l'Amérique* (Paris: L'Harmattan, 2014), 61. From French: "that which inspires the first hieroglyphics, belong to the Mennfarite or Lebu-Bantu. It belongs to the same ensemble which comprises the Lingala, the Kiswahili, the Kongo, the Serer, the Pulaar, the Joola of Casamance, the Chadian Sara, the Dwala, the Miele, the Ngola or the Zulu."

108. *Ibid.,* 25. P. Diagne rightly argues: "*Le Terme Tara et ses variantes Taru, Para, Peru signifie Terre Ta de Ra.*" From French: "The Term Tara and its variations Taru, Para, Peru means Land Ta of Ra."

109. *Ibid.*, 53.

110. *Ibid.*, 42–43. I strongly recommend P. Diagne's work for a personal appraisal of his evidence by the reader.

111. Cheikh Anta Diop, *Civilisation ou Barbarie, op. cit.*, 29.

112.*Ibid.*, 58–81.

113. Constantin-François Volney, *The Ruins or, Meditation on the Revolutions of Empires* (Boston: Josiah P. Mendum, 1869), 19–20.

114. Jean-François Champollion, *Grammaire Égyptienne ou Principes Généraux de l'Ecriture Sacrée Égyptienne Appliquée à la Représentations de la Langue Parlée* (Paris: Typographie de Firmin Didot Frères, 1981), xxij–xxiij. From French: "The interpretation of the monuments of Egypt will highlight even more the Egyptian

origin of the sciences and main philosophic doctrines of Greece; the Platonic school is but Egyptianism, taken from the sanctuaries of Sais."

115. Annex 2.

116. Annex 5.

117. Philippe Laburthe-Tolra, *Initiations et Sociétés Secrètes au Cameroun. Essai sur la religion beti, op. cit*, 37.

118. Cheikh Anta Diop, *L'Unité Culturelle de l'Afrique Noire, op. cit.*

119. Cheikh Anta Diop, *Parenté Génétique de l'Egyptien Pharaonique et des Langues Négro-Africaines, op. cit.*

120. Cheikh Anta Diop, *Civilisation ou Barbarie, op. cit*., 271–81.

121. Kwame Nkrumah, *Consciencism. Philosophy and Ideology for De-colonization* (New York: Monthly Review Press, 1970), 103.

122. Cheikh Anta Diop, "Origin of the ancient Egyptians" in G. Mokhtar (Ed.), *General History of Africa, Vol. II., op. cit*., 41–42.

123. There are four main philosophic systems in the Kemetic cosmology, which I will not examine in detail in the present discussion: the Hermopolitan, the Heliopolitan, the Memphite, and the Theban. These systems are documented in the Pyramid Texts dated 2600 BCE. See: Cheich Anta Diop, *Civilisation ou Barbarie, op. cit.*, 388–477. These pages are instructive, especially as CAD respectively compares the Kemtiyu's cosmogony with that of the contemporary Dogon of West Afrika, with Plato's texts, namely the *Timaeus*, as well as with Aristotle's *Physics.*

124. Cheikh Anta Diop, *Civilisation ou Barbarie, op. cit*., 415 and 454. *Toum*, explains CAD, is the visionless condition of Ra in the netherworld. In Walaf, *Toum* is the cane that helps blind people navigate the world independently. The latter meaning is also associated with the Beti *Ntum* which, additionally, serves as baton/cane of command for civil, military, and spiritual leaders.

125. Théophile Obenga, *La Philosophie Africaine de la Période Pharaonique, op. cit*., 62–63.

126. Annex 9. Eyo's identity will be revealed after this paragraph.

127. *Ibid.* From French: Bumba "first vomited the sun, then the moon and the stars afterwards; that is how light came into being."

128. The Mvettographer's life, work, and writing are like the chordophone (Mvett) that echoes the all-encompassing Web and vital Energy Eyo (Being). The Mvettographer participates in Eyo's eternal presence in all things by a constant rational quest for wisdom, equity, and truth. See: Alain Elloué-Engoune, *Du Sphinx au Mvett, op. cit*., 103.

129. Tsira Ndong Ndoutoume, *Le Mvett. L'Homme, la Mort et l'Immortalité* (Paris: L'Harmattan, 1993), 22. The translation from Beti into English is mine.

130. Alain Elloué-Engoune, *Du Sphinx au Mvett, op. cit*., 117. From French: "Eyo is immortal and powerful, and the relation with him is the only possibility to become immortal, free, intelligent: the intelligence of necessity."

131. Adriaan de Buck, *Coffin Texts*, Vol. VII, Spell 1130, 461–65; Théophile Obenga, *La philosophie Africaine de la Période Pharaonique, op. cit*., 97–98. These are texts from the Pharaonic Middle Kingdom Period (2060–1785 BCE).

132. Raymond O. Faulkner, *The Papyrus Bremner-Rhind. British Museum No. 10188* (Bruxelles: Édition de la Fondation Égyptologique Reine Élisabeth, 1933); Théophile Obenga, *La philosophie Africaine de la Période Pharaonique, ibid.*, 55–56. The text is from the fourth century BCE.

133. Théophile Obenga, *La philosophie Africaine de la Période Pharaonique, ibid.*, 55–63.

134. Cheikh Anta Diop, *Ibid.,* 390.

135. Théophile Obenga, *La philosophie Africaine de la Période Pharaonique, op. cit.,* 56. From French: "I dilated myself in him. I tied my own hand, all alone."

136. Annex 8.

137. Cheikh Anta Diop, *Civilisation ou Barbarie, op. cit*., 429–30. From French: "In effect, the primordial *noun*, under the action of the god of becoming, engenders Ra, who is the first 'eye,' the first consciousness which observes the world, and which becomes aware of its own existence. The *noun* is the father of Ra, and in fact, Ra calls him so in the Heliopolitan cosmogony. It is therefore the son of the *noun,* Ra, who, once appeared, completes creation as demiurge, while his father, the *noun*, returns to his initial rest and no longer intervenes in creation."

138. Philosophers like G. Yancy also attempt to unravel this very question. See: George Yancy (Ed.), *The Philosophical I. Personal Reflections on Life in Philosophy* (New York: Rowman & Littlefield Publishers, Inc., 2002), 152.

139. Against CAD, one may argue for de-historicized subjectivities, but I wonder what that could mean in practical terms.

140. Cheikh Anta Diop, Civilisation ou Barbarie, op. cit., 12–13. From French: "No philosophy can develop out of its historical terrain. Our young philosophers must understand that and quickly equip themselves with the necessary intellectual means to reconnect with the home of philosophy in Africa . . . One must therefore stop with the a-temporal structural study of African cosmogonies."

141. From this vantage point, philosophy itself is a cultural experience. See: Cheikh Anta Diop, *Civilisation ou Barbarie, op. cit.,* 12–13; Molefi Kete Asante and Ama Mazama (Ed.), *Egypt vs. Greece and the American Academy. The debate over the birth of civilization* (Chicago: African American Images, 2002), 129; Michel Foucault, *The Government of Self and Others. Lectures at the Collège de France 1982–1983* (Trans. Graham Burchell, New York: Palgrave Macmillan, 2010), 12–13.

142. In the Mvett, the Beti initiates address the sun (*vian*) as Tara (Ptah-Ra?), meaning Father. *Vian (iunu*?) is the male principle of the hierogamic union of the sun with the earth, the female enlivening principle. *Ta(g)* in Beti means to rejoice, arrange, program, or put things in order. See: S. B. Atangana Ondigui, *Le Nouveau Dictionnaire Ewondo, op. cit.,* 194.

143. *Ibid.* 197. The Beti verb *tot* means to gather things with both hands, to recollect, or to awaken. Jehuti (Thot), according to Plato in *Phaedrus,* 274c–275e, is the Kemetic god of writing, measuring, and calculation.

144. The Kemtiyu called Heliopolis (City of the Sun) Iunu. This toponym finds striking linguistic similarities with *vian* (sun in Beti) and the Igbo (Nigeria) theonym Dinwenu, meaning "That which owns us/me." The sun is indeed that which "owns" us, since it is the center around which the earth orbits.

145. Cheich Anta Diop, *Civilisation ou Barbarie, op. cit.*, 427.

146. *Ibid.*, 431. CAD rightly sees in this assertion the first historical (written) trinitarian confession in the history of monotheisms (Judaism, Christianity, and Islam).

147. *Ibid.*, 16.

148. Though researching on the field of microphysics, I am not yet well equipped to appraise the accuracy of CAD's views on the subject.

149. Cheikh Anta Diop, *Sciences et Philosophie, op. cit.*, 165. Completeness is the empirical claim that all physical events can be accounted for in purely physical terms. The theory negates any causal interaction between the "metaphysical" and "physical" domains. But I have already called our attention to the Greek prefix "*meta,*" arguing that our semantic focus should not solely be on its beyondness, but rather on its immediateness and mediativeness, as suggested by the English adjective mid, the French noun *milieu*, or the German dative preposition *mit*. Accordingly, the metaphysical would be that which coheres with and dwells veilingly within the physical.

150. *Ibid.*, 165–66. From French: "As we shall see, it is scientific rationalism in its classical form which is called into question: one often talks about a crisis of reason insofar as the principle of causality, determinism, the separability of phenomena and their objectivity which prevail in macrophysics are fundamentally challenged in microphysics . . . In this way, observer, observing instrument and corpuscle or observed phenomenon form an indissoluble whole, which is impossible to separate. That is the reason why the observed physical reality ceases to be independent from the observer, as postulates classical physics . . . Besides, the complementarity wave-corpuscle shows that one cannot perceive through a single 'gaze' at once, all the aspects of this universe: one observes either the undulatory aspect or the corpuscular aspect, never both simultaneously."

151. Cheikh Anta Diop, *Sciences et Philosophie, op. cit.*, 186–87.

152. Cheikh Anta Diop, *L'Unité Culturelle de l'Afrique Noire* (Paris: Présence Africaine, 1962).

153. Cheikh Anta Diop, *Les Fondements Économiques et Culturels d'un Etat Fédéral d'Afrique Noire* (Paris: Présence Africaine, 1960).

154. Cheikh Anta Diop, *Sciences et Philosophie, op. cit.*, 143. In French: "*La description de la nature va du niveau subquantique et quantique à celui de la galaxie, de l'hypergalaxie et de la structure de l'univers.*"

155. Philippe Laburthe-Tolra, *Initiations et Sociétés Secrètes au Cameroun, op. cit.*, 37.

156. Cheikh Anta Diop, *L'Unité Culturelle de l'Afrique Noire, op. cit.*, 186. In French: "*Quinze milliards d'années, la durée de vie que les savants assignent aujourd'hui au système solaire.*"

157. *Ibid.*, 187. From French: " . . . the human being will realize that her/his mission is only starting. She will then discover that it is absolutely in her possibilities long before 15 billion years of reflection, to tame the solar system, and to reign therein up to the peripheric planet of Pluto, in a virtually eternal fashion. Will she achieve it perhaps by nourishing the sun with precarious satellites formed with sidereal matter which end up falling into its mass, or perhaps by returning to the sun the

energy radiated through the acceleration of hydrogen seeds from gigantic artificial electro-magnetic fields? To negate thermodynamic death, stabilize the solar system, protect it from dangerous meteorites, solidify gaseous planets, warm those of the periphery up to make them habitable, prevent the apparition and the proliferation of biological monsters, control climates and the evolution of planets, discover and maintain all the practicable routes of the system, communicate with stars neighboring the galaxy, create a superhuman with a longer lifespan, such will perhaps be the enthusiastic preoccupations of the future thinker. Life would thus in its own way have triumphed over death, the human being would realize an earthly paradise practically eternal, he would triumph by the same token of all the pessimistic metaphysical and philosophic systems, of all the apocalyptic visions of the species' destiny. A grandiose step in the evolution of the human consciousness would be crossed. The human being would appear as a God in becoming . . . "

158. Cheikh Anta Diop, *Sciences et Philosophie, op. cit.*, 125–56.

159. Given the socialness of humans who act and therefore cohere with social events for better or worse.

160. *Ibid.,* 177. From French: "Considering the principle of non-separability, the existence of entities, of independent objects endowed with properties is negated, and the universe appears in new theories as a single piece whose constitutive parts can instantly vibrate in phase."

161. Cheikh Anta Diop, *Civilisation ou Barbarie, op. cit.*, 16. In French: "*animé d'une conscience historique, un vrai créateur, un Prométhée porteur d'une nouvelle civilisation et parfaitement conscient de ce que la terre entière doit à son génie ancestral dans tous les domaines de la science, de la culture et de la religion.*"

162. Marie Rose Abomo-Morin, *Les Pérégrinations des descendants d'Afri Kara* (Paris: L'Harmattan, 2012). Afiri is an anthroponym meaning Hope. The verb *ka* means to save, to rescue, or catch something. Ra/Da is the One. Thus explained, Afiri Kara means the Hope that rescues the One/Unity (the Sun), or the Life-Giver who sustains Hope.

163. Cheikh Anta Diop, *Civilisation ou Barbarie, op. cit.,* 475.

164. From 1960 to 1963, CAD creates a Radiocarbon 14 Dating Laboratory at the Institut Français d'Afrique Noire (IFAN) in Dakar, Senegal. See: Cheikh M'Backé Diop, *Cheikh Anta Diop. L'homme et l'œuvre* (Paris: Présence Africaine, 2003), 74–81.

165. Frantz Fanon, *Peau noire, masques blancs, op. cit.*, 186. Fanon writes: "*Je suis solidaire de l'Être dans la mesure où je le dépasse.*" From French: "I am a part of Being to the degree that I go beyond it."

166. *Ibid.,* 186–87. From French: "I am not a prisoner of History, I should not seek there for the meaning of my destiny . . . The body of History does not determine a single one of my actions."

167. *Ibid.,* 10. From French: "Every human problem must be considered from the standpoint of time."

168. Frantz Fanon, *The Wretched of the Earth, op. cit.,* 15.

169. Kwame Nkrumah, *Consciencism. Philosophy and ideology for decolonization* (New York: Monthly Review Press, 1970), 79.

170. Kwame Nkrumah, *Consciencism. Philosophy and ideology for decolonization* (New York: Monthly Review Press, 1970), 63.

171. *Ibid.*, 103.

172. Alain Badiou et al., *What is a People?* (Trans. Jody Gladding, New York: Columbia University Press, 2016).

173. The concept is formed from the Beti words *adzo* (event, responsibility, debate, dialogue, trial) and *bod* (people). *Bod* is the plural of *mod* (the human being). The *adzo-bod* refers to the entire body politic (children, women, men) of national and international arenas as self-governing entities.

174. Kwame Nkrumah, *Consciencism, Ibid.*, 68. The phrase suggests the presence of further grafted segments on the Afrikan face, namely the (neo)colonial Jesus-Christian, Mohammedan, and Western European traditions.

175. Human being in Beti.

176. Kwame Nkrumah, *Ibid.*

177. Théophile Obenga, *Cheikh Anta Diop, Volney et le Sphinx, op. cit.*, 70 and 360.

178. Philippe Laburthe-Tolra, *Initiations et Sociétés secrètes au Cameroun. Essai sur la religion beti, op. cit.*, 45, 53, 102, 212.

179. *Ibid.*, 159, 213.

180. Plato, *Apology & Phaedo*

181. Cheikh Anta Diop, *Civilisation ou Barbarie, op. cit.*, 416. In French "*Sans doute, l'histoire et les réalisations de chaque peuple sont intimement liées à la façon dont celui-ci résout le problème de la mort, à la philosophie qu'il adopte devant le destin de l'homme.*"

182. Plato, *Phaedo,* 64a.

183. Plato, *Phaedo*, 114c–115b.

184. *Ibid.*, 107d.

185. *Ibid.,* 115a.

186. *Ibid.,* 115b.

187. *Ibid.*, 114c.

188. Philippe Laburthe-Tolra, *Initiations et Sociétés secrètes au Cameroun. Essai sur la religion beti, op. cit.*, 324. From French: *sǒsǒ* corresponds to the French 'rectitude'; "*sǒsǒ mod* is the 'just' human being, . . . , the human being who acts above passions and self-interest according to the sole reason of equity."

189. *Ibid.*

190. Siméon Basile Atangana Ondigui, *Le Nouveau Dictionnaire Ewondo, op. cit.*, 191.

191. Ibid.

192. Annex 10.

193. In the cosmogony of Khemenu (Hermopolis), Jehuti (*dhwt*), called Thoth by the Greeks, is the demiurge who creates the universe through the Word. See: Cheikh Anta Diop, *Civilisation ou Barbarie, Ibid.*, 445. Plato's Socrates considers Thoth to be the "Father" of writing. See: Plato, *Phaedrus*, 274c–275e. I share Socrates' view, considering the striking morphological and semantic similarities between the theonym Je-huti and the Beti substantive for writing *otil/ntil.* See: Siméon Basile Atangana Ondigui, *Le Nouveau Dictionnaire Ewondo, op. cit.*, 164; 183. As we saw

earlier, Nti is the singular form of the patronym, theonym, and ethnonym Beti. In that sense, writing (*ntil*) is a demiurgic act that crystallizes, in literary form, the enlivening and uplifting values from the writer (*ntil*). Thus, in Beti, writer and writing co-share in the same concept *ntil*.

194. Edgar Morin, *Penser Global. L'humain et son univers* (Paris: Éditions Robert Laffont, 2015), 35.

195. Pierre Chantraine, *Dictionnaire étymologique de la langue grecque. Histoire des mots* (Paris: Klincksieck, 2009), 996.

196. Plato, *Cratylus*, 412b.

197. Plato, *Phaedrus*, 274c–275b; *Timaeus*, 21e–24c; *Laws*, 818e–819d.

198. Aristotle, *Metaphysics*, *B.* I, 981b23–24.

199. Cheikh Anta Diop, *Civilisation ou Barbarie, op. cit*., 389–91.

200. Plato, *Republic,* VI, 508b.

201. Cheikh Anta Diop, *L'Unité Culturelle de l'Afrique Noire, op. cit*., 187.

202. Grégoire Biyogo, *Encyclopédie du Mvett. Tome I—Du Haut Nil en Afrique Centrale. Le rêve musical et poétique des Fang Anciens: la quête de l'éternité et la conquête du Logos solaire* (Paris: Menaibuc, 2002).

203. Mbog Bassong, *La Méthode de la Philosophie Africaine* (Paris: L'Harmattan, 2007), 82.

204. Mongo Beti, *Mission to Kala* (Trans. from the French by Peter Green, Devon, England: Mallory Publishing, 2008), 41, 48, 72, etc.

Conclusion

This book is about us, *Femina/Homo sapiens sapiens*. I still speak in the present tense, even as I soon hang up my meditative thinking on the meaning and purpose of our presence in the cosmos. I coined the concept Afrosofia to help present and future generations of philosophers and all humans in general ponder our sapient identity, especially as imperiled by the ferociousness of global alienation/barbarism.

We now witness the burgeoning of a panafrikan renaissance. The second chapter shows that Afrisofia construes Afrika as an ethical trope. It is both the archeological and teleological wheel of sapient humanity. Afrika plays an anamnestic function, reminding us whence we come, and confronting us with our sofian (solarizing) mission in the universe (chapter five). Here, the unknown etymology of philo*sophia* is unveiled in Afro*sofia*. To philosophize, thus, means to be(come) sunny and enlivening in one's thoughts, writing, and living.

That is the purpose of the Antadiopian conciliatory-scientific-philosophy and direct methodology (chapter four). In other words, CAD considers that reasoned living, qua quest for ultimate geo-economic and political principles and purposes, is the path to creativity and progress in the cultural life of a people. Reason enlightens inquiry, providing a deeper understanding of the nature of things, including reason's own self. Reasoning, that is, speculative and applied inquiry (science) makes us hopeful that we can live as civilized beings and venture into the Milky Way and beyond as our possible homelands. The challenge is Herculean, but as the Mvettean apothegm reminds us, "*Bikalik!*,"[1] that is, Let us not despair!

CAD writes that the world to come, in all likelihood, will be permeated with Afrikan optimism.[2] I think that *Afiri*, the Beti anthroponym and concept for an embodied and militant hope, is constitutive of the demiurgic (creative) consciousness, of which the slain South Afrikan civil rights leader Steve Biko (1946–1977) talks about when he writes incisively:

> People must not just give in to the hardship of life, people must develop a hope, people must develop some form of security to be together to look at their problems, and people must in this way build up their humanity. This is the point about conscientization and Black Consciousness.[3]

Without militant hope, individual and communal struggles for freedom and advancement would hardly be undertaken. Without militant hope, prejudices (ethnic, racial, sexual, economic, etc.) could defeat our inner demiurgic consciousness. Without militant hope for a reconciled humanity, Countee Cullen in his poem *Heritage* would perhaps not have addressed our straying minds and hearts, wondering why we do not yet realize that civilization is our existential purpose.[4]

This misguidance is identified and denounced as *kara olere* (colonial alienation) in the third chapter. In today's geo-economic dispensation, its modus operandi is the wrecking corporatocracy, which I call Oku.[5] As we have seen, in-between the polarities of Engong (harmony) and Oku (chaos), sways CAD's antithetic poles of civilization and barbarism.[6]

To become barbaric means to forget to "be human and not inhumane."[7] It means to stray from the truth that humans "are made for cooperation, like feet, like hands, like eyelids, like the rows of the upper and lower teeth."[8] It means to disregard the fact that human life can be reasoned and predicated upon the quality of one's character according to Martin Luther King Jr.[9] Barbarism is the ravine to Oku (civilizational decline) and no sofian human, I presume, would tread that impasse . . .

This book has been laborious, requiring that I weave a creative analytic and trans-linguistic stratum as an image of future humanity, where people join minds to investigate the conundrums of the universe. I still have a long way to achieve CAD's trans-disciplinarian scientific expertise. But I did take to heart his direct methodology, which took me to Senegal and Cameroon for field research. I would have loved to elaborate on the question of the Afrikan renaissance in the first chapter, which CAD examines in *Les Fondements Économiques et Culturels d'un État Fédéral d'Afrique Noire.*[10] But I will make it a priority in my future research. It is a critical concern of our contemporary world if we are to address, in practical terms, the questions of geopolitical peace, freedom, and independence. In this vein, Kwame Nkrumah is sagacious in his pronouncement that *Africa must Unite*,[11] for "the greatest danger at present facing Africa is neo-colonialism and its major instrument, balkanization."[12] I agree with Nkrumah that what is needed is

> a united foreign policy, a common defence plan, and a fully integrated economic programme for the development of the whole continent. Only then can the dangers of neo-colonialism and its handmaiden balkanization be overcome.

> When that has been accomplished, our relations with Europe can enter upon a new phase.[13]

My hope is that present and future generations, in reading these thoughts, will come to terms with the imperativeness of be(com)ing *sosŏ*, that is, sunny humans. We say in Beti: "*Owog na akuma: ve bod,*"[14] meaning that the cipher *akuma* (wealth) should always be construed as a trope for *bod* (human beings). In other words, when you hear "wealth," understand human beings. This perceptive self-image is psychologically crucial, because it can cultivate a sense of communal somebodiness, self-reliance, and self-help. CAD calls this inner self the creator. It makes transcendence, qua limitless mental potential to solve problems and subsequently move beyond the constraining boundaries of the imperium, constitutive of our immanent geo-economic and political struggles.

Transcendence toward a more cohesive and egalitarian world is the very essence of people's struggles for better lives. Hopefully, the discipline of *akuma*logy, that is, the scientific study of the human being as profuse wealth and abundance will someday emerge in the Academy and flesh out the Antadiopian optimistic dream of a conciliatory humanity. It would impact younger generations around the world with a sharpened new self-perception. They will see themselves in America and the world over beyond the Du Boisian "color line," which would have become obsolete through their re-education in pacific and *akuma*logical anthropologies. With this social turn, the world could witness a renewed concerted commitment to more dignified lives. That is the sense of my writing, which is basically congruent with those of Steve Biko, Frantz Faon, and CAD.

Steve Biko (1946–1977), who discusses Fanon[15] in his *I Write What I Like*,[16] wraps his intellectual activity in an anthropological blueprint, stating:

> We have set out on a quest for true humanity, and somewhere on the distant horizon we can see the glittering prize. Let us march forth with courage and determination, drawing strength from our common plight and our brotherhood. In time we shall be in a position to bestow upon South Africa the greatest gift possible—a more human face.[17]

Writing with different emphases from the context of the same geopolitical predicament of human alienation vis-à-vis itself, both Fanon in Algeria and Biko in Azania (South Africa) express convergent views on the need for a renewed humanity shaped by the value of unity. They urge us, humans, to labor for something novel and truthful within us. Fanon addresses everyone, Afrikans, Americans (North and South), and all humans alike, to refrain from the ideologies of division, predation, and racism, and rather nurture our humaneness from cooperative blueprints, arguing:

> [. . .] what we want is to walk in the company of man, every man, night and day, for all times. [. . .] So comrades, let us not pay tribute to Europe by creating states, institutions, and societies that draw their inspiration from it. Humanity expects other things from us than this grotesque and generally obscene emulation. If we want to transform Africa into a new Europe, America into a new Europe, then let us entrust the destinies of our countries to the Europeans. They will do a better job than the best of us. . . . If we want to respond to the expectations of our peoples, we must look elsewhere besides Europe. Moreover, if we want to respond to the expectations of the Europeans we must not send them back a reflection, however ideal, of their society and their thought that periodically sickens even them. For Europe, for ourselves and for humanity, comrades, we must make a new start, develop a new way of thinking, and endeavor to create a new man.[18]

More than Biko and Fanon, however, CAD not only underscores global cooperation (humaneness) as his epistemic ideal, but also instantiates the embodiment of such altruism by a concrete exemplar, Alioune Diop. What philosophic truth did the cultured founder of *Présence Africaine* (Afrikan Presence),[19] Alioune Diop, discover and endeavor to bring forth during his earthly presence? Why did he successively create the Parisian intellectual journal (*1*947), publishing house (1949), and library (1962) *Présence Africaine*? Why the appellation *Présence Africaine*? How was/is Afrika to be present in intellectual milieux such as the famous Quartier Latin, where both *Présence Africaine* and the Parisian Sorbonne University are located?

Alioune Diop, himself, seems to be answering the foregoing questions symbolically. For him, the Afrikan anthropo-zoomorphic ideogram of the human being, construed as bird and crocodile,[20] captures the cultural mission of *Présence Africaine.* Alioune Diop's contention is that humanity unites, within itself, a birdy taste for heights, open space, aerial elevation, and subtleness, as well as an amphibious (crocodilian) thirst for firmness, suppleness, and depths. Thus, with the constant interaction of heavenly and earthly-aquatic elements (air-water-earth-fire) in humans, it is their cosmic nature which is affirmed by the founder of *Présence Africaine.*

CAD's take on A. Diop (and of humanity at large) is equally cosmic but marked by a distinctive gnoseological moment. Alioune Diop knew the purpose of his earthly presence and, consequently, oriented his life toward an unreserved service to humanity. CAD's tribute to him is impressive:

> *Alioune, tu savais ce que tu étais venu faire sur la terre: Une vie entièrement consacrée aux autres, rien pour soi, tout pour autrui, un cœur rempli de bonté*

et de générosité, une âme pétrie de noblesse, un esprit toujours serein, la simplicité personnifiée! Le démiurge voulait-il nous proposer, en exemple, un idéal de perfection, en t'appelant à l'existence?[21]

In asking why and for whom we write ("*Pourquoi et pour qui écrivons-nous?*")[22] in philosophy and in the academe at large, CAD aims at building, through a fourfold perspective, a novel[23] reconciling philosophy for the whole of humanity. But the "*nous,*" the "we" in the question, overflows CAD's individuality. It confronts each writer's objectives and her/his addressees in the academe itself at large. May we endorse the same "*nous*" introducing the forthcoming Antadiopian final contention:

Nous aspirons tous au triomphe de la notion d'espèce humaine dans les esprits et dans les consciences, de sorte que l'histoire particulière de telle ou telle race s'efface devant celle de l'homme tout court. On n'aura plus alors qu'à décrire, en termes généraux qui ne tiendront plus compte des singularités accidentelles devenues sans intérêt, les étapes significatives de la conquête de la civilisation par l'homme, par l'espèce humaine tout entière.[24]

NOTES

1. Steeve Elvis Ella, *Mvett ékang et le projet bikalik, op. cit.*, 232.
2. Cheikh Anta Diop, *L'Unité Culturelle de l'Afrique noire, op. cit.,* 187. In French: "*l'univers de demain, selon toute vraisemblance sera imprégné de l'optimisme africain.*"
3. Steve Biko, *I Write What I Like* (Ed. Aelred Stubbs C. R., New York: Harper & Row, 1986), 114.
4. Alain Locke (Ed.), *The New Negro. Voices of the Harlem Renaissance, op. cit.,* 251.
5. In the Beti Mvett, which is the inner quest of unity with our creative nature named Eyo, Oku represents the chaotic thoughts, words, and actions from individuals/social classes/ lobbies, etc., while Engong embodies all that unites. See: Alain Alloué-Engoune, *Du Sphinx au Mvett: Connaissance et Sagesse de l'Afrique, op. cit.*, 134.
6. Barbarism qua thoughtlessness of one's "sofian" nature can be rendered through the Beti category of *ovoan*, or *oubli* and forgetfulness in French and English respectively. *Ovoan* to think the human monogenetic origin and social nature as expressed by Molefi K. Asante in his introductory excerpt to this chapter, but more importantly *ovoan* to meditate and constantly ascend toward our sapient nature. M. Heidegger, in his ontological questioning, renders this cognitive defect of oblivion in terms of *Vergessenheit* in his restatement of the question of Being (first paragraph of *Sein und Zeit).* See: Martin Heidegger, *Sein und Zeit* (Tübingen: Max Niemeyer Verlag, 1967), 2.

7. Martin Heidegger, *Basic Writings* (Ed. David Farrell Krell, London: Routledge & Kegan Paul, 1977), 200. The quote is from Heidegger's *Letter on Humanism*, 193–242 in Farrell Krell's edition.

8. Marcus Aurelius Antoninus, *The Philosophy of Antoninus*, II.1. This Roman philosopher lived from 121–180 CE.

9. Martin Luther King Jr.'s Speech "I Have a Dream" at the March on Washington in 1963: Martin Luther King, Jr., "I Have a Dream." *National Archives.* Retrieved July 18, 2019. https://www.archives.gov/files/press/exhibits/dream-speech.pdf, 5, paragraph 2.

10. Cheikh Anta Diop, *Fondements Économiques et Culturels d'un État Fédéral d'Afrique Noire, op. cit.*

11. Kwame Nkrumah, *Africa Must Unite* (London: Heinemann Educational Books Ltd, 1963).

12. *Ibid.*, 173.

13. *Ibid.*, 177.

14. Jacques Fulbert Owono, *Pauvreté ou Paupérisation en Afrique. Une étude exegético-ethique de la pauvreté chez les Beti-Fang du Cameroun* (Bamberg: Bamberg University Press, 2011), 81.

15. Steve Biko, *I Write What I Like* (New York: Harper & Row, 1986), 69–72. Biko was an anti-Apartheid hero in South Africa, where he founded and invested his life in the Black Consciousness Movement from the 1960s to his murder in 1977. In the pages referenced here, Biko discusses Fanon's denunciation of the colonial rationale, namely how it distorts, disfigures, and destroys the history of the colonized. A national consciousness, that is, "an attitude of mind and a way of life" that sees the imperativeness of rewriting history (philosophic and scientific) in colonized territories, is therefore to be championed.

16. *Ibid.*, 108.

17. *Ibid.*, 98.

18. Frantz Fanon, *The Wretched of the Earth, op. cit.*, 238–89. The Fanonian new humanism may sound quite sexist to untrained ears, especially with his recurring reference to the generic term "man," which can be mistaken to solely mean a masculine human adult. Besides, Fanon does also use the inclusive concept of "humanity" in the foregoing quote. Surely then, Fanon's aim is not to alienate women from his cultural project of striving for unity among humans. While Fanon articulates his antinomies around old and new ways of thinking, Biko's own dynamic binarism swings from the denunciation of falsehood (alienation/divisiveness) to the advocacy of truthfulness (solidarity) in human relations.

19. *Présence Africaine* is Cheikh Anta Diop's main publisher.

20. Jean Mazel, *Présence du Monde Noir* (Paris: Éditions Robert Laffont, 1975), 33.

21. Cheikh Anta Diop, *Civilisation ou Barbarie, op. cit.*, dedication page. From French: "Alioune, you knew what you came on earth for: A life entirely dedicated to others, nothing for oneself, everything for others, a heart full of goodness and of generosity, a soul made of nobility, a serene mind always, embodied simplicity. Did the demiurge want to suggest to us, as example, an ideal of perfection, by calling you into existence?"

22. Cheikh Anta Diop, *Alerte sous les Tropiques, op. cit.,* 34.

23. The adjective novel suggests something contemporary about the Antadiopian conciliatory philosophy: its novelty will be accounted for by its ethical, scientific, and geopolitical bent.

24. Cheikh Anta Diop, *Antériorité des Civilisations Nègres, op. cit.,* 275. From French: "We all aspire to the triumph of the notion of human species in the minds and in the consciences, such that the particular history of this or that race simply fades before that of the human being. One will only have to describe, in general terms that will no longer consider the fortuitous singularities now without interest, the significant steps of the conquest of civilization by the human being, by the entire human species."

Bibliography

Abomo-Maurin, Marie-Rose. *Les pérégrinations des descendants d'Afri Kara.* Paris: L'Harmattan, 2012.

Agbohou, Nicolas. *Le Franc CFA et L'Euro Contre L'Afrique.* Paris: Éditions Solidarité Mondiale, 1999.

Alexander, Michelle. *The New Jim Crow. Mass Incarceration in the Age of Colorblindness.* New York: The New Press, 2012.

Alexandre, Pierre & Binet, Jacques. *Le Groupe dit Pahouin (Fang-Boulou-Beti).* Paris: Puf, 1958.

Amin, Samir. *The Liberal Virus. Permanent War and the Americanization of the World.* New York: Monthly Review Press, 2004.

Apple, Michael W. *Ideology and Curriculum.* New York: Routledge, 1990.

Aristotle. *The Complete Works of Aristotle: The Revised Oxford Translation, Vol. I & II.* Ed. Jonathan Barnes, Princeton, NJ: Princeton University Press, 1995.

Arnaiz-Villena, A. et al. "HLA genses in Macedonians and the sub-Saharan origin of the Greeks." *Tissue Antigens*, 2001, No. 57, 118–27.

Asante, Molefi Kete & Mazama, Ama (Ed.). *Egypt vs. Greece and the American Academy. The debate over the birth of civilization.* Chicago: African American Images, 2002.

———, *Encyclopedia of African Religion.* Thousand Oaks, CA: Sage Publications, Inc., 2009.

Asante, Molefi Kete & Asante, Kariamu Welsh. *African Culture: The Rhythms of Unity.* Trenton, NJ: Africa World Press, Inc., 1996.

Asante, Molefi Kete. *The Painful Demise of Eurocentrism.* Trenton, NJ: Africa World Press, Inc., 1999.

———. *Afrocentricity: The Theory of Social Change.* Chicago: African American Images, 2003.

———. *Cheikh Anta Diop: An Intellectual Portrait.* Los Angeles: The University of Sankore Press, 2007.

———. *As I Run toward Africa.* Boulder, CO: Paradigm Publishers, 2011.

———. *Revolutionary Pedagogy. Primer for Teachers of Black Children.* Brooklyn, NY: Universal Write Publications LLC, 2017.

Assoumou Ndoutoume, Daniel. *Du Mvett. Essai sur la Dynastie Ekang Nna.* Paris: L'Harmattan, 1986.

———. *Du Mvett. L'Orace: Processus de démocratisation conté par un diseur du Mvett.* Paris: L'Harmattan, 1993.

Atangana Ondigui, Siméon Basile. *Le Nouveau Dictionnaire Ewondo.* Condé-sur-Noireau, France: Les Éditions Terre Africaine, 2007.

Aubame, Jean-Marie. *Les Beti du Gabon et d'Ailleurs, Tome I. Sites, parcours et structures.* Paris: L'Harmattan, 2002.

———. *Les Beti du Gabon et d'Ailleurs, Tome II. Croyances, us et coutumes.* Paris: L'Harmattan, 2002.

Augustine (J. H. S. Burleigh, Ed. & Trans.). *Earlier Writings.* Louisville, KY: Westminster John Knox Press, 2006.

Aurelius Antoninus, Marcus. *The Meditations of the Emperor Marcus Aurelius Antoninus.* Trans. George Long, London & Glasgow: Collins' Clear-Type Press, 1890.

Bachelard, Gaston. *Le Nouvel Esprit Scientifique.* Paris: PUF, [1934] 2009.

Badiou, Alain et al. *What Is a People?.* Trans. Jody Gladding, New York: Columbia University Press, 2016.

Baldwin, James. *The Fire Next Time.* Middlesex, England: Penguin Books Ltd, 1963.

———. "Who is the Nigger?" [Video]. *YoutTube.* Retrieved January 9, 2020. https://www.youtube.com/watch?v=L0L5fciA6AU.

Battalora, Jacqueline. *Birth of a White Nation. The Invention of White People and its Relevance Today.* Houston, TX: Strategic Book Publishing and Rights Co., 2013.

ben-Jochannan, Yosef A. A. *Africa. Mother of Western Civilization.* Baltimore, MD: Black Classic Press, 1988.

Bennett, Jeffrey. *Beyond UFOs: The Search for Extraterrestrial Life and Its Astonishing Implications for Our Future.* Princeton, NJ: Princeton University Press, 2008.

Bernal, Martin. *Black Athena. The Afroasiatic Roots of Classical Civilization, Vol. I: The Fabrication of Ancient Greece 1785–1985.* New Brunswick: Rutgers University Press, 1987.

Bessis, Sophie. *L'Occident et les autres: Histoire d'une suprématie.* Paris: La Découverte, 2003.

Biko, Steve. *I Write What I Like.* Ed. Aelred Stubbs C. R., New York: Harper & Row, 1986.

Bilolo, Mubabinge. *Les Cosmo-Théologies philosophiques de l'Égypte Antique. Problématiques-Prémisses herméneutiques-et-problèmes majeurs.* Kinshasa: Publications Universitaires Africaines, 1986.

Biyogo, Grégoire. *Aux Sources Égyptiennes du Savoir, Vol. I: Généalogie et Enjeux de la Pensée de Cheikh Anta Diop.* Paris: Menaibuc, 2000.

———. *Aux Sources Égyptiennes du Savoir, Vol. II: Système et anti-Système, Cheikh Anta Diop et la Destruction du Logos Classique.* Paris: Menaibuc, 2000.

———. *Encyclopédie du Mvett: Tome I—Du Haut Nil en Afrique Centrale.* Paris: Menaibuc, 2002.

———. *Adieu à Tsira Ndong Ndoutoume: Hommage à L'inventeur de la raison graphique du Mvett.* Paris: L'Harmattan, 2006.

———. *Manifeste pour Lire Autrement l'œuvre de Cheikh Anta Diop* (1923–1986). Paris: L'Harmattan, 2007.

———. *Dictionnaire Comparé Égyptien/Fang-Beti.* Paris: Imhotep, 2013.

Blum, William. *Rogue State. A Guide to the World's Only Superpower.* Monroe, ME: Common Courage Press, 2005.

———. *America's Deadliest Export: Democracy—the Truth about US Foreign Policy and Everything Else.* London: Zed Books Ltd, 2014.

Brock-Utne, Birgit. *Whose Education for All? The Recolonization of the African Mind.* New York: Falmer Press, 2000.

Buck, Adriaan de. *Coffin Texts*, Vol. VII, Spell 1130, 461–65.

Burrell, Tom. *Brainwashed. Challenging the Myth of Black Inferiority.* New York: SmileyBooks, 2010.

Bynum, Edward Bruce. *Dark Light Consciousness. Melanin, Serpent Power, and the Luminous Matrix of Reality.* Rochester, VT: Inner Traditions, 2012.

Carpenter, Nathan Reley and Lawrance, Benjamin N. (Ed.). *Africans in Exile. Mobility, Law, and Identity.* Bloomington, IN: Indiana University Press, 2018.

Central Intelligence Agency (CIA). "Hitler." *CIA.* Retrieved January 11, 2018. https://www.cia.gov/library/readingroom/docs/HITLER%2C%20ADOLF_0003.pdf.

Césaire, Aimé. *Discours sur le colonialisme, Suivi de Discours sur la Négritude.* Paris: Présence Africaine, 2004.

———. *Discourse on Colonialism.* Trans. Joan Pinkham, New York: Monthly Review Press, 2000.

Champollion le Jeune. *Grammaire Égyptienne, ou Principes généraux de l'écriture sacrée égyptienne.* Paris: Imprimeurs de l'Institut de France, 1836, xxij–xxiij.

———. *Grammaire Égyptienne ou Principes Généraux de l'Ecriture Sacrée Égyptienne Appliquée à la Représentations de la Langue Parlée.* Paris: Typographie de Firmin Didot Frères, 1981.

———. "Les Lettres écrites d'Égypte et de Nubie en 1828 et 1829." *Bibliothèque Nationale de France.* Retrieved April 12, 2018. https://www.sapili.org/livros/fr/gu010764.pdf.

Chantraine, Pierre. *Dictionnaire Étymologique de la Langue Grecque.* Paris: Klincksieck, 2009.

Cheru, Fantu. *African Renaissance: Roadmaps to the Challenge of Globalization.* New York: Zed Books, 2002.

Chevrier, Jacques. *Littérature nègre.* Paris: Armand Colin, 1974.

Chinweizu. *The West and the Rest of Us: White Predators, Black Slavers and the African Elite.* New York: Random House, 1975.

Chukwedi Eze, Emmanuel, (Ed.). *Race and the Enlightenment. A Reader.* Malden, MA: Blackwell Publishers Inc., 1997.

Clarke, John Henrik. *Christopher Columbus and the Afrikan Holocaust: Slavery and the Rise of European Capitalism.* New York: EWorld Inc., 1998.

———. *Cheikh Anta Diop and the New Light on African History.* Lexington: Brawtley Press, 2014.

Cress Welsing, Frances. *The Isis Papers. The Keys to the Colors.* Washington, DC: C. W. Publishing, 2004.

Darkwah, Nana Banchie. *The Africans Who Wrote the Bible. Ancient Secrets Africa and Christianity Have Never Told.* Orlando, FL: HBC Publications, 2018.

Davidson, Basil. *The Black Man's Burden: Africa and the Curse of the Nation-State.* New York: Times Books, 1992.

DeGruy, Joy. *Post Traumatic Slave Syndrome. America's Legacy of Enduring Injury and Healing.* Portland, OR: Joy DeGruy Publications Inc., 2017.

Deleuze, Gilles & Guattari, Félix. *A Thousand Plateaus. Capitalism and Schizophrenia.* Trans. from French by Brian Massumi, Minneapolis: University of Minnesota Press, 2001.

Deltombe, Thomas et al. *La Guerre du Cameroun. L'invention de la Françafrique 1948–1971.* Paris: La Découverte, 2016.

Dene Morel, Edmund. *The Black Man's Burden.* Northbrook: Metro Books, 1972.

Derrida, Jacques. "Hospitality." *Angelaki. Journal of the Theoretical Humanities.* No. 3, Vol. 5, 2000, 3–18.

———. *Rogues. Two Essays on Reason.* Stanford, CA: Stanford University Press, 2005.

Descartes, René. *Discours de la méthode pour bien conduire sa raison, et chercher la vérité dans les sciences*. Paris: Librio, 2008.

Diagne, Pathé. *Cheikh Anta Diop et l'Afrique dans l'histoire du monde.* Paris: L'Harmattan, 2008.

———. *Bakari II (1312) et Christophe Colomb (1492). À la rencontre de Tarana ou l'Amérique.* Paris: L'Harmattan, 2014.

Diakité, Tidiane. *L'Afrique malade d'elle-même.* Paris: Karthala,1986.

Diawara, Mantha. "Reading Africa Through Foucault: V. Y. Mudimbe's Reaffirmation of the Subject" in *The MIT Press.* October, Vol. 55, Winter 1990, 79–92.

Diogenes Laertius. *The Lives and Opinions of Eminent Philosophers.* Trans. C. D. Yonge, Lexington, KY, 2016.

Diop, Cheikh Anta. *Nations Nègres et Culture. De l'antiquité nègre égyptienne aux problèmes culturels de l'Afrique Noire d'aujourd'hui.* Paris: Présence Africaine, 1979.

———. *Les Fondements Économiques et Culturels d'un État Fédéral d'Afrique Noire.* Paris: Présence Africaine, 1974.

———. *The African Origin of Civilization. Myth or Reality.* Ed. & Trans. by Mercer Cook, Chicago: Lawrence Hill Books, 1974.

———. *Parenté Génétique de l'Egyptien Pharaonique et des Langues Négro-Africaines.* IFAN-Dakar: Les Nouvelles Éditions Africaines, 1977.

———. *Antériorité des Civilisations Nègres: Mythe ou Vérité Historique?* Paris: Présence Africaine, 1993.

———. *Civilisation ou Barbarie: Anthropologie Sans Complaisance.* Paris: Présence Africaine, 1981.

———. "Origin of the ancient Egyptians." G. Mokhtar (Ed.), *General History of Africa, Vol. II. Ancient Civilizations of Africa.* California: University of California Press, 1981, 41–42.

———. *L'Unité Culturelle de l'Afrique Noire.* Paris: Présence Africaine, 1982.

———. *"L'unité d'origine de l'espèce humaine."* Unesco Symposium on Racism, Science and Pseudo-Science: Proceedings of the Symposium to Examine Pseudo-Scientific Theories Invoked to Justify Racism and Racial Discrimination, Athens, 30 March to 3 April, *Racisme, science et pseudo-science.* Paris: Presses Universitaires de France, 1982, 137–41.

———. *L'Afrique Noire Précoloniale.* Paris: Présence Africaine, 1987.

———. *Alerte sous les Tropiques.* Paris: Présence Africaine, 1990.

———. *Sciences et Philosophie*: Textes 1960–1986. Dakar, Sénégal: IFAN Cheikh Anta Diop, 2007.

Diop, Cheikh M'Backé. *Cheikh Anta Diop, L'homme et l'œuvre.* Paris: Présence Africaine, 2003.

Diop-Maes, Louise Marie. *Afrique Noire. Démographie, Sol et Histoire.* Paris: Présence Africaine, 1996.

Djasso, Djasso. "L'Egyptologue OUM NDIGI nous explique l'œuvre de Wêre Wêre Liking selon le paradigme Kamite" [Video]. *Youtube.* Retrieved January 17 and March 10, 2020. https://www.youtube.com/watch?v=h-ZHnO_fNgI.

Do Nascimento, Abdias, & Larkin Nascimento, Elisa. *Africans in Brazil. A Pan-African Perspective.* Trenton, NJ: Africa World Press, Inc., 1992.

Du Bois, W. E. B. *The Negro.* Radford: Wilder Publications, 2008.

———. *The Souls of Black Folk.* New York: Dover Publications, Inc., 1994.

Eboussi Boulaga, Fabien. *L'Affaire de la Philosophie Africaine: Au-delà des querelles.* Yaoundé: Éditions Terroirs, 2011.

Eco, Umberto. *Semiotics and the Philosophy of Language.* London: The Macmillan Press Ltd, 1984.

Egypt Forever. "The Moscow Papyrus." *Egypt Forever.* Retrieved April 12, 2018. http://www.egyptforever.hu/en/articles/about-ancient-egypt/the-moscow-papyrus.html.

Ela, Jean-Marc. *Le Cri de l'Homme Africain. Questions aux Chrétiens et aux Églises d'Afrique*. Paris: L'Harmattan, 1980.

———. *Cheikh Anta Diop ou l'honneur de penser.* Paris: L'Harmattan, 1989.

Ella, Steeve Elvis. *Mvett ékang et le projet bikalik. Essai sur la condition humaine.* Paris: L'Harmattan, 2011.

———. *Altérité et Transcendance dans le Mvett. Essai de Philosophie Pratique.* Paris: L'Harmattan, 2014.

Elloué-Engoune, Alain. *Du Sphinx au Mvett. Connaissance et sagesse de l'Afrique.* Paris: L'Harmattan, 2008.

Espagnat de, Bernard. *Penser la science ou les enjeux du savoir.* Paris: Bordas, 1990.

Etikkrädet for Statens Pensjonsfond utland. "Recommendation to use the climate criterion to exclude ExxonMobil from the Government Pension Fund Global (GPFG)." *The Norwegian Climate Foundation.* Retrieved April 13, 2018. http://klimastiftelsen.no/wp-content/uploads/2017/03/Letter-to-Council-on-Ethics-Exxon-and-climate-change.pdf.

Fanon, Frantz. *Peau Noire, Masques Blancs.* Paris: Éditions du Seuil, 1952.

———. *The Wretched of the Earth.* Translated from the French by Richard Philcox, New York: Grove Press, 2004.

———. *Toward the African Revolution.* Translated from the French by Haakon Chevalier, New York: Grove Press, 1988.

———. *A Dying Colonialism.* Translated from the French by Haakon Chevalier, New York: Grove Press, 1967.

Faulkner, Raymond O. *The Papyrus Bremner-Rhind. British Museum No. 10188.* Bruxelles: Édition de la Fondation Égyptologique Reine Élisabeth, 1933.

———. *A Concise Dictionary of Middle Egyptian.* Oxford: Griffith Institute, 1991.

Fauvelle-Aymar, François-Xavier. *L'Afrique de Cheikh Anta Diop.* Paris: Karthala, 1996.

Fauvelle-Aymar, François-Xavier et al. *Afrocentrismes. L'histoire des Africains entre Égypte et Amérique.* Paris: Karthala, 2000.

Firmin, Anténor. *The Equality of the Human Races.* Translated by Asselin Charles, Chicago: University of Illinois Press, 2002.

Foucault, Michel. *The Archaeology of Knowledge & The Discourse on Language.* Translated from the French by A. M. Sheridan Smith, New York: Pantheon Books, 1972.

———. *The History of Sexuality. Vol. I: An Introduction.* Trans. Robert Hurley, New York: Vintage Books, 1978.

———. *Discipline & Punish. The Birth of the Prison.* Trans. from the French by Alan Sheridan, New York: Vintage Books, 1995.

———. *The Government of Self and Others.* Trans. Graham Burchell, New York: Palgrave Macmillan, 2011.

———. "What Are the Iranians Dreaming About?" *Foucault and the Iranian Revolution.* Retrieved September 13, 2018. https://www.press.uchicago.edu/Misc/Chicago/007863.html.

Freeman, Joel A. & Griffin, Don B. *Return to Glory: The Powerful Stirring of the Black Race.* Shippensburgh: Destiny Image, 2003.

Freud, Sigmund. *The Basic Writings of Sigmund Freud.* Trans. A. A. Brill, New York: Random House, Inc., 1995.

Fu-Kiau, Kimbwandende Kia Bunseki. *Self-Healing Power and Therapy. Old Teachings from Africa.* Baltimore, MD: Inprint Editions, 2003.

Gassama, Makhily (Dir.). *L'Afrique répond à Sarkozy. Contre le discours de Dakar.* Paris: Philippe Rey, 2008.

Gbadegesin, Segun. *African Philosophy: Traditional Yoruba Philosophy and Contemporary African Realities.* New York: Peter Lang, 1991.

Glissant, Édouard. *Poetics of Relation.* Trans. Betsy Wing, Ann Arbor: The University of Michigan Press, 2010.

Gobineau, Arthur Comte De. *The Inequality of Human Races.* Trans., by Adrian Collins, Burlington: Ostara Publications, 2011.

Gnonsea, Doue. *Cheikh Anta Diop, Théophile Obenga: Combat pour la Re-naissance africaine.* Paris: L'Harmattan, 2003.

Gray, Chris. *Conceptions of History: Cheikh Anta Diop and Théophile Obenga.* London: Karnak House, 1989.

Greenhouse, Joel B. "[Replication and Meta-Analysis in Parapsychology]: Comment: Parapsychology—On the Margins of Science?" *Statistical Science,* Vol. 6, No. 4, Nov. 1991, 386–89.

Greenpeace France. "Africa's forests under threat: Socfin's plantations in Cameroon and Liberia." *Greenpeace.* Retrieved April 13, 2018. https://www.greenpeace.org/africa/Global/africa/publications/forests/2016/AFRICA%27S_FORESTS_UNDER_THREAT_1.pdf.

Guillaumin, Collette. *L'idéologie raciste. Genèse et langage actuel.* Paris: Gallimard, 2002.

Hamdun, Said & King, Noël. *Ibn Battata In Black Africa.* Princeton, NJ: Markus Wiener Publishers, 1998.

Hamidou Kane, Cheikh. *L'Aventure Ambiguë.* Paris: Union générale d'éditions, 1971.

Hebga, Meinrad. *Afrique de la raison, Afrique de la foi.* Paris: Karthala, 1995.

Heidegger, Martin. *Discourse on Thinking.* Trans. John M. Anderson and E. Hans Freund, New York: Harper & Row, 1966.

———. *Sein und Zeit.* Tübingen: Max Niemeyer Verlag, 1967.

———. *Poetry, Language, Thought.* Trans. Albert Hofstadter, New York: Harper Colophon Books, 1975.

———. *Basic Writings.* Ed. David Farrell Krell, New York: Harper & Row, 1977.

———. *Being and Time.* Trans. By John Macquarrie & Edward Robinson, Oxford: Blackwell, 1978.

Heredia de, José-Maria. "Les Conquérants." *Étudeslittéraires.* Retrieved April 15, 2018.

http://poesie.webnet.fr/lesgrandsclassiques/poemes/jose_maria_de_heredia/les_conquerants.html.

Hilliard III, Asa G. et al., (Ed.). *The Teachings of Ptahhotep. The Oldest Book in the World.* Atlanta: Blackwood Press, 1987.

Hilliard III, Asa G. "Lefkowitz and the Myth of the Immaculate Conception of Western Civilization: The Myth Is Not Out of Africa" in Molefi Kete Asante & Ama Mazama (Ed.), *Egypt vs. Greece and the American Academy. The debate over the birth of civilization.* Chicago: African American Images, 2002, 51–66.

Hitler, Adolf. *My Struggle.* London: The Gainsborough Press, 1988.

Hochschild, Adam. *King Leopold's Ghost. A story of greed, terror, and heroism in colonial Africa.* New York: A Mariner Book, 1998.

Hunter-Gault, Charlayne. *New news out of Africa: Uncovering Africa's Renaissance.* Oxford: Oxford University Press, 2008.

Huntington, Samuel P. *The Clash of Civilizations and the Remaking of World Order.* New York: Touchstone, 1997.

Husserl, Edmund. *The Crisis of European Sciences and Transcendental Phenomenology.* Trans. by David Carr, Evanston, IL: Northwestern University Press, 1970.

———. *Cartesian Meditations. An Introduction to Phenomenology.* Trans. Dorion Cairns, Hingham, MA: Kluwer Boston. Inc., 1982.

Jackson, John G. *Christianity Before Christ.* Cranford, NJ: American Atheist Press, 2002. James, George G. M., *Stolen Legacy: The Greeks were not the authors of*

Greek Philosophy, but the people of North Africa, commonly called the Egyptians were. Chicago: African American Images, 2001.

Jung, Carl Gustav. *Dreams.* Trans. R.F.C. Hull, Princeton, NJ: Princeton University Press, 1974.

Kä Mana. *L'Afrique va-t-elle mourir? Bousculer l'imaginaire africain: Essai d'éthique politique.* Paris: Cerf, 1991.

———. *L'Afrique notre projet.* Yaoundé: Terroirs, 2009.

Kabou, Axelle. *Et si l'Afrique refusait le développement?.* Paris: L'Harmattan, 1991.

Kaku, Michio. *Quantum Field Theory. A Modern Introduction.* New York: Oxford University Press, Inc., 1993.

———. *Hyperspace. A Scientific Odyssey Through Parallel Universes, Time Warps, and the Tenth Dimension.* New York: Doubleday, 1995.

Kamer Lyrics. "Donny Elwood: Négro et Beau" [Video]. *Youtube.* Retrieved May 10, 2019. https://www.youtube.com/watch?v=zRgrgyq9BKs.

Kant, Immanuel. *Critique of Pure Reason.* Trans. Paul Guyer & Allen W. Wood, New York: Cambridge University Press, 2009.

Karenga, Maulana. "Afrocentricity and Multicultural Education: Concept, Challenge and Contribution." Ama Mazama (Ed.), *The Afrocentric Paradigm.* Trenton, NJ: Africa World Press, Inc., 2003, 79–81.

Keita, Maghan. *Race and the Writing of History: Riddling the Sphinx.* Oxford: Oxford University Press, 2000.

King Jr., Martin Luther. "I Have a Dream." *National Archives.* Retrieved July 18, 2019. https://www.archives.gov/files/press/exhibits/dream-speech.pdf., 5, paragraph 2.

Kodena, François. "'I Can't Breathe!': Eric Garner's Salutary Verdict to the Racist Euro-American World and Its Implications for the African Worldwide." *APA Newsletter on Philosophy and the Black Experience,* Vol. 14, No. 2, Spring 2015, 12–17.

Knitter, Paul F. *No Other Name? A critical survey of Christian attitudes toward the world religions.* Quezon City: Claretian Publications, 1985.

Kum'a N'dumbe III, Alexandre. *Hitler Voulait l'Afrique. Les plans secrets pour une Afrique fasciste 1933–1945.* Paris: L'Harmattan, 1980.

Laburthe-Tolra, Philippe. *Initiations et Sociétés Secrètes au Cameroun. Essai sur la religion beti.* Paris: Karthala, 1985.

Lamb, David. *The Search for Extraterrestrial Intelligence. A Philosophical Inquiry.* New York: Routledge, 2005.

Lampert, Jay. "Hegel and Ancient Egypt: History and Becoming." *International Philosophical Quarterly,* Vol. XXXV, No. 1, Issue No. 137, March 1995, 55–56.

Lapouge, Georges Vacher de. *L'Aryen. Son Rôle Social.* Paris: Albert Fontemoing [Ed.], 1899.

Leakey, Louis Seymour Bazett. *By the Evidence: Memoirs, 1932–1951.* New York: A Harvest Book, 1974.

Lefkowitz, Mary. *Not Out of Africa: How Afrocentrism Became an Excuse to Teach Myth as History.* New York: BasicBooks, 1996.

Leloup, Jean-Yves. *Introduction aux « vrais philosophes ». Les Pères grecs: un continent oublié de la pensée occidentale.* Paris: Albin Michel, 1998.

Le MondeAfrique. "Le Discours de Dakar de Nicolas Sarkozy." *Le Monde.* Retrieved December 11, 2018. https://www.lemonde.fr/afrique/article/2007/11/09/le-discours-de dakar_976786_3212.html.

Lenin, V. I. *Imperialism. The Highest Stage of Capitalism.* New York: International Publishers Co., Inc., 2011.

Lévinas, Emmanuel. *Totalité et Infini. Essai sur l'Extériorité.* Paris: Brodard et Taupin, 1971.

Lévi-Strauss, Claude. *Tristes Tropiques. The Complete Translation of the Classic Work by the Dean of Structural Anthropology.* Trans. from the French by John and Doreen Weightman, New York: Penguin Books, 1992.

Lewin, Kurt. *The Conceptual Representation and the Measurement of Psychological Forces.* Durham, NC: Duke University Press, 1938.

Locke, Alain. *The New Negro. Voices of the Harlem Renaissance.* New York: A Touchstone Book, 1997.

Lu, Kelvin. "Kemtiyu Cheikh Anta Full Movie" [Video]. *YouTube.* Retrieved April 26, 2019. https://www.youtube.com/watch?v=tJ9573ExAvg.

Lucretius. *The Nature of Things.* Trans. A. E. Stallings, New York: Penguin Books, 2007.

Luke, Don. "Preserving the Eurosupremacist Myth." Molefi Kete Asante and Ama Mazama (Ed.), *Egypt vs. Greece and the American Academy. The debate over the birth of civilization.* Chicago: African American Images, 2002, 91–120.

Lyons, Len. *The 101 Best Jazz Albums. A History of Jazz on Records.* New York: William Morrow and Company, Inc., 1980.

Malcolm X. *By Any Means Necessary.* New York: Pathfinder Press, 2012.

Malcomson, Scott L. *One Drop of Blood. The American Misadventure of Race.* New York: Farrar Straus Giroux, 2001.

Martins, Nuno R. B. et al. "Human Brain/Cloud Interface." *Frontiers in Neuroscience,* March 2019, Vol. 13, Article 112, 1–24.

Masson-Oursel, Paul. *Comparative Philosophy.* New York: Brace & Company, 1926.

Mazama, Ama (Ed.). *The Afrocentric Paradigm.* Trenton, NJ: Africa World Press, Inc., 2003.

Mazel, Jean. *Présence du Monde Noir.* Paris: Éditions Robert Laffont, 1975.

Mbelek, Jean Paul. *"Le Déchiffrement de l'Os d'Ishango." ANKH,* No. 12/13, 2003–2004, 118–37.

Mbembe, Achille. *Critique de la Raison Nègre.* Paris: La Découverte, 2013.

Mbog Bassong. *La Méthode de la Philosophie Africaine.* Paris: L'Harmattan, 2007.

———. *La Religion Africaine. De la Cosmologie Quantique à la Symbolique de Dieu.* Québec: Kiyikaat Editions, 2013.

———. *Le Savoir Africain. Essai sur la théorie avancée de la connaissance.* Québec: Kiyikaat Editions, 2013.

———. *Les Fondements de la Philosophie Africaine.* Québec: Kiyikaat Editions, 2014.

Mboli, Jean-Claude. *Origine des Langues Africaines.* Paris: L'Harmattan, 2010,

Menu, Bernadette. *Egypte pharaonique, Nouvelles recherches sur l'histoire juridique, économique et sociale de l'ancienne Egypte.* Paris: L'Harmattan, 2004.

Mignolo, Walter D. *Local Hitories/Global Designs: Coloniality, Subaltern Knowledges, and Border Thinking.* Princeton, NJ: Princeton University Press, 2000.

Miller, Joaquin. "Africa." *Poetry Atlas.* Retrieved April 10, 2018. http://www.poetryatlas.com/poetry/poem/4501/africa.html.

Minko Bengone, Laurent, *Comprendre autrement le Mvett.* Paris: L'Harmattan, 2008.

Moffa, Claudio. *L'Afrique à la périphérie de l'Histoire.* Paris: L'Harmattan,1995.

Mokhtar, G., (Ed.). *General History of Africa, Vol. II. Ancient Civilizations of Africa.* California: University of California Press, 1981.

Mongo Beti. *Mission to Kala.* Trans. from the French by Peter Green, Devon, England: Mallory Publishing, 2008.

Morel, Edmund Dene. *The Black Man's Burden.* Northbrook, IL: Metro Books, 1972.

Morin, Edgar. *Introduction à la pensée complexe.* Paris: Éditions du Seuil, 2005.

———. *Penser Global. L'humain et son univers.* Paris: Robert Laffont, 2015.

Moyo, Dambisa. *Edge of Chaos. Why Democracy Is Failing to Deliver Economic Growth—and How to Fix It.* New York: Basic Books, 2018.

Mudimbe, Valentin-Yves. *The Invention of Africa.* Bloomington and Indianapolis: Indiana University Press, 1988.

Mveng, Engelbert. *L'art d'Afrique noire. Liturgie cosmique et langage religieux.* Yaoundé: Clé, 1994.

Ndebi Biya, Robert. *L'Être Comme Génération. Essai critique d'une ontologie d'inspiration africaine.* Strasbourg: Cérit, 1995.

Ndinga, Gabriel & Ndumba, Georges. *Relecture critique des origines de la philosophie et ses enjeux pour l'Afrique.* Bonneuil: Menaibuc, 2005.

Nietzsche, Friedrich. *The Birth of Tragedy or Hellenism and Pessimism.* Trans. WM. A. Haussmann, New York: The Macmillan Company, 1910.

———. *Beyond Good and Evil. Prelude to a Philosophy of the Future.* Trans. Walter Kaufmann, New York: Vintage Books, 1966.

Ngũgĩ wa Thiong'o. *Something Torn and New. An African Renaissance.* New York: Basic*Civitas* Books, 2009.

Njoh Mouelle, Ébénézer. *De la médiocrité à l'excellence: Essai sur la signification humaine du développement.* Yaoundé: CLE, 1972.

Nkrumah, Kwame. *Africa Must Unite.* London: Heinemann, 1963.

———. *Consciencism: Philosophy and Ideology for Decolonization.* New York: Monthly Review Press, 1964.

———. *Neo-colonialism. The Last Stage of Imperialism*. London: Panaf Books, 2004.

Nyerere, Julius K. *Ujamaa: Essays on Socialism.* London: Oxford University Press, 1971.

Obenga, Théophile. *La philosophie africaine de la période pharaonique. 2780–330 avant notre ère.* Paris: L'Harmattan, 1990.

———. *Origine Commune de l'Egyptien Ancien, du Copte et des Langues Négro-Africaines Modernes. Introduction à la Linguistique Historique Africaine.* Paris: L'Harmattan, 1993.

———. *La géométrie égyptienne. Contribution de l'Afrique antique à la mathématique mondiale.* Paris: L'Harmattan, 1995.

———. *Cheikh Anta Diop, Volney et le Sphinx: Contribution de Cheikh Anta Diop à l'Historiographie mondiale.* Paris: Présence Africaine, 2000.

———. *Le sens de la lutte contre l'africanisme eurocentriste.* Paris: L'Harmattan, 2001.

———. "Egypt: Ancient History of African Philosophy." Kwasi Wiredu (Ed.), *A Companion to African Philosophy.* Malden, MA: Blackwell Publishing Ltd, 2004, 33–35.

———. *L'État Fédéral d'Afrique Noire: La Seule Issue.* Paris: L'Harmattan, 2012.

Okumu, Washington A. J. *The African Renaissance: History, Significance and Strategy.* Trenton, NJ: Africa World Press, Inc., 2002.

Omotunde, Jean-Philippe. *L'Origine négro-africaine du savoir grec.* Bonneuil: Menaibuc, 2000.

Ondo, Angèle Christine. *Mvett Ekang: Forme et Sens. L'épique dévoile le sens.* Paris: L'Harmattan, 2014.

Online Etymology Dictionary. "Philosophy." *Online Etymology Dictionary*. Retrieved, April 20, 2018. https://www.etymonline.com/search?q=wisdom.

Owono, Jacques Fulbert. *Pauvreté ou Paupérisation en Afrique. Une étude exegético-ethique de la pauvreté chez les Beti-Fang du Cameroun.* Bamberg: Bamberg University Press, 2011.

Parenti, Michael. *The Face of Imperialism.* Boulder, CO: Paradigm Publishers, 2011.

———. *Profit Pathology and Other Indecencies.* Boulder, CO: Paradigm Publishers, 2015.

Peet, Richard. *Unholy Trinity. The IMF, World Band and WTO.* New York: Zed Books Ltd, 2010.

Perkins, John. *Confessions of an Economic Hit Man.* New York: Plume, 2004.

———. *The Secret History of the American Empire. The Truth About Economic Hit Men, Jackals, and How to Change the World.* New York: A Plume Book, 2008.

Plato. *Complete Works.* John M. Cooper (Ed.), Indianapolis, IN: Hackett Publishing Company, Inc., 1997.

Plotinus. *The Six Enneads.* Trans. By Stephen MacKenna and B. S. Page, Chicago: Encyclopaedia Britannica, 1952.

Plumelle-Uribe, Rosa Amelia. *La Férocité Blanche. Des non-Blancs aux non-Aryriens: génocides occultés de 1492 à nos jours.* Paris: Albin Michel, 2001.

Pondi, Jean-Emmanuel. *Barack Obama. De l'interrogation à l'admiration.* Yaoundé: Clé, 2009.

Powell, Corey S. "Will Human Teleportation Ever Be Possible?" *The Sciences.* Retrieved February 13, 2020. https://www.discovermagazine.com/the-sciences/will-human-teleportation-ever-be-possible.

Prince Dika Akwa Nya Bonambela (Dir.). *Hommage du Cameroun au Professeur Cheikh Anta Diop.* Dakar Fann, Sénégal: Éditions Panafrika/Silex/Nouvelles du Sud, 2006.

Ricœur, Paul. *Le Conflit des interprétations.* Paris: Seuil, 1969.

———. *The Symbolism of Evil.* Trans. Emerson Buchanan, Boston: Beacon Press, 1969.

Rogers, Joel Augustus. *Nature Knows No Color-Line.* Middletown, Connecticut, CT: Wesleyan University Press, 2014.

———. *From Superman to Man.* Ocean Shores, WA: Watchmaker Publishing, 2015.

Russell, Bertrand. *The Problems of Philosophy.* Oxford: Oxford University Press, 1976.

Sartre, Jean-Paul. *Black Orpheus.* Paris: Présence Africaine, 1976.

Sauneron, Serge. *Les Prêtres de l'ancienne Égypte.* Paris: Éditions du Seuil, 1998.

Schoener, Allon, (Ed.). *Harlem On My Mind. Cultural Capital and Black America 1900–1978.* New York: Dell Publishing Co., Inc., 1979.

Smiley, Tavis & West, Cornel. *The Rich and the Rest of Us. A Poverty Manifesto.* New York: SmileyBooks, 2012.

Société Africaine de Culture. *La Civilisation de la Femme dans la Tradition Africaine.* Paris: Présence Africaine, 1972.

Somet, Yoporeka. *L'Afrique dans la philosophie.* Gif-sur Yvette: Khepera, 2005.

Spengler, Oswald. *The Decline of the West. Vol. 1. Form and Actuality.* New York: Charles Francis Atkinson, 1927.

Spero Adotevi, Stanislas. *Négritude et Négrologues.* Bègles: Le Castor Astral, 1998.

SpringerLink. "Asmara Declaration (2000)." *Springer Nature.* Retrieved May 15, 2018. https://www0.sun.ac.za/taalsentrum/assets/files/Asmara%20Declaration.pdf.

Stannard, David E. *American Holocaust. The Conquest of the New World.* New York: Oxford University Press, 1992.

Stringer, Christopher & McKie, Robin. *African Exodus: The Origins of Modern Humanity.* New York: Henry Holt and Company, 1997.

Sun, Degang & Zoubir, Yahia H. "The Eagle's Nest in the Horn of Africa: US Military Strategic Deployment in Djibouti." *Africa Spectrum,* 1/2016, 111–124.

Tchundjang Pouemi, Joseph. *Monnaie, Servitude et Liberté. La répression monétaire de l'Afrique.* Yaoundé: MENAIBUC, 2000.

Tempels, Placide. *La philosophie bantoue.* Paris: Présence Africaine, 1949.

Tété-Adjalogo Têtêvi, Godwin. *La question nègre.* Paris: L'Harmattan, 2003.

The Editors of Encyclopaedia Britannica. "Kepler's laws of planetary motion." *Encyclopaedia Britannica.* Retrieved April 13, 2018 & January 30, 2020. https://www.britannica.com/science/Keplers-laws-of-planetary-motion.

Thomas, Louis-Vincent & Luneau, René. *La Terre Africaine et ses Religions.* Paris: L'Harmattan, 2015.

Tiziano et al. "The bilocated mind: new perspectives on self-localization and self-identification." *Frontiers in Human Neuroscience*, March 2013, Vol. 7, Article 71.

Tonme, Shanda. *Fondements culturels du retard de l'Afrique Noire.* Paris: L'Harmattan, 2009.

Towa, Marcien. *Essai sur la problématique philosophique dans l'Afrique actuelle.* Yaoundé: CLE, 1971.

Tsira Ndong Ndoutoume. *Le Mvett. L'homme, la Mort et l'Immortalité.* Paris: L'Harmattan, 1993.

Turse, Nick. "The US military's best kept secret." *The Nation.* Retrieved March 1, 2018. https://www.thenation.com/article/the-us-militarys-best-kept-secret/.

UNESCO. *Race and Science.* New York: Columbia University Press, 1961.

United Nations. "Voting System." *United Nations Security Council*. Retrieved January 22, 2020. https://www.un.org/securitycouncil/content/voting-system.

United Nations. *The United Nations Today*. New York: United Nations Publication, 2008.

Van Sertima, Ivan. *They Came Before Columbus: The African Presence in Ancient America*. New York: Random House, 1976.

Van Sertima, Ivan & Williams Obadele, Larry. *Great African Thinkers: Cheikh Anta Diop*. New Jersey: The Journal of African Civilization Ltd., 2000.

Vattel, Emer de. *The Law of Nations*. Ed. Knud Haakonssen, Carmel, Indiana: Liberty Fund, Inc., 2008.

Verharen, Charles. "In and Out of Africa: Misreading Afrocentricity." Molefi Kete Asante & Ama Mazama (Ed.), *Egypt vs. Greece and the American Academy. The debate over the birth of civilization*. Chicago: African American Images, 2002, 67–90.

Volney Chasseboeuf De. *History and Geography: Travels through Syria and Egypt, in the years 1783, 1784, and 1785. Containing the present natural and political state of those countries, . . . Translated from the French. In two volumes. . . . Volume 1 of 2*. Dublin: Ecco Print Editions, 1788.

———. *The Ruins or, Meditation on the Revolutions of Empires*. Boston: Josiah P. Mendum, 1869.

———. *Œuvres Complètes*. Paris: Bossange Frères, 1921.

Wago N., Jean Baptiste. *L'Afrique face à son destin*. Paris: L'Harmattan, 1997.

Wallis Budge, Ernest A. *Easy Lessons in Egyptian Hieroglyphics*. New York: Dover Publications, Inc., 1983.

———. (Trans.), *The Egyptian Book of the Dead. The Papyrus of Ani*. Scotts Valley, CA: IAP, 2009.

Washington, Booker T. *Up from Slavery*. New York: Dover Publications, Inc., 1995.

Westphal, Jonathan. & Levenson, Carl. (Ed.). *Time*. Indianapolis, IN: Hackett Publishing Company, Inc., 1993.

WikiLeaks. "The New Dirty War for Africa's uranium and mineral rights." *WikiLeaks*. Retrieved April 13, 2018. https://wikileaks.org/car-mining/.

Williams, Chancellor. *The Destruction of Black Civilization: Great Issues of a Race from 4500 B. C. To 2000 A. D.* Chicago: Third World Press, 1987.

Wiredu, Kwasi, (Ed.). *A Companion to African Philosophy*. Malden, MA: Blackwell Publishing Ltd, 2004.

Wobogo, Vulindlela I. *Cold Wind from the North: The Prehistoric European Origin of Racism Explained by Diop's Two Cradle Theory*. Charleston, SC: Books on Demand, 2011.

Woodson, Carter G. *The Mis-Education of the Negro*. Chicago: African American Images, 2000.

Yancy, George (Ed.). *The Philosophical I. Personal Reflections on Life in Philosophy.* New York: Rowman & Littlefield Publishers, Inc., 2002.

———. *Backlash. What Happens When We Talk Honestly about Racism in America.* Lanham, MA: Rowman & Littlefield, 2018.

Ziegler, Jean. *Les vivants et la mort. Essai de sociologie.* Coll. Esprit, Paris: Seuil, 1975.

Index

Page references for figures are italicized.

About the Author

François Ngoa Kodena, PhD in geopolitics and ethics from Duquesne University (Pittsburgh, Pennsylvania, USA), is an Afrikan-Kam(h)erunian (Cameroonian) Afrosofer-philosopher. Inventor of the epistemic paradigm "Afrosofia," his research focuses on Afrikological studies, Black theologies, geo-ethics, and politics. Ngoa Kodena is a skilled translingual, strategic, and interdisciplinary thinker in the Imhotepian revolutionary-innovative traditions, who investigates racial and gender related philosophies, and promotes corrective thinking in diverse-inclusive educational programs in academe and beyond, including Afrikan-world histories, politics, cultures and civilizations, literatures, musical genres, and arts in Pan-Afrikan renascent movements. Involved in conflict resolutions as a *Ka*tholic *fara*/priest, he advocates the key role of spiritualities like the Beti Mvett in the shaping of demiurgic and ecological mindsets. Ngoa Kodena's research extends also to Afro-Asian relations, geo-economic, social, and public policy analyses, strategic and security studies, NGO management, sustainable lifestyles, lasting peace, and leadership-oriented projects with youth in transcultural environments. These wide-ranging issues have constituted the ebullient biotope of his worldwide lectures for almost two decades now.